Project Scheduling
with Time Windows

Contributions to Management Science

Ulrich Dorndorf

Project Scheduling with Time Windows

From Theory to Applications

With 21 Figures and 17 Tables

Physica-Verlag

A Springer-Verlag Company

Series Editors
Werner A. Müller
Martina Bihn

Author
Dr. Ulrich Dorndorf
INFORM – Institut für Operations Research
und Management GmbH
Pascalstraße 23
52076 Aachen
Germany
udorndorf@acm.org

ISSN 1431-1941
ISBN 3-7908-1516-0 Physica-Verlag Heidelberg New York

Cataloging-in-Publication Data applied for
Die Deutsche Bibliothek – CIP-Einheitsaufnahme
Dorndorf, Ulrich: Project scheduling with time windows: from theory to applications; with
17 tables / Ulrich Dorndorf. – Heidelberg; New York: Physica-Verl., 2002
   (Contributions to economics)
   ISBN 3-7908-1516-0

Zugl. Diss., TU Darmstadt, Kennziffer D17

Physica-Verlag Heidelberg New York
a member of BertelsmannSpringer Science+Business Media GmbH

© Physica-Verlag Heidelberg 2002
Printed in Germany

The use of general descriptive names, registered names, trademarks, etc. in this publication
does not imply, even in the absence of a specific statement, that such names are exempt from
the relevant protective laws and regulations and therefore free for general use.

Softcover Design: Erich Kirchner, Heidelberg

SPIN 10885915   88/2202-5 4 3 2 1 0 – Printed on acid-free and non-aging paper

Acknowledgements

In the preparation of this work I am greatly indebted to the following people who have given freely of their time and shared their insights to assist in this effort. I am grateful to my advisors Prof. Dr. Wolfgang Domschke and Prof. Dr. Erwin Pesch, whose exceptional encouragement and support, kindness and patience have made this research a most valuable experience. I am indebted to Toàn Phan Huy for many helpful, inspiring and enjoyable discussions, which helped improve this work considerably, and for carefully reading drafts of several chapters. I am also indebted to Werner Siemes for his help in the evaluation of the gate scheduling algorithm. I also want to thank Thomas Schmidt for his kind support. Most importantly, my special thanks goes to my family, without whose support this book could never have been completed.

Frankfurt am Main, May 2002   U. Dorndorf

Contents

Chapter 1

Introduction

1.1 Motivation and Objectives

Project scheduling is concerned with the allocation of resources over time to perform a collection of activities. The decision models that fit within this framework cover a multitude of practical problems that arise, for example, in such diverse areas as research and development, software engineering, construction engineering, repair and maintenance, as well as make-to-order and small batch production planning.

A project is a one-of-a-kind undertaking with specific objectives that has to be performed within a certain time-frame and with limited resource supply. Its management roughly consists of (1) a project definition and data acquisition phase, (2) a scheduling phase and (3) an execution and termination phase during which the schedule is realised and the performance is analysed.

This work deals with the scheduling aspect. The aim is to develop methods for finding an optimal schedule for a project; this involves the assignment of activities to resources and the definition of exact activity start and completion times, a task that is generally difficult whenever multiple activities simultaneously compete for the same resources. We will not address the topics related to the conception, selection, and definition of a project, but will rather assume that the project structure is given, including data on resource availabilities and requirements as well as the necessary processing times. Likewise, we will not deal with the issues that typically arise during the realisation phase of a project.

We shall investigate a very general class of deterministic project scheduling problems that is expressive enough to capture many features commonly found in practical problems, such as precedence constraints, activity time windows, fixed activity start times, synchronisation of start or finish times, maximal or minimal activity overlaps, non-delay execution of activities, setup times, or time varying resource supply and demand.

In the basic model, technological or organisational requirements are represented through generalised precedence constraints that allow to specify minimal and/or maximal time lags, or *time windows*, between any pair of activities. An activity may require different amounts of several resource types. Resource requirements and availabilities may vary in discrete steps over time. While we usually consider the objective of minimising the overall completion time of a project, most of the results apply at least for any performance measure that is a non-decreasing function of the completion or start times of the activities. We will also address multi-mode scheduling, i.e., the situation where a choice must be made between several modes in which an activity may be processed, reflecting time-resource or resource-resource tradeoffs. Due to its generality, the basic model also covers many difficult special problems that have been extensively studied in scheduling research, for example, shop scheduling problems (Błażewicz et al. 1996).

Throughout this work, we study deterministic project scheduling problems, where all parameters that define a problem instance are known with certainty in advance. Deterministic scheduling models are best suited if any possible random influences in the project execution phase can be expected to be low, and if the problem parameters can thus be estimated with high accuracy. This may, for instance, be the case if the activities of a project show a high degree of similarity with previous projects. In situations where the problem parameters are difficult to estimate and are subject to significant random influences, the use of deterministic scheduling techniques may, however, be problematic. As a typical example, deterministic scheduling in the presence of stochastic activity processing times generally leads to an underestimation of the expected project duration, as already observed by Fulkerson (1962).

The first models and methods for dealing with large scale projects have been devised in the late 1950's and early 1960's. The well known Critical Path Method (CPM, Kelley 1961) and the Metra Potential Method (MPM, Roy 1962) have been designed for deterministic project scheduling with ordinary or generalised precedence constraints, respectively, while the Project Evaluation and Review Technique (PERT, Malcolm et al. 1959) considers probabilistic activity processing times; the Graphical Evaluation and Review Technique (GERT, Pritsker and Happ 1966) additionally takes probabilistic precedence relations into account. These approaches have received great attention in the following years. In the early 1970's, Davis (1973) already reported more than 15 books and 300 papers on the subject.

The original models and methods simplified the problem by concentrating only on temporal constraints, i.e., by assuming that the availability of resources is not a limiting factor. Beginning in the late 1960's, the models were extended by additionally considering scarcity of resources. In order to distinguish between the classic CPM, MPM, and PERT or GERT models on the one hand and models that consider limited resource availability on the other hand, the latter are usually referred to as *resource-constrained*. The underlying problems are much more difficult to solve, as the computational effort for finding an optimal solution usually grows exponentially with the problem size. For a long time, this has prohibited the use of exact algorithms for scheduling large practical projects with resource constraints.

In the past years, interest and research efforts in the field of resource-constrained project scheduling have strongly increased, and many new modelling concepts and algorithms have been developed. Overviews of the advances in models and solution methods are given in the survey papers of Brucker et al. (1999), Herroelen et al. (1998), Kolisch and Padman (2001), Drexl et al. (1997), Elmaghraby (1995), Özdamar and Ulusoy (1995), Icmeli et al. (1993), or Domschke and Drexl (1991). A gentle introduction to network models for project planning and control is given by Elmaghraby (1977). Descriptions of the basic classic project scheduling models for the temporal analysis of projects can be found in many introductory Management Science textbooks (e.g. Domschke and Drexl 1998). Applications within the area of production planning have been described, e.g., by Hax and Candea (1984) and Günther and Tempelmeier (2000); Drexl et al. (1994) discuss a special type of project scheduling software, called Leitstand system, for make-to-order manufacturing management.

The resource-constrained project scheduling problems studied in this work can be understood as extensions of the basic problem covered by the Metra Potential Method. Due to the general form of the temporal constraints, the resource-constrained version of the problem is particularly difficult to solve. Even the question for the existence of a feasible schedule can in general only be answered with exponentially growing effort. This may be one the main reasons why, despite the expressiveness and high practical relevance of the models, very few attempts have so far been made to design solution procedures for this class of problems.

The main objective of this work is to help overcome this deficiency by developing effective and efficient solution methods. The focus will be on the design and evaluation of exact branch-and-bound algorithms for finding optimal schedules, but we shall also study the performance of heuristics based upon truncated versions of these procedures.

The scheduling methods that will be developed make use of a general purpose problem solving paradigm that originated in the area of Artificial Intelligence. *Constraint propagation* is an elementary technique for simplifying difficult search and optimisation problems by exploiting implicit constraints that are discovered through the repeated analysis of the domains of decision variables and the interrelation between the variables and domains that is induced by the constraints. In the past years, constraint propagation techniques have been applied with growing success for solving a number of difficult, idealised scheduling problems, mostly in the area of machine scheduling. The successful application for solving special cases of the general problem class studied here suggests that the approach may also be valuable in this context. As a second objective of this work, we shall therefore study the application of constraint propagation techniques in project scheduling.

A third objective is to demonstrate the practical relevance of the approach taken in this work. To this end we shall describe possible applications of the models and methods and extensions thereof in the area of airport operations management.

1.2 Outline

The presentation of the results is organised as follows.

Chapter 2 introduces a decision model for deterministic project scheduling with generalised precedence constraints, the basic problem considered in this work. The chapter starts with a description of the entities that make up a project scheduling problem: activities, resources, precedence relations or time windows, and performance measures. After presenting a formal optimisation model, the concept of domains, i.e., sets of possible values of decision variables, is introduced. The general problem is then related to some well known special cases that are obtained if certain assumptions about the resource availability and requirements and/or the structure of the precedence relations are made. Finally, the generalisation to multiple activity execution modes is described.

Chapter 3 gives a general introduction to constraint propagation. Constraint propagation is a search space reduction technique that tries to remove inconsistent values from the variable domains, i.e., values that cannot participate in any feasible solution, by repeated applying a set of consistency tests. The chapter discusses different *concepts of consistency* that have been developed in the literature on the constraint satisfaction problem, and which may serve as a theoretical background for the propagation techniques that will be employed. *Consistency checking* methods are described that control the repeated application of the tests until a fixed point is reached, i.e., until no further reductions are possible. The chapter concludes by pointing to constraint programming environments that build upon the concepts that have been introduced.

Chapter 4 is devoted to consistency tests for project scheduling that may be applied within the general framework introduced in the preceding chapter. It first describes simple tests that analyse the precedence constraints of a problem. The emphasis of the chapter is on *interval consistency tests* that are based upon the comparison of the resource supply and demand within certain time intervals. Previous research has shown that difficult project scheduling problem instances are frequently characterised by a low resource availability, which leads to the existence of many *disjunctive* sub-problems, i.e., sub-problems with unit resource availabilities and requirements. The chapter shows how disjunctive sub-problems can be identified and selected. Consistency tests that have been proposed in the literature for disjunctive (machine) scheduling problems are then reviewed and presented within a unifying framework using numerous examples. Previous results are generalised and related to the concept of *interval work*, i.e., the minimum amount of work that must be performed within a time interval. The search space reduction that is achieved by applying the tests within a fixed point propagation method is analysed and related to the theoretical concepts of consistency presented in Chapter 3. The results for disjunctive sub-problems are then extended for the case of arbitrary resource availabilities and requirements. The chapter finally shows how the results can be used for multimode project scheduling by considering a mode-minimal problem instance, where all mode-dependent problem parameters are replaced with the minimum possible values.

Chapter 5 describes a new time-oriented branch-and-bound procedure for the basic single-mode project scheduling problem, in which the constraint propagation techniques are embedded. The solution method enumerates possible activity start times by scheduling activities as early as possible or delaying them by reducing their start time domains in such a way that the construction of non-active (dominated) schedules is avoided. The procedure heavily relies upon the application of constraint propagation techniques at the nodes of the search tree. The algorithm is evaluated for the problem with generalised precedence constraints as well as for the special case of ordinary (finish-start) precedence constraints, using many large sets of benchmark test problems from the literature with up to five hundred activities per problem instance. The results are compared to those of other exact procedures that have recently been proposed as well as to heuristic results; a detailed analysis of the influence of certain parameters that characterise a problem instance is given.

Chapter 6 extends the branching scheme for the case of multi-mode project scheduling. The basic idea is to integrate a time-oriented branching over activity start times with a branching over mode assignments or restrictions.

Chapter 7 discusses applications of the models and methods in the area of airport operations management. We first describe an application of single-mode project scheduling with time windows in ground handling, where activities required for servicing an aircraft while on the ground have to be scheduled. The focus of the chapter then is on the development of a model and solution procedure for gate scheduling, i.e., the problem of assigning flights (activities) to airport terminal gates or parking positions (modes) and scheduling the start and end times of the assignments. The chapter demonstrates how this problem can be modelled as a special multi-mode project scheduling problem with time windows. A solution procedure based on the concepts and techniques developed in the preceding chapters is described and evaluated on large practical test-cases.

This work finishes with a summary and some concluding remarks in Chapter 8.

Chapter 2

Optimisation Model

This chapter describes an optimisation model for deterministic resource-constrained project scheduling with generalised precedence constraints. It introduces the basic elements of project scheduling models such as activities, resources, precedence constraints, as well as performance measures for evaluating the cost or utility of a schedule.

We are concerned with scheduling a set of activities subject to constraints on the availability of several shared resources and temporal constraints that allow to specify minimal and maximal time lags between the start of two activities. The objective considered in this work usually is to minimise the *makespan*, i.e., the maximum of the completion times of all activities, although most of the results hold for any regular objective function and are frequently also useful for optimising non-regular objective functions[1]. The rationale behind the makespan criterion is that an early completion of the project is advantageous in the sense that it frees resources for other tasks and reduces the risk of deadline violations and associated penalties; furthermore, significant payments are often linked to the project completion, and an early completion thus tends to increase the net present value of a project.

Sometimes, a choice can be made between several *modes* in which an activity can be processed. The modes may differ with respect to resource requirements and processing time, and they can influence the tightness of the temporal constraints; the modes reflect time-resource and resource-resource tradeoffs. Models with multiple possible execution modes per activity are called *multi-mode* models; otherwise we speak of *single-mode* models.

Using the classification scheme for project scheduling proposed by Brucker et al. (1999), which extends the well known three-field classification scheme for machine scheduling introduced by Graham et al. (1979), we will denote the main single-mode problem considered in this work with $PS|temp|C_{max}$, for (α) project scheduling with

---

[1]Chapter 7 develops a special project scheduling model for a specific application with a non-regular objective function.

(β) general temporal constraints and (γ) the objective of minimising the maximum completion time. In the alternative classification scheme developed by Herroelen et al. (1999) the problem can be characterised as $m, 1|gpr|C_{\max}$. The multi-mode extension of the problem will be denoted with $MPS|temp|C_{max}$.

The problem $PS|temp|C_{max}$ is sometimes referred to as resource-constrained project scheduling problem (RCPSP) with time windows (e.g. Bartusch et al. 1988), RCPSP with generalised precedence relations (e.g. De Reyck and Herroelen 1998), or RCPSP with minimal and maximal time lags (RCPSP/max, e.g. Schwindt 1998b).

While the classic resource-constrained project scheduling problem with simple precedence constraints, i.e. the problem $PS|prec|C_{max}$, has been extensively studied, algorithms for solving the problem $PS|temp|C_{max}$ or its multi-mode generalisation have only recently received growing attention in the literature, as documented by the recent surveys by Brucker et al. (1999), Herroelen et al. (1998), and Kolisch and Padman (2001). This may to some extent have been caused by the fact that the problem $PS|prec|C_{max}$ itself is intractable and belongs to the class of NP-hard optimisation problems (Błażewicz et al. 1983). As an extension, the problem $PS|temp|C_{max}$ is, of course, also NP-hard, and even the question whether a problem instance has a feasible solution is NP-complete in the strong sense (Bartusch et al. 1988)[2]. As a generalisation of the problem $PS|temp|C_{max}$, the multi-mode problem $MPS|temp|C_{max}$ and its corresponding feasibility problem belong to the same complexity class.

In the following, we will first describe the single-mode project scheduling problem $PS|temp|C_{max}$ in detail in Section 2.1 and then introduce its multi-mode version in Section 2.2.

2.1   The General Single-Mode Model

2.1.1   Activities and Resources

The basic entities of the project scheduling problem considered are the activities or jobs. A set of activities $\mathcal{V} = \{1, \ldots, n\}$ has to be processed with the objective of minimising the makespan, which is the maximum of the completion times of all activities. Each activity $i \in \mathcal{V}$ has a specific processing time p_i and a start time S_i. While the former is fixed in advance, the latter is a decision variable. The completion time of an activity is denoted with C_i. Because the processing times are fixed and deterministic, the completion time of an activity follows from its start time. By choosing sufficiently small time units we can always assume that the processing and start and completion times are non-negative integer values. We study the *non-preemptive* version of the problem, which means that activities must not be interrupted during their processing.

---

[2]NP-completeness of the feasibility problem is shown by transformation of an NP-complete unit-time scheduling problem Q. NP-completeness in the strong sense follows from the fact that Q is not a number-problem.

An activity i requires $r_{ik} \in \mathbb{N}_0$ units of one or several resources $k \in \mathcal{R}$, where $\mathcal{R}$ denotes the set of all resources. For the sake of simplicity we assume that resource k is available in constant amount R_k, although the results derived in the subsequent sections also apply if we consider variable resource supply instead: for constant R_k, time varying resource supply can easily be modelled by introducing fictitious activities (Bartusch et al. 1988). Resources may not be shared and are exclusively assigned to an activity during its processing. They are reusable, i.e., they are released when they are no longer required by an activity and are then available for processing other activities. More precisely, an activity uses exactly r_{ik} units of resource k in any interval of width one starting at time $t = S_i, \ldots, S_i + p_i - 1$, at which these units are not available for other activities, and releases them at time $t = S_i + p_i$. The set of activities which require resource k is denoted with $\mathcal{V}_k := \{i \in \mathcal{V} \mid r_{ik} > 0\}$.

A resource $k \in \mathcal{R}$ with supply $R_k > 1$ is also called *cumulative* resource; in the special case where $R_k = 1$ we speak of *disjunctive* or *unary* resources, which are sometimes also referred to as *machines*.

Resource constraints ensure that in any processing period the resource demand never exceeds the resource supply. It is possible to define these resource constraints in a quite elegant way using the concept of a *slack function*, which will be introduced in Chapter 4. For the time being it is sufficient to define the auxiliary set $\mathcal{V}(t)$ of activities in process at time t, or more precisely, in the right-open interval $[t, t + 1[$. The resource constraints can then be stated as follows:

$$\sum_{i \in \mathcal{V}(t)} r_{ik} \leq R_k, \quad \forall t \in \mathbb{N}_0, \forall k \in \mathcal{R}. \tag{2.1}$$

A schedule, i.e., an assignment of activity start times $S_i, \ldots, S_n$, is *resource feasible* if it satisfies the above constraint.

2.1.2 Temporal Constraints

In general, activities cannot be processed independently from each other due to scarcity of resources and additional technological requirements. Technological requirements will be modelled by *temporal constraints* or, as synonyms, *generalised precedence constraints* or *time windows*. Many classic scheduling models such as the well known resource-constrained project scheduling problem, which is a special case of the model described here, only use minimal time lags between activities; the lags reflect finish-start precedence relations between activities and are thus assumed to be equal to activity processing times. Arbitrary minimal and maximal time lags are an important generalisation, as they allow to model many characteristics commonly found in practical scheduling problems. The temporal constraints can for instance be used to model activity time windows, fixed activity start times, synchronisation of start or completion times, maximal or minimal activity overlaps, non-delay execution of activities, setup times, or time varying resource supply and demand (Bartusch et al. 1988, Elmaghraby and Kamburowski 1992, Neumann and Schwindt 1997).

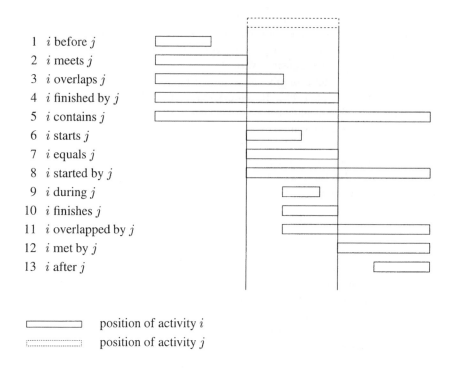

1   i before j
2   i meets j
3   i overlaps j
4   i finished by j
5   i contains j
6   i starts j
7   i equals j
8   i started by j
9   i during j
10 i finishes j
11 i overlapped by j
12 i met by j
13 i after j

position of activity i
position of activity j

Figure 2.1: Possible temporal relations between two activities

Figure 2.1 shows the thirteen possible temporal relations between a pair of activities (Allen 1983)[3]. We will see that generalised precedence constraints can selectively enforce or admit any of these relations; this stands in contrast to precedence constraints with minimal time lags only and simple completion-start precedence constraints.

A generalised precedence constraint (i, j) specifies a minimal or maximal time lag between two activities i and j and has the general *standardised form*:

$$S_i + d_{ij} \leq S_j. \tag{2.2}$$

As for the activity start and processing times, we will assume without loss of generality that all time lags d_{ij} are integer values. If $d_{ij} > 0$ then the constraint (i, j) can be interpreted as: activity j must start at least d_{ij} time units after the start of i (*minimal time lag*). If $d_{ij} \leq 0$, then the following interpretation applies: j must start at most d_{ij} time units before the start of i (*maximal time lag*). The set of all generalised precedence constraints is denoted with $\mathcal{E}$.

---

[3]By swapping the roles of activities i and j in Figure 2.1 the number of relations is reduced to seven.

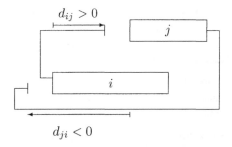

Figure 2.2: Visualisation of temporal constraints as forward and backward arcs

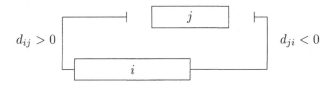

Figure 2.3: Visualisation of temporal constraints as time window of j relative to i

Temporal constraints between two activities can always be formulated in the standardised form (2.2) as start-start relations. Because the activity processing times are fixed and deterministic, all other possible relations, i.e. start-completion, completion-start, and completion-completion, can be trivially transformed into start-start relations.

For example, Relation 2 shown in Figure 2.1 (i meets j) can be enforced by imposing the two constraints $C_i \leq S_j$ and $S_j \leq C_i$. By substituting $C_i := S_i + p_i$, these constraints can be transformed into the standardised form $S_i + p_i \leq S_j$ and $S_j - p_i \leq S_i$.

Figures 2.2 and 2.3 visualise the temporal constraints between a pair of activities i and j; the activities are shown as solid rectangles with a horizontal length corresponding to the processing time. Figure 2.2 shows a constraint $S_i + d_{ij} \leq S_j$ with a strictly positive time lag as a forward arc of length d_{ij} starting at time S_i; the constraint requires that j starts *at least* d_{ij} units of time after the start of i. The figure also shows a constraint $S_j + d_{ji} \leq S_i$ with strictly negative time lag as a backward arc of length d_{ji} starting at time S_j; this constraint requires that j starts *at most* d_{ji} units of time after the start of i. The constraints can also be visualised in the form shown in Figure 2.3, i.e., as time window of activity j relative to activity i, or vice versa. By changing the values of d_{ij} and d_{ji} the length of the "handles" shown in

Figure 2.3 can be adjusted and the size or position of the relative time window is changed. For simplicity, Figures 2.2 and 2.3 use only two activities for visualising minimal and maximal time lags. In general, the time lags may lead to cycles involving an arbitrary number of activities.

Many special cases of the problem $PS|temp|C_{max}$ do not allow for negative time lags and cyclic temporal constraints. In the terms of Figure 2.3 this corresponds to removing the right handle labelled d_{ji}.

Using the time window visualisation, it is easy to see that any of the thirteen possible relations shown in Figure 2.1 can either be selectively enforced or be admitted or ruled out by choosing suitable minimal and maximal time lags (and, of course, processing times).

The set of all temporal constraints can be visualised in an activity-on-node network or digraph $G(\mathcal{V}, \mathcal{E})$ with vertex set $\mathcal{V}$ and edge set $\mathcal{E}$ with edge weights d_{ij}, where minimal lags are usually represented as forward edges and maximal lags as backward edges[4]. The vertices of G correspond to the activities of the project, and there are edges between any two activities (vertices) i and j that are linked by a precedence constraint $(i, j) \in \mathcal{E}$. Frequently, two fictitious activities 0 and $n + 1$ that represent the start and end of a project are added as source and sink of the network, with edges from the source to all real activities and from all real activities to the sink, with edge weights $d_{0,i} = 0$ and $d_{i,n+1} = p_i$, for $i = 1, \ldots, n$. For the remainder of this section we will assume that G contains the fictitious start and end activities.

A *time feasible* schedule, i.e., one that satisfies all temporal constraints, is an assignment of non-negative numbers to the activity start times $S_1, \ldots, S_n$, or, equivalently, to the vertices of G, such that

$$S_i + d_{ij} \leq S_j, \quad \forall (i, j) \in \mathcal{E}. \tag{2.3}$$

The numbers fulfilling (2.3) are also called *potentials* in graph theory (Berge 1985), and there is a well developed theory about them that also forms the basis of the Metra-Potential-Method (MPM) for project networks (Roy 1962), which deals with start-start time lags and also covers the temporal constraints of the model discussed here.

It is well known that there exists a time feasible schedule (a potential for G) iff G has no directed circle of positive length (Bartusch et al. 1988). Such a cycle would correspond to a logical contradiction in the temporal constraints. For example, consider a cycle involving only two activities that is formed by the constraints $S_i + 3 \leq S_j$ and $S_j - 2 \leq S_i$; the length of the cycle is 1; while the first constraint requires that activity j starts at least 3 units of time after i, the second constraint demands that i starts at most 2 units before j.

The existence of a time feasible schedule can be tested by computing the unique component-wise minimum solution of (2.3), which gives the earliest possible starting

---

[4]For all graph theoretic notions not defined here see Lawler (1976). For an introduction to network representations of projects see Elmaghraby (1977).

times. This schedule, which is usually not resource feasible, is also called the *earliest start* schedule. The earliest start schedule can be efficiently computed by standard graph algorithms, e.g. with effort $0(n^3)$ by the Floyd-Warshall Algorithm (Lawler 1976). Alternatively, the earliest start schedule can be derived through constraint propagation, as shall be explained in the following chapters.

2.1.3 The Model

The problem $PS|temp|C_{max}$ can now conceptually be stated as follows:

$$
\begin{array}{lll}
\min\{\max_{i\in V}\{S_i + p_i\}\} & \text{s.t.} & (i)\\
S_i + d_{ij} \le S_j, & \forall (i,j) \in \mathcal{E}, & (ii)\\
\sum_{i\in V(t)} r_{ik} \le R_k, & \forall t \in \mathbb{N}_0, \forall k \in \mathcal{R}, & (iii)\\
S_i \in \mathbb{N}_0, & \forall i \in V. & (iv)
\end{array}
$$

A schedule $S = (S_1, \ldots, S_n)$ is an assignment of all activity start times. S is *feasible* if it satisfies all precedence constraints (ii) and resource constraints (iii). Reformulating the problem, the task is to find a feasible schedule with minimal makespan.

There are several other ways of formally modelling the problem $PS|temp|C_{max}$ that mainly differ in the way how resource constraints are represented. Many formulations have originally been proposed for the problem $PS|prec|C_{max}$, i.e., the extensively studied variant of the problem $PS|temp|C_{max}$ where all time lags d_{ij} are equal to the activity processing times p_i.

The formulations are frequently based on using *time indexed* binary decision variables x_{it} that take the value one if an activity $i \in V$ finishes in (or is processed in, or starts before, etc.) period t and zero otherwise. The first formulation of this type for the problem $PS|prec|C_{max}$ has been described by Pritsker et al. (1969).

Other formulations are based on the concept of using forbidden sets (Bartusch et al. 1988) to represent the resource constraints. A *forbidden set* of activities is a set $N \subseteq V$ for which

$$
\sum_{i\in N} r_{ik} > R_k, \qquad \text{for some } k \in \mathcal{R}. \tag{2.4}
$$

Condition (2.4) is the negation of (2.1); it is time independent due to the constant resource demands and supplies. Given a set $\mathcal{N}$ of all forbidden sets, a schedule S is resource feasible iff no set $N \in \mathcal{N}$ is scheduled simultaneously in any period t. A disadvantage of the description by forbidden sets is the fact that the number of required (minimal) forbidden sets may grow exponentially with the problem size, although it seems that for many applications this does not cause problems (Stork and Uetz 2000).

Forbidden set formulations have been used, e.g., by Bartusch et al. (1988) and by Alvarez-Valdes and Tamarit (1993). A formulation based on the complementary concept of *compatible sets* of activities has been proposed by Mingozzi et al. (1998).

2.1.4   Schedules and Performance Measures

A schedule $S = (S_1, \ldots, S_n)$ is an assignment of all activity start times. The quality of a schedule is usually measured by a cost or utility function $\kappa : \mathbb{R}^n \to \mathbb{R}$ that transforms the vector of start or completion times onto a one-dimensional scale. The makespan function $C_{\max} := \kappa(S) := \max_{i \in \mathcal{V}} S_i + p_i$ is an example of such a transformation.

When comparing two schedules S and S' we say that $S \leq S'$ if no activity in S starts later than in S':

$$S \leq S' \quad \Longleftrightarrow \quad \forall i \in \mathcal{V} : S_i \leq S_i{}'.$$

Further, $S < S'$ if $S \leq S'$ and additionally at least one activity in S starts earlier:

$$S < S' \quad \Longleftrightarrow \quad S \leq S' \wedge \exists i \in \mathcal{V} : S_i < S_i{}'.$$

A schedule S is *active* if it is feasible and if there exists no other feasible schedule S' such that $S' < S$. In other words, S is active, if no activity can be started earlier without violating either one of the precedence or resource constraints. If a schedule S is not active and some activity i can therefore be started earlier than at time S_i, then we say for short that i can be *left-shifted* in S.

A detailed discussion of active schedules and the related concepts of semi-active and non-delay schedules in the context of project scheduling is given by Sprecher et al. (1995).

The definition of active schedules immediately leads to the following simple and well known observation: any solution method which minimises the makespan function can refrain from generating non-active schedules, since there always exists a corresponding active schedule with a lower or identical makespan. We shall exploit this observation in the branch-and-bound procedure developed in Chapter 5.

The observation can be generalised for the class of *regular measures of performance* (Conway et al. 1967) which is defined as the class of all objective functions that are non-decreasing with respect to the component-wise ordering of $\mathbb{R}^n$, i.e., for which

$$S \leq S' \quad \Longrightarrow \quad f(S) \leq f(S').$$

Regular measures of performance cover the standard objective functions used in scheduling such as makespan, weighted flowtime, or tardiness costs. The condition is general enough to allow for many cost terms that occur in practical applications.

2.1.5 Domains of Decision Variables

We will now introduce the concept of domains of decision variables, which will prove useful in the following chapters. Each activity start time variable S_i has a *current domain* $\Delta_{S_i} \subseteq \mathbb{N}_0$ of possible values. Because the activity start times are the only decision variables in the single-mode model, we will also use the shorter notation Δ_i instead of Δ_{S_i} when no confusion is possible and simply speak of the domain of activity i; we shall use the explicit notation when dealing with multi-mode models. We will later assume that some real or hypothetical upper bound UB on the optimal makespan is known or given, so that even $\Delta_i \subseteq [0, UB - p_i]$ holds. This is necessary, since most of the constraint propagation methods that will be applied can only deduce a domain reduction if the current domains are finite. If no initial upper bound is given we use the trivial upper bound

$$\sum_{i \in \mathcal{V}} \max\{p_i, \max_{(i,j) \in \mathcal{E}} d_{ij}\}.$$

The set of current domains of all activities is denoted with $\Delta := \{\Delta_i \mid i \in \mathcal{V}\}$. For an activity $i \in \mathcal{V}$, $ES_i(\Delta) := \min \Delta_i$ is the earliest start time, $LS_i(\Delta) := \max \Delta_i$ the latest start time, $EC_i(\Delta) := ES_i(\Delta) + p_i$ the earliest completion time and $LC_i(\Delta) := LS_i(\Delta) + p_i$ the latest completion time of i. If no confusion is possible, then we will write ES_i, LS_i, etc., for short.

A schedule S is called *domain feasible* with respect to a set Δ of current domains if the current domain of each activity still contains the start time of this activity in S, i.e., if we can arrive at S by repeatedly reducing the current domains.

Given a set Δ of current domains, the set of all activities $\mathcal{V}$ can be naturally partitioned into a set of *scheduled* and non-scheduled, or *free*, activities. Clearly, if the current domain of an activity i contains exactly one entry, then i must start at that time and can be considered as scheduled. Hence

$$\mathcal{V}^s(\Delta) := \{i \in \mathcal{V} \mid |\Delta_i| = 1\}$$

is the set of scheduled activities, and

$$\mathcal{V}^f(\Delta) := \{i \in \mathcal{V} \mid |\Delta_i| > 1\}$$

is the set of free activities. For all scheduled activities $i \in \mathcal{V}^s(\Delta)$, the start time is defined through $S_i(\Delta) := ES_i(\Delta) = LS_i(\Delta)$.

2.1.6 Special Cases

The general problem $PS|temp|C_{max}$ contains several special cases that are obtained if the admissible precedence constraints are restricted in certain ways or if the resource supply takes a special form.

A first class of simple problems is obtained if the resource constraints are relaxed, i.e., if resource supply is unlimited. This first leads to a (resource-un-constrained) project scheduling problem with generalised precedence constraints, a problem that is addressed by the well known Metra-Potential Method (MPM) for the temporal analysis of project networks. The problem covered by the famous Critical Path Method (CPM) is obtained if, additionally, only simple precedence constraints are allowed, i.e., if the time lags d_{ij} between a pair of activities i and j are equal to the processing time of the preceding activity i: $d_{ij} = p_i, \forall (i, j) \in \mathcal{E}$.

In contrast to the simple problems with unlimited resource supply, problems with resource constraints are generally difficult to solve.

One of the best studied special cases of the problem $PS|temp|C_{max}$ is the classic RCPSP with simple precedence constraints, i.e., the problem $PS|prec|C_{max}$, which generalises the problem covered by the CPM method by adding resource constraints.

It has been shown that several seemingly unrelated optimisation problems can be formulated as instances of the problem $PS|prec|C_{max}$. Examples include the bin packing (Garey et al. 1976) and the assembly line balancing problem (Elmaghraby 1977, Sprecher 1994). The relation of the multi-mode problem $MPS|prec|C_{max}$ to the knapsack packing problem as well as to two- and three-dimensional packing and cutting problems has been discussed by Hartmann (1999).

The problem $PS|prec|C_{max}$ with ordinary precedence constraints is in turn a generalisation of several well known, difficult optimisation problems studied in *machine scheduling*, where unary, or disjunctive, resources are considered. Examples include shop scheduling problems such as the job shop, flow shop, and open shop problems (Błażewicz et al. 2001) as well as many other, more special problems. We will see in the following chapters that some solution techniques originally developed for shop scheduling can be successfully applied for solving project scheduling problems.

A special problem that has been called Generalised RCPSP (Demeulemeester and Herroelen 1997a, Klein 2000b) is obtained if the RCPSP is extended by allowing for arbitrary minimal time lags, combined with the assumption that the precedence constraints are acyclic.[5]

2.2   Extension to Multiple Execution Modes

2.2.1   Modes

In *multi-mode scheduling*, an activity may be processed in one of multiple possible execution modes, which differ with respect to the necessary processing time and the resource requirements. Furthermore, the time lag between a pair of activities may

---

[5]The fact that time lags of value zero are legal would otherwise allow for cycles of length zero, corresponding to a synchronisation of start times; this would slightly complicate the design of enumeration schemes.

vary depending on the chosen mode. The modes reflect tradeoffs between required processing time and resource consumption on the one hand as well as tradeoffs between the consumption of different types of resources on the other hand; additionally the time lags between activities may vary depending on the chosen modes.

The mode M_i in which an activity $i \in V$ is processed thus becomes an additional decision variable, which can take values from the associated set $\mathcal{M}_i$ of all admissible modes. The current domain of M_i is denoted with Δ_{M_i}, and initially $\Delta_{M_i} = \mathcal{M}_i$.

As the processing time and resource requirements of an activity now depend on the chosen mode, they are indexed accordingly: $p_{i\mu}$ is the time required for processing activity i in mode $\mu \in \mathcal{M}_i$, and $r_{i\mu k}$ is the amount of resource $k \in \mathcal{R}$ needed for executing activity i in mode μ. The mode dependent time lag that must pass between the start of two activities $i, j \in V$ if i is performed in mode $\mu \in \mathcal{M}_i$ and j in mode $\nu \in \mathcal{M}_j$ is denoted with $d_{i\mu j\nu}$.

The initial mode domain of an activity can be reduced by removing inefficient modes. In multi-mode models with simple finish-start precedence constraints, a mode is called *inefficient* if its processing time is not shorter and its resource requirement is not less than that of another mode of the same activity. If generalised precedence constraints are allowed, this condition must be strengthened by additionally considering the mode-dependent time lags: A mode $\mu \in \Delta_{M_i}$ of activity i is inefficient if its processing time is not shorter and its resource requirement is not less than that of another mode of i *and* if the time lags $d_{i\mu j\nu}$ and $d_{j\nu i\mu}$ associated with mode μ and activity i are not less than for another mode of i, for all $j \in V$, for which $(i, j) \in \mathcal{E}$ or $(j, i) \in \mathcal{E}$, and all $\nu \in \Delta_{M_j}$.

2.2.2 Resources

In multi-mode project scheduling it is common practice to distinguish between *renewable* and *non-renewable* resources, as originally proposed by Slowinski (1980) and Węglarz (1981).

So far, we have only introduced *renewable* resources, which are constrained on a per period basis. The required number of units of a renewable resource are assigned to an activity during its processing; upon completion of the activity, the resource units are released again and are then available for processing other activities. Examples of renewable resources include manpower and machines.

Non-renewable resources are globally constrained for the entire planning horizon. In contrast to renewable resources, they are consumed by processing an activity and cannot be reused. Money is an example for a non-renewable resource. Non-renewable resources can thus be used to model budget constraints for a project. A non-renewable resource is *redundant* and may be removed if the mode-dependent maximal total demand for the resource is at most equal to the resource supply. Non-renewable resources need only be considered in multi-mode problems as they must always be redundant in instances of single-mode problems (or the problem instance does not have a solution).

Resources that are constrained per period as well as for the entire project are called *doubly constrained*. A doubly constrained resource can be modelled by introducing a renewable and a non-renewable resource.

Another type of resource that allows to model resource supply restrictions for a sub-set of periods and that is called *partially renewable* has recently been proposed by Böttcher et al. (1999).

In the following we will distinguish between the set $\mathcal{R}^\rho$ of renewable and the set $\mathcal{R}^\nu$ of non-renewable resources, i.e., $\mathcal{R} = \mathcal{R}^\rho \cup \mathcal{R}^\nu$, and denote the supply of a renewable (non-renewable) resource $k \in \mathcal{R}$ with R_k^ρ (R_k^ν).

2.2.3 The Model

The problem $MPS|temp|C_{max}$ can now conceptually be stated as follows:

$$
\begin{array}{lll}
\min\{\max_{i\in\mathcal{V}}\{S_i + p_{iM_i}\}\} & \text{s.t.} & (i) \\
S_i + d_{iM_i jM_j} \leq S_j, & \forall(i,j) \in \mathcal{E}, & (ii) \\
\sum_{i\in\mathcal{V}(t)} r_{iM_i k} \leq R_k^\rho, & \forall t \in \mathbb{N}_0, \forall k \in \mathcal{R}^\rho, & (iii) \\
\sum_{i\in\mathcal{V}} r_{iM_i k} \leq R_k^\nu, & \forall t \in \mathbb{N}_0, \forall k \in \mathcal{R}^\nu, & (iv) \\
S_i \in \mathbb{N}_0, & \forall i \in \mathcal{V}. & (v) \\
M_i \in \mathcal{M}_i, & \forall i \in \mathcal{V}. & (vi)
\end{array}
$$

A schedule $(S, M) = (S_1, \dots, S_n, M_1, \dots, M_n)$ is an assignment of all activity start times and modes. (S, M) is *feasible* if it satisfies all precedence constraints (ii) and constraints for renewable (iii) and non-renewable (iv) resources.

The multi-mode project scheduling problem $MPS|temp|C_{max}$ can be conceptually divided into two sub-problems. The *mode assignment problem* consists of finding a mode vector that satisfies constraints (iv) and (vi); it is NP-complete for problems with at least two non-renewable resources (Kolisch 1995). Given a mode-assignment, the *scheduling sub-problem* defined by (i) – (iii) and (v) is of the type $PS|temp|C_{max}$.

Chapter 3

Constraint Propagation

The branch-and-bound algorithms that will be developed in the following chapters rely to a great extent on efficient constraint propagation techniques. Constraint propagation is a problem reduction technique that transforms problems into equivalent problems that are hopefully easier to solve. The basic idea is to reduce the search space of a problem instance through the repeated analysis and evaluation of variables, their domains, and the interdependence between the variables that is induced by the set of constraints. The goal is to detect and remove inconsistent assignments that cannot participate in any feasible solution. A whole theory is devoted to the definition of different concepts of consistency, which may serve as a theoretical background for the propagation techniques that we will employ. This theory has been developed for the *constraint satisfaction problem* (CSP) or *constraint optimisation problem* (COP); the project scheduling problems examined in this work can be understood as special subclasses of the CSP or COP.

In this chapter we shall introduce the standard CSP and COP and the important concepts related to it. Section 3.1 gives a short introduction to these problem classes; Section 3.2 then describes different concepts of consistency, and Section 3.3 addresses consistency checking algorithms. Section 3.4 points to some software systems and languages that have been developed based on concepts from CSP research and help in the formulation and solution of CSPs.

3.1 Constraint Satisfaction and Optimisation

A CSP is composed of a finite set of *variables*, each of which is associated with a finite *domain*, and a set of *constraints* that restrict the values that the variables can simultaneously take. The task is to assign a value from its domain to each variable so that all constraints are satisfied. The COP additionally requires that the solution optimises some objective function. The problem $PS|temp|C_{max}$ introduced in Chapter 2 is an example of a COP. Any COP can be transformed into a related CSP by replacing the objective function with a constraint on the objective value. By repeatedly restricting the value, e.g. through bi-section over the interval defined by a bound on the objective function value and an initial guess for the optimal value, a COP can be solved by repeatedly solving related CSPs.

The CSP was first formalised and studied by Huffman (1971), Clowes (1971) and Waltz (1975) in vision research for solving line-labelling problems. Haralick and Shapiro (1979, 1980) and Mackworth (1992) discuss general algorithms and applications of CSP solving. Hentenryck (1992) and Cohen (1990) tackle the CSP from a constraint logic programming viewpoint. Comprehensive introductions to the CSP are provided by Meseguer (1989), Kumar (1992) and Dorndorf et al. (2000b). An exhaustive overview of the theory of constraint satisfaction and optimisation is given by Tsang (1993). We will only present the necessary aspects and start with some basic definitions.

The finite *domain* of a variable is the set of all values that can be assigned to the variable. For many interesting problems, the assumption that the domains are finite is not a serious restriction. For example, for the project scheduling problems introduced in Chapter 2 the domains of the start and completion times can easily be made finite by imposing a bound on the makespan. The domain associated with the variable x is denoted with Δ_x. If $V = \{x_1, \ldots, x_n\}$ is a set of variables and $\Delta = \{\Delta_{x_1}, \ldots, \Delta_{x_n}\}$ the set of their domains, then an *assignment* $a = (a_1, \ldots, a_n)$ is an element of the Cartesian product $\Delta_{x_1} \times \ldots \times \Delta_{x_n}$; in other words, an assignment instantiates each variable x_i with a value $a_i \in \Delta_{x_i}$ from its domain.

A *constraint* c on Δ is a function $c : \Delta_{x_{i_1}} \times \ldots \times \Delta_{x_{i_k}} \to \{\text{true, false}\}$, where $V' := \{x_{i_1}, \ldots, x_{i_k}\}$ is a non empty set of variables. The cardinality $|V'|$ is also called the *arity* of c. If $|V'| = 1$ or $|V'| = 2$ then we speak of unary and binary constraints, respectively. An assignment $a \in \Delta_{x_1} \times \ldots \times \Delta_{x_n}$ satisfies c if $c(a_{i_1}, \ldots, a_{i_k}) = \text{true}$.

Given a set of current domains Δ, a constraint is called *resolved* if it is satisfied for all assignments $a \in \Delta_{x_1} \times \ldots \times \Delta_{x_n}$, otherwise it is (still) *unresolved*.

3.1.1   The Constraint Satisfaction Problem

An instance P of the *constraint satisfaction problem* (CSP) is defined by a tuple $P = (V, \Delta, C)$, where V is a finite set of variables, Δ the set of associated domains and C a finite set of constraints on Δ. An assignment a is *feasible* if it satisfies all constraints in C. A feasible assignment is also called a *solution* of P. We denote with $\mathcal{F}(P)$ the set of all feasible assignments (solutions) of P.

Given an instance P of the CSP, the associated task is to find a solution $a \in \mathcal{F}(P)$ or to prove that P has no solution.

The goal of constraint propagation is to transform a problem P into a reduced but equivalent problem P' that is easier to solve. The reduced problem P' usually differs from P in the sense that the variable domains are reduced or that new, redundant constraints, which may help in deducing future domain reductions, have been added. Problem reduction is an iterative process; we will generally assume that Δ and $\mathcal{C}$ refer to the *current* domain set and constraint set of the current reduced problem. Whenever we must explicitly refer to the original domain set and constraint set in $\mathcal{P}$ to avoid confusion, we will use the notation Δ^0 and $\mathcal{C}^0$.

3.1.2 The Constraint Optimisation Problem

As distinguished from the constraint satisfaction problem, the constraint optimisation problem searches for a solution which optimises a given objective function. We will only consider the case of minimisation, as maximisation can be handled symmetrically.

An instance of the *constraint optimisation problem* (COP) is defined by a tuple $\mathcal{P} = (\mathcal{V}, \Delta, \mathcal{C}, z)$, where $(\mathcal{V}, \Delta, \mathcal{C})$ is an instance of the CSP and z an objective function $z : \Delta_{x_1} \times \ldots \times \Delta_{x_n} \to \mathbb{R}$. Defining

$$z_{min}(\mathcal{P}) := \begin{cases} \min_{b \in \mathcal{F}(\mathcal{P})} z(b) & \mathcal{F}(\mathcal{P}) \neq \emptyset, \\ \infty & \text{otherwise,} \end{cases}$$

an assignment a is called an *optimal solution* of $\mathcal{P}$ if a is feasible and $z(a) = z_{min}(\mathcal{P})$.

Given an instance $\mathcal{P}$ of the COP, the associated task is to find an optimal solution of $\mathcal{P}$ and to determine $z_{min}(\mathcal{P})$.

The project scheduling problems introduced in Chapter 2 can be seen as special COPs.

It is not hard to see that the CSP and the COP are intractable and belong to the class of NP-hard problems. For a more detailed discussion, which exceeds our needs, we refer to Garey and Johnson (1979) or Tsang (1993).

3.1.3 Constraint Graphs

An instance of the CSP can be represented by means of a *constraint graph* which visualises the interdependencies between variables that are induced by the constraints. If we restrict our attention to unary and binary constraints then the definition of a constraint graph $\mathcal{G}$ is quite straightforward. The vertex set of $\mathcal{G}$ corresponds to the set of all variables $\mathcal{V}$, while the edge set is defined as follows: two vertices $x_i, x_j \in \mathcal{V}$, $i \neq j$, are connected by an undirected edge if there exists a constraint $c(x_i, x_j) \in \mathcal{C}$. This can be generalised to constraints of arbitrary arity using the concept of hypergraphs (Tsang 1993).

For a resource-*un*-constrained project scheduling problem that contains only precedence constraints the constraint graph of the problem has the same structure as the activity-on-node precedence network but is undirected.

3.2 Concepts of Consistency

As the domains of a CSP instance $\mathcal{P}$ are finite, $\mathcal{P}$ can in principle be solved by a simple generate-and-test algorithm that enumerates all assignments $a \in \Delta_{x_1} \times \ldots \times \Delta_{x_n}$, verifies whether a satisfies all constraints $c \in \mathcal{C}$, and stops if the answer is "yes". The COP can be solved by enumerating all feasible assignments and storing the one with minimal objective function value.

Of course, this method is not practicable due to the size of the search space which grows exponentially with the number of variables. In the worst case, all assignments of a CSP instance have to be tested which cannot be carried out efficiently except for problem instances too small to be of any practical value. It is thus worth to look for methods that can reduce the search space prior to starting (or during) the search process.

One such method of search space reduction which only makes use of simple inference mechanisms and which is not problem specific is known as *constraint propagation*. The origins of constraint propagation go back to Waltz (1972) who almost three decades ago developed a now well-known filtering algorithm for labelling three-dimensional line diagrams.

The basic idea of constraint propagation is to make implicit constraints more visible through the repeated analysis and evaluation of the variables, domains and constraints describing a specific problem instance. This makes it possible to detect and remove *inconsistent* variable assignments that cannot participate in any solution by a merely partial problem analysis.

Over the years, different concepts of *consistency* have been developed that allow to identify inconsistent assignments. In this context, the term consistency with regard to certain properties must be understood in the following way: variable assignments, whose presence would cause these properties to be false, have been ruled out. The different types of consistency guarantee different properties. Roughly speaking, a concept of consistency defines the maximal search space reduction that is possible regarding some specific properties. It is worth pointing out that the term consistency as used here is neither a necessary nor a sufficient condition for a problem to be solvable.

3.2.1 k-Consistency

The first concepts of consistency have been formalised by Montanari (1974) who introduced *node-*, *arc-* and *path-consistency*. Roughly speaking, these concepts are based on the examination of constraints containing k variables, where $k = 1, 2, 3$, with their names being derived from the presentation of a CSP instance as a constraint graph. These concepts have been generalised by Freuder (1978) to the notion of k-*consistency*. We will describe the basic ideas of k-consistency in an informal way; a detailed analysis is given by Tsang (1993).

In order to define k-consistency we have to introduce the notion of k-*feasibility*. Let $a = (a_1, \ldots, a_n)$ be an assignment of a given CSP instance. A partial assignment of k variables $(a_{i_1}, \ldots, a_{i_k})$ is k-*feasible* iff it satisfies all constraints which at most contain these variables[1]. The motivation of the definition of of k-consistency is based on the following observation: a can only be feasible if, for a given k, any partial assignment $(a_{i_1}, \ldots, a_{i_k})$ is k-feasible. Inversely, any partial assignment of k variables that is not feasible is not interesting and hints at an inconsistent state.

In the words of Freuder (1978), k-*consistency* is established if, for any $(k - 1)$-feasible assignment of a set of $k - 1$ variables (taken from a set $\Delta_{x_{i_1}} \times \ldots \times \Delta_{x_{i_{k-1}}}$) and any choice of a k-th variable, there exists an assignment of the k-th variable (taken from the set Δ_{x_k}) such that the assignment of the k variables taken together is k-feasible.

It is tempting to believe that k-consistency as defined above implies $(k - 1)$-consistency, but, as Freuder (1982) has pointed out, a CSP which is k-consistent needs not be $(k - 1)$-consistent. This can be seen by observing that k-consistency only requires that any $(k - 1)$-feasible assignment can always be extended to a k-th variable such that the assignment of all k variables is k-feasible; however this does not rule out the possible existence of $(k - 1)$-infeasible assignments. In view of this weakness, Freuder (1982) has introduced the concept of *strong k-consistency*, which additionally requires j-consistency for $1 \leq j \leq k$.

The property of k-consistency is always relative to the sets of possible assignments $\Delta_{x_{i_1}} \times \ldots \times \Delta_{x_{i_{k-1}}}$ and $\Delta_{x_{i_k}}$. To establish k-consistency, starting from an inconsistent state, thus implicitly requires a $(k - 1)$-dimensional administration of these sets. In the beginning, the sets contain all assignments; inconsistent assignments, i.e., tuples $(a_{i_1}, \ldots, a_{i_k - 1})$, are then eventually discarded until k-consistency is reached.

1-consistency is quite easy to achieve: if $x_i \in V$ is a variable and $c(x_i)$ a unary constraint then all assignments $a_i \in \Delta_{x_i}$ for which $c(a_i) = \text{false}$ are removed. In order to establish 2-consistency, pairs of variables $x_i, x_j \in V$ and binary constraints $c(x_i, x_j)$ have to be examined: an assignment $a_i \in \Delta_{x_i}$ can be removed if $c(a_i, a_j) = \text{false}$ for all $a_j \in \Delta_{x_j}$. Analogously, 3-consistency requires the examination of triples of variables $x_i, x_j, x_k \in V$ and removes pairs of assignments $(a_i, a_j) \in \Delta_{x_i} \times \Delta_{x_j}$, etc. As already mentioned, 1- and 2-consistency coincide with the notions of node- and arc-consistency, whereas 2- and 3-consistency taken together are equivalent to path-consistency (Tsang 1993). 1-, 2- and 3-consistency have also been summarised under the name of *lower-level* consistency as opposed to *higher-level* consistency, since only small subsets of variables, domains and constraints are evaluated simultaneously.

An optimal algorithm for achieving k-consistency has been described by Cooper (1989). The algorithm requires testing all subsets of $(k - 1)$-feasible assignments

---

[1] k-feasibility depends on the chosen set of variables. We therefore assume that a partial assignment always identifies the corresponding set of variables.

which is only practicable for small values of k. We therefore describe two weaker concepts of consistency.

3.2.2 Domain-Consistency

The first concept is based on only storing the 1-dimensional sets Δ_{x_i} for all variables $x_i \in V$. For reasons near at hand, Δ_{x_i} is also called the *current domain* of x_i. Intuitively, we can at most discard all values $a_i \in \Delta_{x_i}$ for which there exist no assignments $a_j \in \Delta_{x_j}, j \neq i$, such that $(a_1, \ldots, a_i, \ldots, a_n)$ is feasible. Alternatively, the feasibility condition can be replaced with the sufficient condition of k-feasibility which leads to a lower level of consistency. We refer to this concept of consistency as *domain-consistency* or *k-d-consistency*. Domain-consistency has been used, among others, by Nuijten (1994).

Formally, k-d-consistency for a CSP instance $\mathcal{P} = (V, \Delta, C)$ can be defined as follows:

1. The set of current domains Δ is *k-d-consistent* for $1 \leq k \leq n$ if, for all subsets $V' := \{x_{i_1}, \ldots, x_{i_{k-1}}\}$ of $k - 1$ variables and any k-th variable $x_{i_k} \notin V'$, the following condition holds:

$$\forall a_{i_k} \in \Delta_{x_{i_k}},$$
$$\exists a_{i_1} \in \Delta_{x_{i_1}}, \ldots, \exists a_{i_{k-1}} \in \Delta_{x_{i_{k-1}}} : (a_{i_1}, \ldots, a_{i_k}) \text{ is } k\text{-feasible.}$$

2. The set of current domains Δ is *strongly k-d-consistent* for $1 \leq k \leq n$ if Δ is k'-d-consistent for all $1 \leq k' \leq k$.

The following naive algorithm establishes k-d-consistency: start with $\Delta_{x_i} := \Delta^0_{x_i}$ for all $x_i \in V$; choose a variable x_{i_k} and an assignment $a_{i_k} \in \Delta_{x_{i_k}}$; test whether there exists a subset of $k-1$ variables $V' := \{x_{i_1}, \ldots, x_{i_{k-1}}\}$ which does not contain x_{i_k}, so that $(a_{i_1}, \ldots, a_{i_{k-1}}, a_{i_k})$ is not k-feasible for all $a_{i_1} \in \Delta_{x_{i_1}}, \ldots, a_{i_{k-1}} \in \Delta_{x_{i_{k-1}}}$; if the answer is "yes" then remove the assignment a_{i_k} from $\Delta_{x_{i_k}}$; repeat this process with other assignments and/or variables until no more domain reductions are possible.

We did not yet discuss how to establish n-d-consistency other than to apply the naive algorithm, so an important question is whether there exists an efficient implementation after all. Before we deal with this issue, however, we will first present another concept of consistency.

3.2.3 Bound Consistency

Storing all values of the current domains $\Delta_{x_1}, \ldots, \Delta_{x_n}$ still might be too costly. An interval oriented encoding of Δ_{x_i} provides an alternative if Δ_{x_i} is totally ordered, for instance, if $\Delta_{x_i} \subseteq \mathbb{N}_0$. In this case, we can identify Δ_{x_i} with the interval $[l_i, r_i] := \{l_i, l_i + 1, \ldots, r_i - 1, r_i\}$, so that only the "left" and "right" bounds of Δ_{x_i} have to be stored. Therefore, this concept of consistency is usually referred to as *bound-consistency* or *k-b-consistency*. Bound-consistency has been discussed, among others, by Moore (1966), Davis (1987), van Beek (1992) and Lhomme (1993).

Formally, k-b-consistency for a CSP instance $\mathcal{P} = (\mathcal{V}, \Delta, \mathcal{C})$ can be defined as follows:

1. The set of current domains Δ is *k-b-consistent* for $1 \leq k \leq n$ if, for all subsets $\mathcal{V}' := \{x_{i_1}, \ldots, x_{i_{k-1}}\}$ of $k - 1$ variables and any k-th variable $x_{i_k} \notin \mathcal{V}'$, the following condition holds:

$$\forall a_{i_k} \in \{l_{i_k}, r_{i_k}\},$$
$$\exists a_{i_1} \in \Delta_{x_{i_1}}, \ldots, \exists a_{i_{k-1}} \in \Delta_{x_{i_{k-1}}} : (a_{i_1}, \ldots, a_{i_k}) \text{ is } k\text{-feasible.}$$

2. The set of current domains Δ is *strongly k-b-consistent* for $1 \leq k \leq n$ if Δ is k'-b-consistent for all $1 \leq k' \leq k$.

A naive algorithm for establishing k-b-consistency is obtained by slightly modifying the naive k-d-consistency algorithm: instead of choosing $a_{i_k} \in \Delta_{x_{i_k}}$, we may only choose (and remove) $a_{i_k} \in \{l_{i_k}, r_{i_k}\}$.

As a negative side effect, only the bounds l_i and r_i, but no intermediate value $l_i < a_i < r_i$ can be discarded except if, due to the repeated removal of other assignments, a_i eventually becomes the left or right bound of the current domain. Bound-consistency therefore is a weaker concept than domain-consistency. However, establishing n-b-consistency for the CSP still is an NP-hard problem.

3.3 Consistency Checking

In general, establishing k-consistency is ruled out due to the complex data structures that are necessary for the administration of the k-feasible subsets. In the last subsection we have further seen that establishing the weaker n-d- or n-b-consistency still is an NP-hard problem. Consequently, using constraint propagation in order to solve the CSP is only sensible if we content ourselves with approximations of the concepts of consistency that have been introduced.

An important task is to derive simple rules which lead to efficient search space reductions, but at the same time can be implemented efficiently with a low polynomial time complexity. These rules are called *consistency tests*.

3.3.1 Consistency Tests

Consistency tests are generally described through a condition–instruction pair $\mathcal{A}$ and $\mathcal{B}$. Intuitively, the semantic of a consistency test is as follows: whenever condition $\mathcal{A}$

is satisfied, $\mathcal{B}$ has to be executed. $\mathcal{A}$ may be, for instance, an equation or inequation, while $\mathcal{B}$ may be a domain reduction rule. We will often use the shorthand notation $\mathcal{A} \Longrightarrow \mathcal{B}$ for consistency tests.

Example 1. (Consistency Tests)
Let us derive a simple consistency test for the constraint $x_1 - 6 \leq x_2$. Given an assignment a_1 of x_1, we can remove a_1 from Δ_{x_1} if there exists no assignment $a_2 \in \Delta_{x_2}$ satisfying $a_1 - 6 \leq a_2$. However, we do not really have to test all assignments in Δ_{x_2}, because if the constraint is not satisfied for $a_2 = \max \Delta_{x_2}$ then it is not satisfied for any other assignment in Δ_{x_2} and vice versa. Hence, for any $a_1 \in \Delta_{x_1}$,

$$a_1 - 6 > \max \Delta_{x_2} \Longrightarrow \Delta_{x_1} := \Delta_{x_1} \setminus \{a_1\}$$

defines a consistency test.   □

Of course, this example is quite simple and it may not seem clear whether any advantages can be drawn from such elementary deductions. Surprisingly, however, an analogously simple analysis will allow us to derive powerful consistency tests, as we will see in the following chapters.

Consistency tests lead to the deduction of additional constraints. Frequently, though not necessarily, the newly discovered constraints are unary and allow to directly reduce individual variable domains and can thus be stated in the form of a domain reduction rule, as in the example above. Consistency tests of this type are also called *domain consistency tests*.

Let us derive a formal definition of domain consistency tests. Let $\Theta := 2^{\Delta^0_{x_1}} \times \ldots \times 2^{\Delta^0_{x_n}}$, where $2^{\Delta^0_{x_i}}$ denotes the set of all subsets of $\Delta^0_{x_i}$. Given $\Delta, \Delta' \in \Theta$, that is, $\Delta = \{\Delta_{x_i} \mid x_i \in \mathcal{V}\}$ and $\Delta' = \{\Delta'_{x_i} \mid x_i \in \mathcal{V}\}$, we say that

1. $\Delta \subseteq \Delta'$ iff $\Delta_{x_i} \subseteq \Delta'_{x_i}$ for all $x_i \in \mathcal{V}$,

2. $\Delta \subsetneq \Delta'$ iff $\Delta \subseteq \Delta$, and there exists $x_i \in \mathcal{V}$, such that $\Delta_{x_i} \subsetneq \Delta'_{x_i}$.

Domain consistency tests have to satisfy two conditions. Firstly, current domains are either reduced or left unchanged. Secondly, only assignments $a_i \in \Delta_{x_i}$ are removed for which no feasible assignment $a = (a_1, \ldots, a_i, \ldots, a_n)$ exists. Since we do not need the second condition in the following examination, only the first one is formalised:

A *domain consistency test* γ is a function $\gamma : \Theta \to \Theta$ satisfying $\gamma(\Delta) \subseteq \Delta$ for all $\Delta \in \Theta$.

3.3.2 Consistency Checking Algorithms

Given a set of consistency tests, these tests have to be applied in an iterative fashion rather than only once in order to obtain the maximal domain reduction possible. The

---

Algorithm 1 Computing the fixed point $CP(\Delta)$

Require: Γ is a set of consistency tests.
  repeat
    $\Delta_{old} := \Delta$;
    for all $(\gamma \in \Gamma)$ **do**
      $\Delta := \gamma(\Delta)$;
    end for
  until $(\Delta = \Delta_{old})$.

---

reason for this is that, after reducing several domains, additional domain adjustments can possibly be derived using some of the tests which previously failed in deducing any reductions. Therefore, the reduction process is carried out until no more up-dates are possible. Algorithm 1 shows the basic reduction principle. Given a set of consistency tests Γ and a set of current domains Δ, the algorithm computes $CP(\Delta)$. Obviously, $CP(\Delta)$ is a fixed point. This point does not have to be unique and in general depends upon the order of the application of the consistency tests. However, we will only study consistency tests which result in a unique fixed point. These tests satisfy a monotony condition described below, which, as we will see, is sufficient for the uniqueness of the fixed point.

The major problem with Algorithm 1 is that the revision of even a single domain in some iteration forces all consistency tests to be re-applied for all variables in the next iteration, even though only a small number of constraints and variables are affected by this reduction. Variations of Algorithm 1 overcome this drawback by only applying the tests for those constraints and variables that are possibly affected by a previous revision.

Efficient algorithms for establishing 1-, 2- and 3-consistency and an analysis of their complexity have been presented, among others, by Montanari (1974), Mackworth (1977), Mackworth and Freuder (1985), Mohr and Henderson (1986), Dechter and Pearl (1988), Han and Lee (1988), Cooper (1989) and Van Hentenryck et al. (1992). Improved arc-consistency algorithms AC-6 and AC-7 have been presented by Bessière (1994) and Bessière et al. (1999). Chen (1999) has recently proposed a new arc-consistency algorithm, AC-8, which requires less computation time and space than AC-6 and AC-7. Cooper (1989) developed an optimal algorithm which achieves k-consistency for arbitrary k. Jeavons et al. (1998) have identified a number of constraint classes for which some fixed level of local consistency is sufficient to ensure global consistency. They characterise all possible constraint types for which strong k-consistency guarantees global consistency, for each $k \geq 2$. Other methods for solving the CSP through the sole application of constraint propagation (*solution synthesis*) have been proposed by Freuder (1978), Seidel (1981) and Tsang and Foster (1990). The deductive approach proposed by Bibel (1988) is closely related to solution synthesis.

The basic constraint propagation algorithm that is actually used in our implementations is a variant of the AC-5 arc-consistency algorithm described by Van Hentenryck et al. (1992). Like all improved consistency algorithms, it works with a queue containing elements to reconsider. A queue element consists of a constraint and a value (or a set of values) that has been removed from the domain of some variable appearing in the constraint and justifies the need to reconsider the constraint. In each iteration of the propagation algorithm, a constraint/value pair is removed from the queue and all consistency tests are evaluated that are associated with this constraint. If any of these tests removes a value a_i from a domain, say from Δ_{x_i}, then all constraints which contain the variable x_i and which are not yet resolved are stored in the queue, together with the information that a_i has been removed from Δ_{x_i}. This process is repeated until the queue is empty and the fixed point is reached. The reason for storing a value together with a constraint is that this may allow to use a more efficient algorithm in a consistency test.

Intuitively, each constraint/value pair can, and needs to, enter the queue only once, if at all, and the maximum number of elements enqueued and dequeued by the algorithm therefore depends on (1) the number of constraints and (2) the number of variables per constraint and their domain sizes. If $d := \max_{x_i \in \mathcal{V}} |\Delta_{x_i}|$ is the size of the largest domain, then we obtain at most $O(|\mathcal{C}| \cdot |\mathcal{V}| \, d)$ enqueueing and dequeueing operations, with $|\mathcal{V}|$ as an upper bound on the highest possible arity of a constraint. Given the number of queue operations, the overall worst case complexity of the propagation algorithm can then be deduced from the complexity of the consistency tests. It is worth mentioning that the worst case in terms of computational effort is also a best case in the sense that it corresponds to reducing the domains until all variables are instantiated; the average propagation effort is usually much lower.

3.3.3 Uniqueness of the Fixed Point

It is important to mention that the fixed point computed by the propagation algorithm does not have to be unique and usually depends upon the order of the application of the consistency tests. However, we will only study monotonous consistency tests for which the order of application does not affect the outcome of the domain reduction process. This result will be derived in the following (cf. Dorndorf et al. 2000b).

A consistency test γ is *monotonous* iff the following condition is satisfied:

$$\forall \Delta, \Delta' \in \Theta : \Delta \subseteq \Delta' \implies \gamma(\Delta) \subseteq \gamma(\Delta').$$

Let us first define the fixed point mentioned above. Let Γ be a set of monotonous domain consistency tests. For practical reasons we will always assume that Γ is finite. Let $\gamma_\infty = (\gamma_g)_{g \in \mathbb{N}} \in \Gamma^{\mathbb{N}}$ be a series of domain consistency tests in Γ, such that

$$\forall \gamma \in \Gamma, \forall h \in \mathbb{N}, \exists g > h : \gamma_g = \gamma. \tag{3.1}$$

The series γ_∞ determines the order of application of the consistency tests. The last condition ensures that every consistency test in Γ is (a priori) infinitely often applied. Starting with an arbitrary set Δ of current domains, we define the series of current domain sets $(\Delta_{(g)})_{g \in \mathbb{N}}$ induced by γ_∞ through the following recursive equation

$$\Delta_{(0)} := \Delta,$$
$$\Delta_{(g)} := \gamma_g(\Delta_{(g-1)}).$$

Since all domains Δ_{x_i} are finite and $\Delta_{(g)} \subseteq \Delta_{(g-1)}$ due to the definition of domain consistency tests, there obviously exists $g^* \in \mathbb{N}$, such that $\Delta_{(g)} = \Delta_{(g^*)}$ for all $g \geq g^*$. We can therefore define $\gamma_\infty(\Delta) := \Delta_{(g^*)}$. The next question to answer is whether $\gamma_\infty(\Delta)$ really depends on the chosen series γ_∞.

Theorem 1 (Unique Fixed Points). *If Γ is a set of monotonous domain consistency tests and $\gamma_\infty, \gamma'_\infty \in \Gamma^\mathbb{N}$ are series satisfying Condition (3.1) then $\gamma_\infty(\Delta) = \gamma'_\infty(\Delta)$.*

Proof. For reasons of symmetry we only have to show $\gamma_\infty(\Delta) \subseteq \gamma'_\infty(\Delta)$.

Let $(\Delta_{(g)})_{g \in \mathbb{N}}$ and $(\Delta'_{(g')})_{g' \in \mathbb{N}}$ be the series induced by γ_∞ and γ'_∞ respectively. It is sufficient to prove that for all $g' \in \mathbb{N}$, there exists $g \in \mathbb{N}$, such that $\Delta_{(g)} \subseteq \Delta'_{(g')}$. This simple proof will be carried out by induction.

The assertion is obviously true for $g' = 0$. If $g' > 0$, we have $\Delta'_{(g')} = \gamma'_{g'}(\Delta'_{(g'-1)})$. By the induction hypothesis, there exists $h \in \mathbb{N}$, such that $\Delta_{(h)} \subseteq \Delta'_{(g'-1)}$. Further, Condition (3.1) implies that there exists $g > h$ satisfying $\gamma_g = \gamma'_{g'}$. Since $g > h$, we know that $\Delta_{(g-1)} \subseteq \Delta_{(h)}$. Using the monotony property of γ_g, we can conclude

$$\Delta_{(g)} = \gamma_g(\Delta_{(g-1)}) \subseteq \gamma_g(\Delta_{(h)}) \subseteq \gamma_g(\Delta'_{(g'-1)}) = \gamma'_{g'}(\Delta'_{(g'-1)}) = \Delta'_{(g')}.$$

This completes the induction proof. □

3.4 Constraint Programming

The generality of the CSP has motivated the development of *constraint proramming* languages and software sytems that offer built-in functions for describing common types of constraints and include techniques developed in CSP research. The idea is to facilitate the development of CSP solution algorithms by letting the user specify models and algorithms on a high level while hiding the details of the constraint solution techniques. The solution algorithms are most often based on (truncated) search tree traversal.

The earliest approaches for constraint programming were based on the constraint logic programming paradigm. Examples for constraint programming systems and languages are CLP (Jaffar et al. 1986) and CLP($\mathcal{R}$) (Jaffar et al. 1992), PROLOG III (Colmerauer 1990), CHIP (Aggoun et al. 1987) and CLAIRE (Caseau and Laburthe

1996a). PROLOG III and CHIP have been developed into commercial systems and have been demonstrated to be effective and elegant in problem solving.

The success of CHIP has lead to the development of other commercial systems, e.g. CHARME, PECOS, and ILOG, that largely use the same solution techniques and mainly differ in their programming languages and implementation efficiency.

Several constraint programming systems include extensions specifically designed for scheduling applications, e.g., ILOG Scheduler (Le Pape 1994b, 1995, Nuijten and Le Pape 1998), CHIP (Aggoun and Beldiceanu 1993), or CLAIRE Schedule (Le Pape and Baptiste 1996a). A detailed review of the early historic development of the application of constraint programming for scheduling is given by Le Pape (1994a).

Chapter 4

Consistency Tests

Consistency tests are logical tests that serve to reduce the current domains of the decision variables and thus reduce the search space of a problem instance. The tests may be iteratively applied within a fixed point constraint propagation algorithm.

The purpose of this chapter is to present classes of consistency tests that are useful for solving project scheduling problems. These tests allow to reduce activity start time domains by ruling out inconsistent start time assignments or inconsistent activity sequences; additionally, they may help reduce activity mode domains by detecting inconsistent mode assignments.

The consistency tests and the constraint propagation algorithm in which they are applied are independent of the actual solution procedure and can be applied in algorithms such as list scheduling heuristics or branch-and-bound procedures. The benefit of the tests is that they can reduce the search space and direct an algorithm towards good solutions. In this chapter, we are only interested in the tests themselves and do neither address the constraint propagation algorithm which controls their application nor any scheduling algorithms in which the resulting constraint propagation procedure can be embedded. Since the tests only eliminate solutions incompatible with the constraints and current variable domains, they are independent of the overall objective function to be optimised.

The remainder of this chapter is organised as follows. Section 4.1 introduces some basic concepts and briefly reviews the relevant parts of the optimisation model in order to keep this chapter mostly self-contained. Section 4.2 discusses some simple consistency tests which are based on the temporal constraints.

Sections 4.3 to 4.6, which form the major part of this chapter, present interval capacity consistency tests that are based on the resource constraints. These tests consider the resource capacities available and required within certain time intervals. In the literature, activity start time domains are often approximated by start time windows, and this approximation is then referred to as activity release times and due dates, or heads and tails. The domain reduction process may then be called adjustment of heads and tails or time bound adjustment. Specific interval consistency tests have become known under the names immediate selection, edge finding, and energetic reasoning. It seems fair to say that the advances in modern branch and bound algorithms for difficult disjunctive scheduling problems, such as the job shop problem, that have been made in the last decade can to a large extent be attributed to the effect of interval consistency tests. Sections 4.3 to 4.6 present these tests within a unified framework, using numerous examples for illustration. The state of the art is reviewed and new results for disjunctive and cumulative scheduling are derived.

Section 4.3 first introduces the general concept of *interval consistency* which serves as a framework for the tests. As several powerful interval consistency tests may be applied for the special case of *disjunctive* scheduling with unit resource capacities and requirements, Section 4.4 explains how disjunctive sub-problems of a project scheduling problem instance can be identified. The tests that may be applied for these sub-problems are discussed in Section 4.5. Section 4.6 then addresses *cumulative* scheduling with arbitrary resource capacities and requirements; the section generalises some of the results obtained for disjunctive scheduling and introduces additional tests for cumulative scheduling.

Throughout most of this chapter, we will consider the single-mode project scheduling problem $PS|temp|C_{max}$ and the goal of reducing activity start time domains. Section 4.7 finally explains how the tests developed for this problem may be applied for the more general multi-mode problem $MPS|temp|C_{max}$ by considering a single-mode relaxation associated with a multi-mode problem instance; the section also introduces consistency tests for reducing activity mode domains. Section 4.8 summarises the results of this chapter.

4.1 Basic Concepts

For the rest of this chapter, except for Section 4.7, we will consider instances of the problem $PS|temp|C_{max}$ introduced in Chapter 2. In this section we briefly review the relevant aspects of the optimisation model in order to keep this chapter self-contained, and introduce some additional concepts and notation.

An activity i is characterised by its processing time p_i and resource requirements r_{ik}: for each of p_i time units, it requires r_{ik} units of a renewable resource k, which is available in constant amount R_k, and it releases the resource units again upon completion. An activity i has an associated start time decision variable S_i. Activities must be processed without preemption. Two activities i and j may be linked by a generalised precedence or temporal constraint (i, j) of the form $S_i + d_{ij} \leq S_j$, and the set of all temporal constraints is denoted with $\mathcal{E}$.

Each activity i has a current domain Δ_i of possible start times.[1] We assume that some upper bound UB on the makespan is known or given, so that $\Delta_i \subseteq [0, UB - p_i]$ holds. We will generally interpret Δ_i as the interval defined by the earliest and latest possible start times of i, i.e., $\Delta_i := [ES_i, LS_i] = \{ES_i, ES_i + 1, \ldots, LS_i\}$, although we will sometimes also refer to the set oriented interpretation.

The set of all activities is denoted with $\mathcal{V}$; the subset of all activities to be processed by a resource k is $\mathcal{V}_k := \{i \in \mathcal{V} \mid r_{ik} > 0\}$. We will frequently consider subsets $\mathcal{A} \subseteq \mathcal{V}_k$ of activities. To deduce domain reductions for the activities in $\mathcal{A}$ we often try to show that an activity $i \in \mathcal{A}$ must start before or finish after all other activities in $\mathcal{A}$. Using the shorthand notation $\mathcal{A}_i := \mathcal{A} \setminus \{i\}$, this is denoted by $i \to \mathcal{A}_i$ if i must start first, and $\mathcal{A}_i \to i$ if i must finish last. We also use the notation $\mathcal{A} \to \mathcal{A}'$ to express that all activities in set $\mathcal{A}$ must start before all activities in set $\mathcal{A}'$. It is convenient to introduce the total processing time $P(\mathcal{A})$ of a set $\mathcal{A}$ of operations, defined by $P(\mathcal{A}) := \sum_{j \in \mathcal{A}} p_j$. Given a set $\mathcal{A}$ of activities the time interval $[t_1, t_2[$ defined by the minimal earliest start time $t_1 = \min_{j \in \mathcal{A}} ES_j$ and the maximal latest completion time $t_2 = \max_{j \in \mathcal{A}} LC_j$ of two different activities in $\mathcal{A}$ is called *activity interval* of $\mathcal{A}$. Many consistency tests operate on activity intervals.

For illustration and motivation of the consistency tests, we use examples in the style of Figure 4.1, which shows two activities that must be processed by the same resource; the style is similar to the one used by Nuijten (1994). Unless stated otherwise, we will assume that the resource has a capacity of 1. Consider activity j

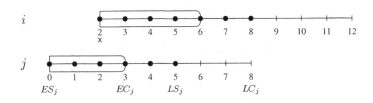

Figure 4.1: Two activities i and j with $p_i = 4$ and $p_j = 3$

where several points on the time scale have been annotated for illustration. The figure shows the time between the earliest start of j, ES_j, and its latest completion, LC_j, as a horizontal line segment. The processing time p_j is depicted as a hollow bar beginning at ES_j with rounded right end at $EC_j = ES_j + p_j$; the length of this bar is, of course, equal to $LC_j - LS_j$. Admissible start times, i.e., the values in Δ_j, are shown as black circles. Times in the interval $[LS_j + 1, LC_j[$ at which j may be in process, but at which it cannot start, are marked with tick marks. Scheduling an activity can be intrepreted as positioning the processing time bar at one of the admissible start times. Activity i in Figure 4.1 appears in the usual style without an-

---

[1] Recall that instead of Δ_{S_i} we usually use the notation Δ_i for the start time domain of activity i for simplicity.

notations. Initially, possible start times of i are in the interval $[2, 8]$. The x appearing under the scale of i at time 2 indicates that we have, by applying a test described below, deduced that i cannot start at time 2.

4.2   Consistency Tests for Temporal Constraints

A temporal or precedence constraint (i, j) of the form $S_i + d_{ij} \leq S_j$ determines the minimal or maximal time lag that must pass between the start of two activities i and j. Clearly, the left side of the constraint is minimal for ES_i, and a lower bound on the earliest possible start of activity j is thus given by $ES_i + d_{ij}$. Likewise, the right side of the constraint is maximal for LS_j, and $LS_j - d_{ij}$ is an upper bound on the latest possible start of i. This leads to the following well known test:

Consistency Test 1 (Precedence Consistency). *For a precedence constraint (i, j) the following domain reduction rules apply:*

$$(i, j) \in \mathcal{E}(\Delta) \implies \begin{cases} \Delta_i & := & \Delta_i & \setminus &]LS_j - d_{ij}, \infty[, \\ \Delta_j & := & \Delta_j & \setminus & [0, ES_i + d_{ij}[. \end{cases}$$

As some of the consistency tests discussed below may discover new precedence constraints, which must hold in addition to those given in the original problem instance, the set $\mathcal{E}$ of all precedence constraints depends on the set Δ of current start time domains and is denoted with $\mathcal{E}(\Delta)$.

When used within the constraint propagation algorithm, Consistency Test 1 naturally leads to the same result (fixed point) as a traditional temporal analysis of the project network (see, e.g., Elmaghraby 1977). A logical contradiction in the precedence constraints, corresponding to a cycle of positive length in the project network, will lead to an empty domain for some activity.

It is interesting to note that if only the precedence consistency test is applied in the constraint propagation algorithm, the resulting algorithm is very similar to label correcting algorithms for solving longest path problems in graphs, for instance the algorithm of Moore and Bellman (see e.g. Lawler 1976). It is therefore no surprise that, as with label correcting algorithms, the worst case time complexity for graphs with positive and negative edge weights cannot be polynomially bounded in the size of the graph. The complexity can be derived as follows. For a given precedence constraint, Consistency Test 1 can be applied with constant effort. The worst case propagation effort caused by the precedence constraints is therefore determined by the $O(|\mathcal{E}| d)$ possible enqueueing and dequeueing operations, where d is the size of the largest domain. We will shortly see that the same fixed point could indeed be calculated with polynomially bounded worst case effort $O(|\mathcal{V}|^3)$. However, due to the good average time complexity, the application of Consistency Test 1 within the propagation algorithm is advantageous.

A temporal constraint (i, j) is *resolved*, i.e., always satisfied given the current set of domains[2], if the maximal value of the left side is smaller than or equal to the minimal value of the right side, i.e., if $LS_i + d_{ij} \leq ES_j$; otherwise the constraint is unresolved.

Clearly, the precedence consistency test, as any consistency test, can only lead to domain reductions for unresolved constraints. The question whether a precedence constraint is resolved will play a role in the branching scheme described in Chapter 5.

Additional domain reductions may be deduced by considering the transitive minimal time lags between two *disjunctive* activities. We will discuss the question when two activities are disjunctive in detail in Section 4.4.1; for the time being it is sufficient to assume that two activities are in disjunction if they must not be processed in parallel because their combined resource requirement is too high.

Let $D' := (d'_{ij})$ be the matrix of transitive minimal temporal distances (longest paths) between activities that is induced by the set of temporal constraints $\mathcal{E}(\Delta)$. D' can be calculated with effort $O(|\mathcal{V}|^3)$ with the Floyd-Warshall Algorithm (Lawler 1976). The domain reductions obtained by applying Consistency Test 1 can also be derived from the matrix D' by simply setting ES_i to the distance of i from the source node and LS_i to the distance of i to the sink node of the project network, assuming a unique source and sink node have been added to the project network.

Using the transitive time lags d'_{ij}, we can state the following observation (Brucker et al. 1998, De Reyck and Herroelen 1998):

Consistency Test 2 (Lag Based Disjunctive Consistency). *Let $i, j \in \mathcal{V}$ be in disjunction. If $d'_{ij} > -p_j$, then i must precede j.*

Note that the condition $d'_{ij} > -p_j$ means that j cannot finish before the start of i; as i and j must not be processed in parallel this implies that i must precede j. Also observe that the test depends only on the "relative" lag between i and j, but not on the "absolute" start time domains of the two activities. Clearly, the test is only useful if $d'_{ij} < p_i$. We add any precedence constraint resulting from the application of this test to the set $\mathcal{E}(\Delta)$, and the corresponding domain reduction then follows from the precedence consistency test. The test also detects infeasibilities that occur if the temporal constraints require that two activities i and j which are in disjunction must be processed in parallel for some time. In this case two contradicting precedence constraints are added, and the precedence consistency test consequently leads to an empty domain.

The matrix D' depends upon the temporal constraints $\mathcal{E}(\Delta)$. Whenever a disjunctive consistency test adds a new precedence constraint to $\mathcal{E}(\Delta)$, the matrix can be updated with effort $O(|\mathcal{V}|^2)$ by exploiting the fact that any increased longest path between two activities must pass through the edge corresponding to the new precedence constraint.

---

[2] See Section 3.1, page 20.

4.3   Interval Consistency

This section introduces a general framework for *interval consistency tests*. These tests are based on the resource constraints and consider the resource availability and requirements within certain time intervals.

An activity i requires an amount of work $w_{ik} := r_{ik}p_i$ from resource k that depends upon the resource requirement r_{ik} and processing time p_i. A time interval is capacity consistent if the amount of work requested by all activities within this time interval can be matched by the amount of work supplied.

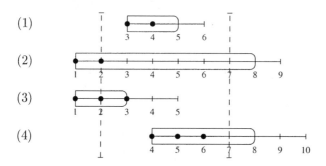

Figure 4.2: Types of intersections between an activity and a time interval

Let us consider the work of an activity i that must fall into a time interval $[t_1, t_2[$. The *interval processing time* $p_i(t_1, t_2)$ is the smallest amount of time during which i has to be processed within $[t_1, t_2[$. There are five possible situations: The activity can be (1) completely contained within the interval, (2) completely overlap the interval when started as early (left-shifted) or as late (right-shifted) as possible, (3) have a minimum processing time within the interval that is realised when started as early as possible, or (4) have a minimum processing within the interval that is realised when started as late as possible. These four situations are shown in Figure 4.2. The fifth situation applies whenever i does not have to be processed — neither completely nor partially — within the given time interval. Consequently,

$$p_i(t_1, t_2) := \max\left\{0, \min\left\{p_i, t_2 - t_1, EC_i - t_1, t_2 - LS_i\right\}\right\}. \tag{4.1}$$

The corresponding *interval work* is $w_{ik}(t_1, t_2) := r_{ik}p_i(t_1, t_2)$. The interval work of a subset of activities $A \subseteq V$ is defined through $W_k(A, t_1, t_2) := \sum_{i \in A} w_{ik}(t_1, t_2)$. Using this definition of interval work we can now define the slack of a time interval with respect to a resource k and a set of activities as the difference between work supply and demand within the interval:

$$slack(A, k, t_1, t_2) := R_k \cdot (t_2 - t_1) - W_k(A, t_1, t_2). \tag{4.2}$$

Observe that the slack function depends on the actual set Δ of current domains, so we will write $slack_\Delta(\mathcal{A}, k, t_1, t_2)$ whenever necessary. An interval $[t_1, t_2[$ is *capacity consistent* if it has non-negative slack for all resources and activities that require the resource:

$$slack_\Delta(\mathcal{V}, k, t_1, t_2) \geq 0, \qquad \forall k \in \mathcal{R}. \tag{4.3}$$

Given a domain set Δ, we can only develop a solution if this necessary condition holds for all resources and all time intervals.

The basic idea behind all interval consistency tests described in this chapter now is as follows: We consider an additional, hypothetical constraint H and try to show that if H is satisfied then Constraint (4.3) is violated for some resource and time interval; in this case we can conclude: $\neg H$. This leads to two main questions which we will try to answer in the following sections:

1. How should H be chosen so that the conclusion $\neg H$ leads to useful domain reductions?

2. For which intervals $[t_1, t_2[$ should Constraint (4.3) be tested?

The notion of interval capacity consistency as defined here has to the best of our knowledge first been suggested by Lopez (1991) (see also Lopez et al. 1992) under the name *energetic reasoning*; the area of the rectangle defined by an activity processing time and a resource requirement can be interpreted as work or energy, and we use the terms interchangeably. Special cases of this concept have been known for a long time (see e.g. Zaloom 1971). Schwindt (1998b) has independently developed a concept of interval work. He and, independently, Baptiste et al. (1999) were the first to answer Question 2.

Although our focus is primarily on the use of interval consistency tests for deducing domain reductions, it is worth mentioning that Constraint (4.3) can, of course, also be used to derive bounds for optimisation problems, e.g., lower bounds for makespan minimisation problems, in the following way: Impose a hypothetical upper bound UB on the makespan; if this leads to a violation of Constraint (4.3) then $UB + 1$ is a lower bound. This approach, for which Klein and Scholl (1999a) have introduced the intuitive name *destructive improvement* due to the principle of repeatedly refuting hypothetical constraints, has for example been used by Nuijten (1994), Pesch and Tetzlaff (1996), Heilmann and Schwindt (1997) and Schwindt (1998b). Test values for UB are usually chosen through a dichotomising search. A violation of Constraint (4.3) can be detected through the repeated application of a temporal analysis and of any of the tests described in the following sections; the constraint is violated if a test causes a domain to become empty.

Resource capacity constraints in the form of Constraint (4.3), but mostly limited to intervals defined by earliest start and latest completion times of activities, have also been used in constraint logic based scheduling; see, e.g., the description of solving a famous bridge scheduling problem (an instance of the problem $PS|temp|C_{max}$) by

Van Hentenryck (1989) or the implementation of the cumulative constraint in CHIP (Aggoun and Beldiceanu 1993).

4.4   Disjunctive Sub-Problems

Two activities i and j are disjunctive if, for instance due to limited resource availability, i and j cannot be processed simultaneously. Difficult project scheduling problem instances are typically characterised by a low resource supply, which causes many pairs of activities to be disjunctive. This motivates a closer study of consistency checking techniques for disjunctive scheduling. These techniques may be applied to disjunctive sub-problems of a project scheduling problem, i.e., sub-problems in which all activities are pair-wise disjunctive.

This section explains how such disjunctive sub-problems can be isolated. It first deals with the question when two activities are in disjunction and then discusses how all disjunctive sub-problems can be found and the most promising ones heuristically selected.

The difficulty of problem instances with very low resource supply has first been systematically analysed by Kolisch et al. (1995) for the problem $PS|prec|C_{max}$. Several authors have subsequently suggested the application of disjunctive consistency checking techniques for the problem $PS|prec|C_{max}$ (Brucker et al. 1998, Klein and Scholl 1999a, Baptiste et al. 1999) and the problem $PS|temp|C_{max}$ (Schwindt 1998b). The importance of disjunctive sub-problems is also underlined by the fact that a very successful lower bound for the problem $PS|prec|C_{max}$, which has been proposed by Mingozzi et al. (1998) and is often referred to as LB_3 or node packing bound, is based on the idea of solving a relaxation of a disjunctive sub-problem. The bound is an important component of most newer branch-and-bound algorithms for the problem (see e.g. Sprecher 2000, Demeulemeester and Herroelen 1997b, Brucker et al. 1998, Klein and Scholl 1999a).

4.4.1   Disjunctive Activity Pairs

Two activities $i, j \in \mathcal{V}$ are *disjunctive* if they cannot be processed simultaneously, i.e., if either i has to finish before j can start, or j has to finish before i can start, which means that the following disjunctive constraint must hold:

$$\underbrace{S_i + p_i \leq S_j}_{i \rightarrow j} \quad \vee \quad \underbrace{S_j + p_j \leq S_i}_{j \rightarrow i},$$

We will denote the fact that i and j are disjunctive with $i \leftrightarrow j$ for short. Obviously, $i \leftrightarrow j$ must hold if (1) the temporal constraints either require that $i \rightarrow j$ or require that $j \rightarrow i$, or (2) the start time domains allow to rule out the possibility that i and j are performed in parallel, or (3) the resource availability is too low to perform i and

j in parallel. In this section, we are most interested in those disjunctive activity pairs for which the (transitive) temporal constraints or the start time domains do *not* immediately imply which part of the disjunction must hold.

Let us therefore consider in more detail when limited resource availability causes the two activities i and j to be in disjunction. This is obviously the case if their combined resource requirements exceed the available capacity, i.e., if $r_{ik} + r_{jk} > R_k$ for some resource k. However, this condition can be relaxed by only considering the slack for a small time interval that depends on the current domains of i and j.

Lemma 1 (Disjunctive Activities). *Consider two activities $i, j \in V$ and an interval $[t_1, t_2[$ defined by*

$$
\begin{aligned}
t_1 &:= \max\{\min\{EC_i, EC_j\} - 1, \max\{ES_i, ES_j\}\}, \\
t_2 &:= \min\{\max\{LS_i, LS_j\} + 1, \min\{LC_i, LC_j\}\}.
\end{aligned}
$$

Activities i and j are in disjunction ($i \leftrightarrow j$), if there is a resource $k \in \mathcal{R}$ required by both i and j and if

$$
slack_\Delta(V \setminus \{i, j\}, k, t, t + 1) < r_{ik} + r_{jk}, \qquad \forall t \in [t_1, t_2[. \tag{4.4}
$$

Proof. If Condition (4.4) is satisfied for the interval $[t_1, t_2[$ then either i or j must finish before t_1 or start after t_2, i.e.

$$
S_i + p_i \leq t_1 \quad \vee \quad S_j + p_j \leq t_1 \quad \vee \quad S_i \geq t_2 \quad \vee \quad S_j \geq t_2, \tag{4.5}
$$

or the two activities must be in disjunction:

$$
S_i + p_i \leq S_j \quad \vee \quad S_j + p_j \leq S_i. \tag{4.6}
$$

It is now easy to show that whenever Condition (4.5) holds then Condition (4.6) must also be satisfied. $\qquad \square$

Simple as it may seem, the condition of Lemma 1 has often been missed and replaced with the stronger condition $r_{ik} + r_{jk} > R_k$ which discovers fewer disjunctions.

The Lemma is useful because (1) it only considers a limited time interval $[t_1, t_2[$ and (2) the slack in this interval is at most equal to but may be less than the resource supply R_k. The second point deserves some further explanation: Recall that the slack function depends upon the start time domains, as it is defined in terms of the interval work and hence in terms of interval processing times. Even if no activity is scheduled, we may, by reducing the start time domains through constraint propagation, be able to deduce that certain activities must be processed and consume resources at some time within the interval $[t_1, t_2[$ and thus reduce the slack. These conclusions will usually be stronger if a tight initial upper bound is given.

4.4.2   Selection of Disjunctive Sub-Problems

A disjunctive sub-problem of a cumulative scheduling problem is defined by a set $\mathcal{V}^c \subseteq \mathcal{V}$ of activities which are pairwise disjunctive. Such a set $\mathcal{V}^c$ is also called *disjunctive clique*. From an algorithmic point of view, disjunctive cliques play an important role as they may allow to deduce the order or at least a partial order in which the activities in a clique must be sequenced.

An intuitive interpretation of the sub-problem defined by a disjunctive clique $\mathcal{V}^c$ is obtained if we think of an associated *redundant disjunctive resource*: We introduce a fictitious resource with capacity one that is required by all activities in the clique; the sub-problem defined by $\mathcal{V}^c$ then is to find a (partial) sequence in which the activities in $\mathcal{V}^c$ must be processed by the resource.

Generally, there are many possibilities for choosing $\mathcal{V}^c$. An obvious example are the two element sets of disjunctive activity pairs. However, due to the way in which the consistency tests described in Section 4.5 below work, we are interested in choosing maximal disjunctive cliques $\mathcal{V}^c$, i.e., sets which have the property that there exists no true superset of pairwise disjunctive activities.

These possible choices of $\mathcal{V}^c$ can be determined by considering an undirected graph $G(\mathcal{V}, \mathcal{E}^{disj})$ with nodes corresponding to the set of activities and edges between any pair of disjunctive activities, i.e., edge set $\mathcal{E}^{disj} := \{(i,j) \mid i,j \in \mathcal{V}, i \neq j, i \leftrightarrow j\}$. A decomposition of G into all maximal cliques then gives all possible choices of $\mathcal{V}^c$.[3] Although already the problem of finding a single largest maximal clique of G is *NP*-hard (Garey and Johnson 1979) and the number of all maximal cliques may in general be exponential in the size of the graph, the decomposition can for practical purposes be quickly calculated with the algorithm of Bron and Kerbosch (1973).

Nevertheless, the number of maximal cliques may still be large and many of these cliques may be overlapping. As the gain of information deduced by the consistency tests may be outweighed by the computational effort for applying the tests, if this is done too frequently, it is reasonble to restrict the attention to a small number of maximal cliques chosen at the beginning of the search according to a heuristic suggested by Phan Huy (2000):

> Phase 1: Given the decomposition of G into all maximal cliques, repeatedly select a maximal clique which contains the largest number of edges that are not already covered by some previously chosen clique, until all edges are covered.
>
> Phase 2: Repeatedly choose an additional clique in order of decreasing size, if the new clique does not overlap with any previously chosen clique for more than two thirds.

---

[3]Observe that the maximal clique decompostion of G in general depends on the set of current start time domains Δ, since, according to Lemma 1, the question whether two activities are disjunctive or not may depend on Δ. However, since we will generally only determine a maximal clique decomposition once during the solution of a problem instance, we will write $\mathcal{V}^c$ instead of $\mathcal{V}^c(\Delta)$.

Other heuristics for choosing some (usually significantly fewer) disjunctive cliques have been described by Brucker et al. (1998), Baptiste et al. (1999) and Baptiste and Le Pape (2000); in contrast to the approach described here, these procedures are not based on an initial decomposition into all maximal cliques but heuristically construct some promising cliques.

4.5 Disjunctive Interval Consistency Tests

The idea behind all consistency tests described in this section is to consider subsets $A \subseteq \mathcal{V}^c$ of disjunctive activities that belong to the same disjunctive clique. Within these subsets, all possible activity sequences with a particular property are examined, e.g. the property that the sequence does not start with an activity $i \in A$. If all such sequences are infeasible, then we can draw the conclusion that the sequence must *not* have this property and deduce that i must be first in A. Using the shorthand notation $A_i := A \setminus \{i\}$, this will be denoted by $i \rightarrow A_i$.

Consistency tests which try to draw conclusions about the (partial) sequence in which some activities must be processed are called *sequence consistency tests*. Given information about a (partial) sequence, associated *domain consistency tests* then try to reduce the activity start time domains.

The consistency tests are presented in order from strongest to weakest condition. While a stronger condition allows a stronger conclusion, it is at the same time more likely to be inapplicable. After developing the individual tests in Sections 4.5.1 to 4.5.3 we generalise the results in Section 4.5.4 and show how they relate to the concept of interval consistency in Section 4.5.5. Sections 4.5.6 and 4.5.7 relate the domain reductions achieved by the consistency tests to the different notions of consistency introduced in Chapter 3.

4.5.1 Input/Output Test

Figure 4.3 shows an example with a set $A = \{i, j, k\}$ of three activities to be processed by the same disjunctive resource. We can deduce that i must be scheduled first in the following way: Suppose i does not start first. Then all three operations must be processed in the interval $[2, 9[$. This means that a total processing time of $8 = 3 + 2 + 3$ must be scheduled in $7 = 9 - 2$ available time units, which is a contradiction. Thus we can conclude that i must start first; we can then deduce that start times of i greater than 1 can be removed from Δ_i. Note that this conclusion cannot be drawn by separately considering any two of the three activities.

Carlier and Pinson (1989) have formalised the observation made in the example and have derived conditions under which it can be concluded that an operation $i \in A$ must be scheduled first or last in A. If i is scheduled before or after A_i we may also

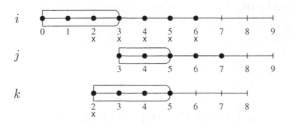

Figure 4.3: Example for the input test

think of i as the input or output of $\mathcal{A}_i$, hence the name of the conditions. We use the shorthand notation $P(\mathcal{A}) := \sum_{i \in \mathcal{A}} p_i$ for the total processing time of $\mathcal{A}$.

Consistency Test 3 (Input/Output). *Let $i \in \mathcal{A} \subseteq \mathcal{V}^c$. If*

$$\max_{u \in \mathcal{A}_i, v \in \mathcal{A}, u \neq v} (LC_v - ES_u) < P(\mathcal{A}) \tag{4.7}$$

then i must precede all activities in $\mathcal{A}_i$ (input condition). Likewise, if

$$\max_{u \in \mathcal{A}, v \in \mathcal{A}_i, u \neq v} (LC_v - ES_u) < P(\mathcal{A})$$

then i must succeed all operations in $\mathcal{A}_i$ (output condition).

Proof. If i does not precede $\mathcal{A}_i$, then all activities in $\mathcal{A}$ must be scheduled within $\max_{u \in \mathcal{A}_i, v \in \mathcal{A}, u \neq v}(LC_v - ES_u)$ time units. If Condition (4.7) holds this is not possible. The second part can be shown symmetrically. $\square$

The special case of the input/output condition where $|\mathcal{A}| = 2$ is also called *disjunctive pair test*.

If the output condition holds, i.e., if we have concluded that $\mathcal{A}_i \rightarrow i$, then we may add precedence constraints $S_j + p_j \leq S_i$ for all $j \in \mathcal{A}_i$ to the set $\mathcal{E}(\Delta)$ of temporal constraints of the original problem instance; a symmetric statement applies for the input condition. The addition of these temporal constraints may obviously cause some domain reductions in a subsequent temporal analysis, i.e., applications of Consistency Test 1, which will for instance ensure that $ES_i \geq \max_{j \in \mathcal{A}_i}(ES_j + p_j)$.

However, a better domain adjustment for activity i may be possible. Assume that we have concluded that $\mathcal{A}_i \rightarrow i$. Clearly, i can only start after the minimum completion time t^* of all activities in $\mathcal{A}_i$. Unfortunately, finding t^* is an $\mathcal{NP}$-hard problem, as it is equivalent to solving the one-machine makespan minimisation problem with release times and due dates (Carlier 1982). Therefore we resort to approximating

t^*. As already mentioned above, a simple and obvious approximation is the maximal earliest completion time in $\mathcal{A}_i$. We can do better by considering the preemptive relaxation of the one-machine problem (preemptive bound). For this problem, an optimal solution known as Jackson's Preemptive Schedule (JPS) can be efficiently obtained by scheduling the activities in $\mathcal{A}_i$ "from left to right" according to the "earliest due date" priority dispatching rule (Jackson 1956):

> Whenever the resource is free, schedule the activity i with minimal LC_i; if an activity j with $LC_j < LC_i$ becomes available while i is in process then interrupt i and start j.

We denote the completion time of JPS for $\mathcal{A}_i$ by $EC^{pr}(\mathcal{A}_i)$. Clearly, $EC^{pr}(\mathcal{A}_i)$ is a lower bound on the earliest start of i, and the same holds true for all subsets $\mathcal{A}' \subseteq \mathcal{A}_i$. However, Carlier (1982) has shown that

$$EC^{pr}(\mathcal{A}_i) = \max_{\mathcal{A}' \subseteq \mathcal{A}_i} \{ \min_{u \in \mathcal{A}'} ES_u + P(\mathcal{A}') \}.$$

This implies that $EC^{pr}(\mathcal{A}') \leq EC^{pr}(\mathcal{A}_i)$, if $\mathcal{A}' \subset \mathcal{A}_i$. We can thus adjust the earliest possible start time of i to $EC^{pr}(\mathcal{A}_i)$.

Symmetrically, we use $LS^{pr}(\mathcal{A}_i)$ as the preemptive bound for the latest start time of $\mathcal{A}_i$, obtained by preemptively scheduling the activities in $\mathcal{A}_i$ "from right to left" as late as possible according to the "maximum latest start" priority dispatching rule. We can now summarise the domain adjustments in the following domain consistency test:

Consistency Test 4 (Input/Output Domain Adjustments). *Let $i \in \mathcal{A} \subseteq \mathcal{V}^c$. Then the following tests apply:*

$$\mathcal{A}_i \rightarrow i \quad \Longrightarrow \quad \Delta_i := \Delta_i \setminus [0, EC^{pr}(\mathcal{A}_i)[. \tag{4.8}$$

$$i \rightarrow \mathcal{A}_i \quad \Longrightarrow \quad \Delta_i := \Delta_i \setminus \,]LS^{pr}(\mathcal{A}_i) - p_i, \infty[. \tag{4.9}$$

Before returning to the initial example, let us point out that Consistency Test 3 is a sequence consistency test while Consistency Test 4 is the associated domain consistency test. Observe that we have not required the sets $\mathcal{A} \subseteq \mathcal{V}^c$ in the two tests to be identical. We will shortly come back to this question.

For the example in Figure 4.3 the maximum of the expression on the left side of the input condition is $9 - 2$, and $P(\mathcal{A}) = 8$; since $9 - 2 < 8$, we can deduce $i \rightarrow \{j, k\}$. With $LS^{pr}(\{j, k\}) = 4$ the domain of i becomes $\Delta_i := [0, 6] \setminus]4 - 3, \infty[= [0, 1]$. Note the effect of using the preemptive bound: By using $LS^{pr}(\{j, k\})$ we have obtained a stronger domain reduction for i than we would have by considering LS_j and LS_k separately, which would have left the value 2 in Δ_i. A subsequent application of Consistency Test 1 for the newly added precedence constraint $i \rightarrow k$ will then reduce the domain of k to $\Delta_k := [2, 5] \setminus [0, 0 + 3[= [3, 5]$. As pointed out above, this reduction in Δ_k could also be achieved through a further application of the input test for $\mathcal{A} = \{i, k\}$.

The input/output test (pair test) also applies in the example in Figure 4.1 on page 33. For activity i and $\mathcal{A} = \{i, j\}$, the output condition gives $8 - 2 < 7$ and deduces $j \rightarrow i$. The domain of j remains unmodified, and the domain of i reduces to $\Delta_i :=$ $\Delta_i \setminus [0, 3[= [3, 8]$.

Let us now consider the question whether the sets $\mathcal{A} \subseteq \mathcal{V}^c$ in the sequence and domain consistency test can always without loss of information be chosen in such a way that they are identical, as seems likely after the previous examples. The example in Figure 4.4 (Dorndorf et al. 2001) demonstrates that this is not the case.

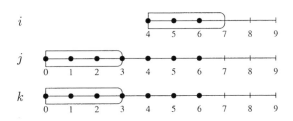

Figure 4.4: Input/output sequence and domain consistency tests

In the example, the input conditions allow to separately conclude $j \rightarrow i$ and $k \rightarrow i$. The output domain adjustment condition then yields: $\{j, k\} \rightarrow i \implies S_i \geq 6$. However, the output condition of Consistency Test 3 is not satisfied for $\mathcal{A} = \{i, j, k\}$ and the distinct activity i, as $9 - 0 \not< 9$. This demonstrates that by independently choosing the set $\mathcal{A}$ for the two tests additional information can be derived.

In branch and bound procedures that branch over disjunctive edges, the tests may be employed to immediately select the orientation of edges, a process often called immediate selection, as first suggested by Carlier and Pinson (1989), or edge finding, a term introduced by Applegate and Cook (1991). The input/output tests have first been described by Carlier and Pinson in the context of a branch and bound algorithm for the job shop problem (JSP); the tests that they actually implemented in their initial algorithm were limited to two-element sets $\mathcal{A}$ and one additional heuristically determined $\mathcal{A}$ and $i \in \mathcal{A}$ for each resource. Using these tests, they were able to optimally solve a notoriously difficult 10×10 JSP instance (Fisher and Thompson 1963) that, despite many attempts, had defied solution for over 25 years.

Efficient algorithms that have later been developed for testing the input/output conditions for all $\mathcal{A}$ and i and performing the corresponding domain reductions based on the preemptive bounds usually use an ordering of activities according to earliest start and latest completion times. The challenging part is to test the input/output conditions and calculate preemptive bounds at the same time. Carlier and Pinson (1990), Martin and Shmoys (1996), and Nuijten (1994) have designed $O(|\mathcal{V}^c|^2)$ algorithms for testing all subsets $\mathcal{A} \subseteq \mathcal{V}^c$. The algorithm of Nuijten has the interesting property that it can be generalised for cumulative scheduling. $O(|\mathcal{V}^c| \log |\mathcal{V}^c|)$ algorithms for testing all subsets have been described by Brucker et al. (1996) and Carlier and Pinson (1994). Caseau and Laburthe (1994, 1995, 1996b) describe an algorithm based on the concept of task or activity intervals for checking all sets $\mathcal{A}$ with effort $O(|\mathcal{V}^c|^3)$. The advantage of their approach is that the consistency conditions can be evaluated incrementally within a search procedure. When used within a branch-and-bound algorithm this means that the effective time complexity for performing the tests at each node of the search tree is usually lower than $O(|\mathcal{V}^c|^3)$ because it is not necessary to test all $\mathcal{A}$; although the worst case complexity for performing the tests at a node is still $O(|\mathcal{V}^c|^3)$, the average complexity is lower. This contrasts with the usual approach of applying the full test at each node of a branch-and-bound tree. All algorithms have in common that they combine the evaluation of Consistency Tests 3 and 4 and thus require the sets $\mathcal{A}$ in both tests to be identical. An $O(|\mathcal{V}^c|^2 \log |\mathcal{V}^c|)$ algorithm which first tries to deduce sequence relations by applying the sequence consistency test and in a second, independent step computes domain adjustments has recently been described by Dorndorf et al. (2001).

As a generalisation of the input/output test, Focacci and Nuijten (2000) have proposed two consistency tests for disjunctive scheduling with sequence dependent setup times between pairs of activities processed by the same resource. A version of the input/output test for preemptive scheduling, i.e., the case where activities can interrupt one another, has been designed by Le Pape and Baptiste (1996b).

Finally, we would like to mention that to our knowledge all algorithms discussed above do not test the input/output conditions in the form of Consistency Test 3, where we have required in the maximum expressions that $u \neq v$, but rather allow for $u = v$, thus actually testing a weaker condition. Although the extension may seem trivial it does lead to additional deductions in certain cases. However, it is not always obvious how to include it in existing algorithms without increasing their time complexity.

4.5.2   Input-or-Output Test

The input/output condition allows to deduce that an operation $i \in \mathcal{A} \subseteq \mathcal{V}_k$ must be scheduled first or last in $\mathcal{A}$. The weaker input-or-output condition can be used to show that a precedence relation $i \rightarrow j$ must exist between a pair of activities i and j from set $\mathcal{A}$.

Figure 4.5 shows an example with a set $\mathcal{A} = \{i, j, k, l\}$ of four activities to be processed by the same resource. The input/output condition does not allow to draw any conclusions about the order in which the activities must be scheduled. However, we can deduce that i must precede j: Suppose i is not scheduled first *and* j is not scheduled last. Then all four activities with a total processing time of $7 = 3+2+1+1$ must be scheduled within the interval $[2, 8]$, which is a contradiction. Hence we can conclude that it is impossible that at the same time i is not first *and* j is not last. If either i must be first or j must be last, then i must precede j, and we can remove the start time 3 from Δ_j. This observation leads to the following consistency test.

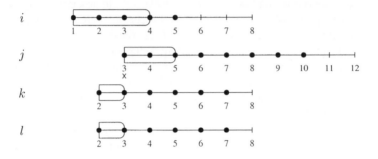

Figure 4.5: Example for the input-or-output test

Consistency Test 5 (Input-or-Output). *Let* $i, j \in \mathcal{A} \subseteq \mathcal{V}^c$. *If*

$$\max_{u \in \mathcal{A}_i, v \in \mathcal{A}_j, u \neq v} (LC_v - ES_u) < P(\mathcal{A}) \tag{4.10}$$

then i *must be scheduled first or* j *must be scheduled last in* $\mathcal{A}$. *If* $i \neq j$ *then* i *must precede* j.

Proof. Suppose neither i is scheduled first nor j is scheduled last. All activities in $\mathcal{A}$ must then be scheduled within $\max_{u \in \mathcal{A}_i, v \in \mathcal{A}_j, u \neq v} (LC_v - ES_u)$ time units. If Condition (4.10) holds, this is impossible and we can conclude that either i must be first or j must be last in $\mathcal{A}$. In both cases i must precede j if $i \neq j$. $\qquad\square$

Comparison to the very similar input/output test shows in what sense the input-or-output test is weaker.

If this condition holds and $i \neq j$ which means that $i{\rightarrow}j$, then we can add the corresponding precedence constraint $S_i + p_i \leq S_j$ to the set $\mathcal{E}(\Delta)$ of temporal constraints. If possible, the start time domains of i and j will then be reduced in a subsequent temporal analysis.

If the condition holds for $i = j$, the domain of i can be reduced in the following way:

$$i{\rightarrow}\mathcal{A}_i \vee \mathcal{A}_i{\rightarrow}i \quad \implies \quad \Delta_i := \Delta_i \setminus\,]LS^{pr}(\mathcal{A}_i) - p_i, EC^{pr}(\mathcal{A}_i)[. \tag{4.11}$$

While any domain reduction in the case that $i \neq j$ can only occur at the domain bounds, domain reduction rule (4.11) may remove values within the domain but leaves the bounds untouched and is thus not useful if only the domain bounds are stored.[4]

For the example in Figure 4.5 we obtain $8 - 2 < 7$ and deduce $i{\rightarrow}j$. By applying a domain reduction rule for the temporal constraint $S_i + p_i \leq S_j$ we can remove the value 3 from Δ_j. Figure 4.6 shows another example where the input-or-output condition can deduce that a single activity must either start first or last; in terms of Consistency Test 5 this is the case where $i = j$. We obtain $5 - 3 < 4$ and conclude that i must start before or after $\{k, l\}$. Domain reduction rule (4.11) allows to remove the values $[2, 4]$ from Δ_i.

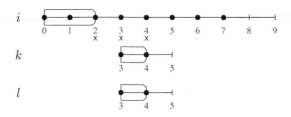

Figure 4.6: Input-or-output condition example: i must be first or last

As a final example, note that the result $i{\rightarrow}\{j, k\}$ that we have obtained with the input/output condition for the example in Figure 4.3 can also be deduced in two steps with the input-or-output condition, resulting in the conclusions $i \rightarrow j$ and $i \rightarrow k$. However, the corresponding reduction in Δ_i is weaker, leaving the value 2 in Δ_i.

To our knowledge, the input-or-output test in its general form has not been discussed in the literature. A similar condition for the special case where $i = j$ has been described by Carlier and Pinson (1990) and Błażewicz et al. (1998). Stronger conditions based on considering all sets $\mathcal{A}$ of cardinality r, hence called r-set conditions, have been discussed by Brucker et al. (1996). They describe an $O(|\mathcal{V}^c|^2)$ 3-set algorithm that checks all activity sets of cardinality three and detects all pairwise ordering relations derivable from triples. The algorithm thus implements the input-or-output test for $|\mathcal{A}| = 3$. Judging from the implementation within their branch-and-bound procedure for the JSP, the efficiency of the 3-set tests is comparable to that of the input/output tests. It is unclear whether a low polynomial time-complexity r-set algorithm could be developed for $r > 3$.

The development of an algorithm with low polynomial time complexity for testing the input-or-output conditions is an open issue. Based on experience with other consistency tests, we conjecture that in order to be of practical value such an algorithm must at most have time complexity $O(|\mathcal{V}^c|^2)$. There is an obvious $O(|\mathcal{V}^c|^4)$ algo-

---

[4]See the discussion of domain-consistency versus bound consistency in Sections 3.2.2 and 3.2.3.

rithm using task or activity intervals, and Phan Huy (2000) has designed an $O(|\mathcal{V}^c|^3)$ algorithm.

4.5.3   Input/Output Negation Test

By further relaxing the condition to be tested, we can still draw additional conclusions in situations where the input-or-output condition and the stronger input/output conditions do not hold. Figure 4.7 shows an example with a set $\mathcal{A} = \{i, j, k\}$ of three activities to be processed by the same resource. Although we cannot conclude that activity i must be last or must precede j or k, we can deduce that i must *not be first*, and therefore remove the value 2 from Δ_i. By generalising the observations

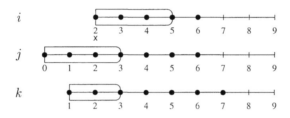

Figure 4.7: Example for the input negation test

made in the example, we arrive at the following consistency test.

Consistency Test 6 (Input/Output Negation). *Let $i \in \mathcal{A} \subseteq \mathcal{V}^c$. If*

$$\max_{v \in \mathcal{A}_i}(LC_v - ES_i) < P(\mathcal{A}) \tag{4.12}$$

then i must not start first in $\mathcal{A}_i$ (input negation: $i \not\to \mathcal{A}_i$). If

$$\max_{u \in \mathcal{A}_i}(LC_i - ES_u) < P(\mathcal{A})$$

then i must not end last in $\mathcal{A}_i$ (output negation: $\mathcal{A}_i \not\to i$).

Proof. If i precedes $\mathcal{A}_i$, all activities in $\mathcal{A}$ must be processed within the interval $[ES_i, \max_{v \in \mathcal{A}_i} LC_v[$. If Condition (4.12) holds, this is not possible. The second part can be shown symmetrically.   □

Again, it is easy to see in which sense these conditions are weaker than in the preceding tests. Domain reduction rules can be based on the observation that i must succeed (input negation) or precede (output negation) at least one other activity in $\mathcal{A}$:

Consistency Test 7 (Input/Output Negation Domain Adjustment). *For $i \in \mathcal{A} \subseteq \mathcal{V}^c$ the following tests apply:*

$$i \not\rightarrow \mathcal{A}_i \quad \Longrightarrow \quad \Delta_i \ := \ \Delta_i \setminus [0, \min_{u \in \mathcal{A}_i} EC_u[,$$

$$\mathcal{A}_i \not\rightarrow i \quad \Longrightarrow \quad \Delta_i \ := \ \Delta_i \setminus] \max_{u \in \mathcal{A}_i} LS_u - p_i, \infty[.$$

For the example in Figure 4.7 the input negation condition yields $9 - 2 < 8$ and we conclude $i \not\rightarrow \{j, k\}$. According to the first domain reduction rule we can therefore remove all values less than 3 from Δ_i.

Conclusions similar to those obtained in the examples for the input/output and input-or-output test could also have been produced through successive application of the input/output negation test. Since the condition to be tested for the input/output negation conclusion is weaker than the preceding conditions, it will of course hold whenever the stronger conditions apply. Consider again the example in Figure 4.3. Here, the input/output negation conditions allows to conclude $j \not\rightarrow \{i, k\} \Leftrightarrow i \rightarrow j \vee k \rightarrow j$ and $k \not\rightarrow \{i, j\} \Leftrightarrow i \rightarrow k \vee j \rightarrow k$, which implies $i \rightarrow \{j, k\}$. However, this implication is not automatically deduced by the input/output negation condition. This demonstrates that input/output negation conditions alone do not deduce all interesting domain reductions. A similar effect can be seen in the example in Figure 4.5. Here, the input/output negation conditions can be used to deduce $\{j, k, l\} \not\rightarrow i$ and $j \not\rightarrow \{i, k, l\}$, but this does not allow to remove the value 3 from Δ_j as in the input-or-output test.

The input/output negation test has first been suggested by Carlier and Pinson (1989). Most authors working on consistency tests have considered the test in some form. However, an algorithm that tests all interesting $\mathcal{A}$ and i with effort $O(|\mathcal{V}^c|^2)$ has only recently been developed by Baptiste and Le Pape (1996). Another $O(|\mathcal{V}^c|^2)$ algorithm has been described by Dorndorf et al. (2001). Nuijten and Le Pape (1998) have derived consistency tests similar to the input/output negation tests with tighter time bound adjustments; the corresponding algorithms have a complexity $O(|\mathcal{V}^c|^3)$ and $O(|\mathcal{V}^c|^2 \log |\mathcal{V}^c|)$.

Other researchers have often applied the tests in an incomplete way, testing only some $\mathcal{A}$ and i (Carlier and Pinson 1989, 1990, Nuijten 1994, Baptiste and Le Pape 1995). Caseau and Laburthe (1994, 1995) have integrated the tests in their task interval algorithm which tests input/output conditions and the negation conditions with effort $O(|\mathcal{V}^c|^3)$.

4.5.4 Summary and Generalisation

All disjunctive interval sequence consistency tests that we have discussed can be derived from the following theorem.

Theorem 2 (Sequence Consistency). *Let $\mathcal{A}', \mathcal{A}'' \subset \mathcal{A} \subseteq \mathcal{V}^c$. If*

$$\max_{u\in A\backslash A',v\in A\backslash A'',u\neq v} (LC_v - ES_u) < P(A) \tag{4.13}$$

then an activity in A' must start first or an activity in A'' must end last in A.

Proof. If none of the activities in A'' succeeds $A\backslash A''$ *and* none of the activities in A' precedes $A \backslash A'$, then A must be processed within $\max_{u\in A\backslash A',v\in A\backslash A'',u\neq v}(LC_v - ES_u)$ units of time. If Condition (4.13) holds this is a contradiction.   □

Test	$A \backslash A''$	$A \backslash A'$	Conclusion ($\neg H$)
input	A	A_i	$i \to A_i$
output	A_i	A	$A_i \to i$
input-or-output	A_j	A_i	$i \to A_i \vee A_j \to j$
input negation	A_i	$\{i\}$	$i \not\to A_i$
output negation	$\{i\}$	A_i	$A_i \not\to i$

Table 4.1: Summary of disjunctive interval consistency tests, $A', A'' \subset A \subseteq V^c$

The results of the preceding sections are summarised in Table 4.1. For each consistency test, the table shows the values of $A \backslash A'$ and $A \backslash A''$ that, when used in Theorem 2, yield the test. The conclusions of Theorem 2 have been reformulated to match the tests presented above. Note that the conclusion is always the negation of the hypothesis H falsified by the test.

4.5.5   Relation to Interval Consistency

We will now relate the Sequence Consistency Theorem to the general concept of interval consistency introduced in Section 4.3. For disjunctive scheduling and a given set of disjunctive activities V^c, the Interval Capacity Constraint (4.3) reduces to

$$t_2 - t_1 \geq P(V^c, t_1, t_2),$$

where $P(V^c, t_1, t_2) := \sum_{i\in V^c} p_i(t_1, t_2)$ is the total interval processing time within $[t_1, t_2[$. Inversely, we denote the set of all activities in V^c that must be processed completely or partially within an interval $[t_1, t_2[$ as $V^c(t_1, t_2) := \{i \in V^c \mid p_i(t_1, t_2) > 0\}$. The following theorem shows how we can efficiently test violations of the Interval Capacity Constraint.

Theorem 3 (Sufficiency of Activity Interval Consistency). *If, for some time interval $[t_1, t_2[$,*

$$t_2 - t_1 < P(V^c, t_1, t_2), \tag{4.14}$$

then

$$\max_{i,j\in V^c(t_1,t_2),i\neq j} (LC_j - ES_i) < P(V^c(t_1, t_2)). \tag{4.15}$$

Proof. From Equation (4.1) we know that $0 < t_2 - t_1 < P(\mathcal{V}^c, t_1, t_2)$ implies that $|\mathcal{V}^c(t_1, t_2)| \geq 2$. We consider two activities $i, j \in \mathcal{V}^c(t_1, t_2), i \neq j$, and start to transform Condition (4.14) into Condition (4.15) by rewriting the left hand side of (4.14):

$$LS_j + t_2 - LS_j - t_1 < P(\mathcal{V}^c, t_1, t_2).$$

By observing that $t_2 - LS_j \geq p_j(t_1, t_2) \geq 0$, according to Equation (4.1), we can approximate the left side. We rewrite the right side and obtain:

$$LS_j + p_j(t_1, t_2) - t_1 < p_i(t_1, t_2) + p_j(t_1, t_2) + \sum_{l \in \mathcal{V}^c \setminus \{i,j\}} p_l(t_1, t_2).$$

Again, we know from Equation (4.1) that $EC_i - t_1 \geq p_i(t_1, t_2) \geq 0$. This approximation leads to:

$$LS_j - t_1 < EC_i - t_1 + \sum_{l \in \mathcal{V}^c \setminus \{i,j\}} p_l(t_1, t_2).$$

Next, we approximate the sum on the right hand side, once again using Equation (4.1) which tells us that $p_k \geq p_k(t_1, t_2) \geq 0$, and obtain:

$$LS_j - EC_i < \sum_{l \in \mathcal{V}^c(t_1, t_2) \setminus \{i,j\}} p_l.$$

By adding $p_i + p_j$ on both sides we arrive at:

$$LC_j - ES_i < P(\mathcal{V}^c(t_1, t_2)).$$

As it is always possible to choose i and j in such a way that the maximum difference $LC_j - ES_i$ is realised, Condition (4.15) must hold. □

The theorem tells us two interesting things. First, it states that if an interval capacity constraint is violated for some arbitrary time interval $[t_1, t_2[$, then there will also be a violation for an interval defined by the earliest start and latest completion time of two different activities in $\mathcal{V}^c(t_1, t_2)$. When checking for violations this allows us to restrict our attention to intervals defined by earliest start and latest completion times, called task or *activity intervals* (Caseau and Laburthe 1994), instead of considering all possible time intervals. Any violation of the capacity constraint can thus be detected by testing $O(|\mathcal{V}^c|^2)$ intervals. For disjunctive scheduling, this answers the initial question, posed in Section 4.3 on page 37, what intervals we should test. Second, the theorem states that, as long as we test all activity intervals, there is nothing to be gained from considering *interval* processing time instead of *simple* processing time. If interval processing time has an effect on the test for a given set $\mathcal{A}$ then we can obtain the same effect by considering a different set $\mathcal{A}'$. In summary, this means that an algorithm which tests Condition (4.15) for all activity intervals will detect all violations according to the more general concept of Condition (4.14) which is the negation of the disjunctive version of the general Interval Capacity Constraint (4.3).

It is worth emphasising that this statement is independent of the particular hypothetical constraint H to be tested. This can be seen as follows: For any set of constraints, it is always possible to first add and propagate the constraints, and then test the interval consistency constraints. The particular form of the sequence consistency tests is simply an accelerated version of this "add and propagate, then test" process. For illustration, consider again the example shown in Figure 4.3, where the conclusion $i \rightarrow \{j, k\}$ could also have been obtained in the following way: (1) Add $H : i \not\rightarrow \{j, k\}$, (2) update the domain of i based on H, which yields $\Delta_i := \Delta_i \setminus \{t | t < \min_{u \in \{j,k\}} EC_u\} = [5, 6]$, and (3) test the interval consistency constraint (4.3) for the activity interval defined by $\{i, j, k\}$ which has the left time bound 2 and the right time bound 9. Because $9 - 2 \not\geq 8$ this test fails and we conclude $\neg H \Leftrightarrow i \rightarrow \{j, k\}$.

For disjunctive scheduling, Theorem 3 improves the characterisation of time intervals for which the capacity constraint may be violated, which has been obtained by Schwindt (1998b) and Baptiste et al. (1999) for the cumulative case discussed in Section 4.6. The theorem also reveals that for disjunctive scheduling the "energetic" consistency tests that have been proposed by Baptiste and Le Pape (1995) are not more powerful than their non-energetic counterparts, i.e., the consistency tests that have been presented above.

4.5.6   Lower Level Consistency

This section relates the disjunctive interval consistency tests to the general concept of lower level consistency, in particular 2-consistency and 2- and 3-b-consistency that are commonly used in CSP research and that have been introduced in Chapter 3. We first derive a 2-consistency test and show that the consistency tests described in Sections 4.5.1 to 4.5.3 can be used to achieve 2-b-consistency.

Let us first briefly recall the relevant notions of consistency: Activity start time domains are called 2-consistent if, for any pair $i, j \in V$, and for any value $a_i \in \Delta_i$ there is some value $a_j \in \Delta_j$ such that $S_i = a_i$ and $S_j = a_j$ is permitted by the constraints of the scheduling problem. The weaker definition of bound consistency looks at domain bounds: Activity domains are called 2-bound-consistent, or 2-b-consistent for short, if, for any pair $i, j \in V$, and for every value $a_i \in \{\min \Delta_i, \max \Delta_i\}$ there is a value $a_j \in \Delta_j$ such that $S_i = a_i$ and $S_j = a_j$ is permitted. Clearly, 2-consistency implies 2-b-consistency. A general definition of k-b-consistency is given in Section 3.2.3.

The concept of bound consistency is of interest because, as we have seen, many consistency tests are based on domain bound considerations. In addition, the propagation of temporal constraints depends on domain bounds. Any change in domain bounds can therefore trigger further domain reductions. Finally, if domains are approximated by start time windows — and this is often done for reasons of implementation efficiency — bound-consistency is the only reasonable concept of consistency.

Figure 4.8 shows an example, taken from Nuijten (1994), with a pair of activities $i, j \in V^c$ where any 2-inconsistent value is marked. For example, j cannot start at

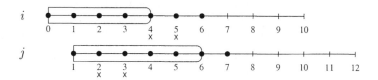

Figure 4.8: 2-consistency

time 2 since this does neither leave enough room for i to be processed before j nor after j. In general, i cannot start in the open interval $]LS_j - p_i, EC_j[$. Note that the interval can be empty if $EC_j \leq LS_j - p_i$. The observation is summarised in the following theorem due to Nuijten (1994).

Theorem 4 (2-consistency). *Let* $i, j \in V^c, i \neq j$. Δ_i *and* Δ_j *are 2-consistent if and only if*

$$\Delta_i \cap]LS_j - p_i, EC_j[= \emptyset. \tag{4.16}$$

Proof. If j is started at time $t \in \Delta_j$ then i is blocked during the open interval $]t - p_i, t + p_j[$. The left bound of the interval is maximal for $t = LS_j$, and the right bound is minimal for $t = ES_j$. Thus the minimal interval during which i cannot start is $]LS_j - p_i, EC_j[$. All other possible start times of j leave possible start times for i. □

The following result shows that the sequence consistency tests based on Theorem 2 can be used to ensure 2-b-consistency.

Theorem 5 (2-b-consistency). *Application of the input/output, input-or-output, or the input/output negation test within a fixed point iteration leads to a 2-b-consistent state.*

Proof. For $\mathcal{A} = \{i, j\}$ all the tests simplify to:

$$LC_j - ES_i < p_i + p_j \implies j \rightarrow i \implies \left\{ \begin{array}{lcl} \Delta_i & := & \Delta_i \setminus [0, EC_j[\, , \\ \Delta_j & := & \Delta_j \setminus]LS_i - p_j, \infty[. \end{array} \right.$$

To achieve 2-b-consistency any 2-inconsistent value must be removed from the domain bounds. According to Equation (4.16), the left domain bound can only be 2-inconsistent if

$$LS_j - p_i < ES_i \iff LC_j - ES_i < p_i + p_j.$$

In this case, the condition of the tests is satisfied and any inconsistent values are removed by the first domain reduction rule above. The proof for the right domain bound is symmetrical. □

We have thus shown that the application of any of the input/output, input-or-output, and input/output negation tests, even if only used for activity pairs, within a fixed point propagation algorithm[5] leads at least to a 2-b-consistent state with respect to the interval capacity, or resource, constraints.[6]

As the example in Figure 4.8 shows, the tests can, however, only ensure 2-b-consistency but not the stronger concept of 2-consistency, because none of the marked values in the domains of i and j can be removed by any of the tests. Of course, it is no surprise that the domain bound-oriented tests can only achieve bound-consistency.

However, a stronger result can be obtained if the the input/output and input/output negation tests are applied *together* within a fixed point algorithm:

Theorem 6 (Strong 3-b-consistency). *Application of the input/output and input/ output-negation tests for all pairs and triples of activities within a fixed point iteration leads to a strongly 3-b-consistent state.*

Proof. A detailed proof is given in Dorndorf et al. (2000b). The proof relies on a technical analysis of the necessary conditions for 3-b-consistency, which are transformed in such a way that it can be seen that these conditions must be satisfied if the input/output and input/output-negation consistency tests are applied at least for pairs and triples of operations.   □

The input/output and input/output negation tests usually, but not necessarily imply more than 3-b-consistency. However, if only pairs and triples of activities are considered, then the application of the tests is equivalent to enforcing strong 3-b-consistency.

4.5.7 Sequence Consistency Does Not Imply k-b-Consistency

Trivial though it may be, it is worth emphasising that the consistency tests only check necessary, but not sufficient conditions for the existence of a feasible schedule. While we could show that the sequence consistency tests always achieve 3-b-consistency, this means that they in general do not achieve k-b-consistency for $k > 3$. The example in Figure 4.9 illustrates these two points.

In the example, $\mathcal{A} = \{i, j, k, l, m\}$. The output condition allows to conclude that $\{j, k, l, m\} \rightarrow i$, since $10 - 0 < 11$. The preemptive bound $EC^{pr}(\mathcal{A}_i)$ for the earliest completion time of $\{j, k, l, m\}$ is 9. According to domain reduction rule (4.8) this leaves the value 9 as the left bound of Δ_i. However, manual inspection shows that the earliest completion time of $\{j, k, l, m\}$ is actually 10. Thus, the input/output test leaves an inconsistent value at the left bound of Δ_i. This demonstrates that the domain reduction rule based on the preemptive bound is heuristic.

---

[5]See Algorithm 1 on page 27.

[6]It is easy to see that if precedence constraints are given in addition to resource constraints, as, e.g., in the problem $PS|temp|C_{max}$, then the additional application of the Precedence Consistency Test 1 will ensure overall 2-b-consistency.

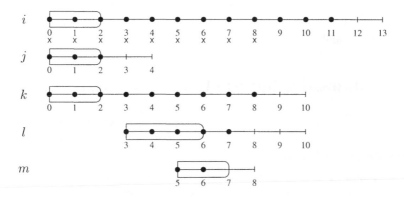

Figure 4.9: When sequence consistency tests fail

Now modify the example by reducing LC_i to 11. The input/output test still yields the same result, and none of the other sequence consistency tests leads to an inconsistency (by producing an empty domain). Again, manual inspection shows that there is no feasible schedule for $\mathcal{A}$.

4.5.8 Shaving

In the tests based on the Sequence Consistency Theorem 2 we have tried to refute hypothetical constraints on the sequence in which activities in a set $\mathcal{A} \subseteq \mathcal{V}^c$ execute. Now, we take a purely time-oriented approach and consider hypothetical constraints on individual activity start times. If we can falsify such a constraint, then we can reduce the corresponding activity domain in an obvious way. The process of reducing activity domains based on this kind of reasoning has been called *shaving* (Martin and Shmoys 1996, Caseau and Laburthe 1996b).

For example, we can test a hypothetical constraint of the type $S_i > t_x$ for some $t_x \in \Delta_i$. If this leads to a contradiction, then we can conclude that S_i must be less than or equal to t_x and remove all values greater t_x from Δ_i. A contradiction may be caused by a direct violation of the interval capacity constraint (4.3) or after propagating the hypothetical constraint by repeatedly applying other consistency tests. Values of t_x can for example be chosen by a dichotomising search over Δ_i.

A shaving approach for disjunctive scheduling has been proposed by Carlier and Pinson (1994) for solving the JSP. Martin and Shmoys (1996) have, independently, applied the technique within a time-oriented branch-and-bound algorithm for the JSP. Using a shaving technique, Caseau and Laburthe (1996b) were able to obtain a proof of optimality for the famous 10×10 job shop problem instance of Fisher and Thompson (1963) with only 7 backtracks. Recently, Dorndorf et al. (2001) have shown how the use of simple shaving techniques can significantly reduce the search effort of a branch-and-bound algorithm for the Open Shop Scheduling Problem, another classic disjunctive scheduling problem.

4.6   Cumulative Interval Consistency Tests

While disjunctive scheduling or sequencing is concerned with unit resource requirements and capacities, cumulative scheduling considers the general case of arbitrary resource supply and demand.

In this section we introduce several consistency tests for cumulative scheduling that are based on the Interval Capacity Constraint (4.3). Section 4.6.1 first deals with the special case of time intervals of width one. Section 4.6.2 then presents tests based on considering activity intervals, i.e., intervals defined by the earliest possible start and latest possible completion time of two activities, while Section 4.6.3 discusses the question which time intervals must in general be tested in order to detect a violation of Constraint (4.3). Finally, Section 4.6.4 briefly describes consistency tests based on the concept of elastic resource relaxations.

4.6.1   Unit-Interval Consistency

An important special case of the general interval capacity constraint (4.3) is obtained if we consider time intervals of width one, also called unit-intervals. If, for a set $\mathcal{V}_k$ of activities to be processed by resource k, some activity $i \in \mathcal{V}_k$ and some time t, the $slack(\mathcal{V}_k \setminus \{i\}, k, t, t+1)$ is less than the required resource amount r_{ik}, then activity i cannot be processed at time t. This leads to the following consistency test, which is also known under the name timetable-based constraint propagation (Le Pape 1994b).

Consistency Test 8 (Unit-Interval Test). *Let $i \in \mathcal{V}_k$. If, for some time t in the interval $[ES_i(\Delta), LC_i(\Delta)[$,*

$$slack_\Delta(\mathcal{V}_k \setminus \{i\}, k, t, t+1) < r_{ik}$$

then the domain of i can be reduced in the following way:

$$\Delta_i := \Delta_i \setminus \,]t - p_i, t].$$

Tests similar or equivalent to the unit-interval consistency test have for instance been described by Le Pape (1994b, 1995), Nuijten (1994), Caseau and Laburthe (1996b), and Klein and Scholl (1999a). For disjunctive scheduling, the unit-interval test is covered by the pair test.

The test can be efficiently implemented through capacity profiles reflecting remaining and used capacity over time; the profiles can be based on a support point representation. A capacity profile can be initialised and updated by using the fact that an activity i must always be in process during its *core time* between its latest start and earliest completion time; observe that it follows from the definition of interval processing time in (4.1) that $p_i(t, t+1) = 1$ for all $t \in [LS_i, EC_i[$, and $p_i(t, t+1) = 0$ otherwise. The capacity profile can therefore only change at points in time corresponding to the latest start or earliest completion time of an activity and can thus be represented using at most $2 \cdot |\mathcal{V}|$ support points.

Let t_k and t_{k+1} be two consecutive support points of the capacity profile, where the capacity value given at time t_k applies in the time interval $[t_k, t_{k+1}[$. Clearly, if an activity cannot be in process at time t_k, then in cannot be processed anywhere in $[t_k, t_{k+1}[$. We therefore only need to test the condition of Consistency Test 8 at the relevant support points and may strengthen the reduction rule by removing all times in the interval $]t_k - p_i, t_{k+1}[$. The worst case effort for checking all activities against the complete remaining capacity profile obviously is $O(|\mathcal{V}|^2)$. However, the average effort is often lower because usually not all activities have a non-zero core time and we need only check against the support points within the start time domain of an activity.

The capacity profile can be updated as part of the constraint propagation process. Whenever the start time domain of an activity is reduced, an update of the capacity profile may be required as the domain reduction may have led to a new or modified core time of i. Since the core time modification may overlap the entire profile, the worst case updating effort is $O(|\mathcal{V}|)$.

4.6.2 Activity Interval Consistency

The disjunctive sequence consistency tests developed in Section 4.5 can be generalised for cumulative scheduling in a straightforward way by considering available and required work instead of time spans and processing times. This relation was first pointed out by Nuijten (1994) (see also Nuijten and Aarts 1996). The following theorem extends the Sequence Consistency Theorem 2 for cumulative scheduling. In analogy to the total processing time $P(\mathcal{A})$ of the activities in a set $\mathcal{A}$, we define the total work with respect to a resource k as $W_k(\mathcal{A}) := \sum_{j \in \mathcal{A}} r_{jk} p_j$. As the time intervals considered are activity intervals that are defined by activity sets, we have chosen the name activity interval consistency.

Theorem 7 (Activity Interval Consistency). *Let* $\mathcal{A}', \mathcal{A}'' \subset \mathcal{A} \subseteq \mathcal{V}_k$. *If*

$$R_k \cdot \max_{u \in \mathcal{A} \setminus \mathcal{A}', v \in \mathcal{A} \setminus \mathcal{A}''} (LC_v - ES_u) < W(\mathcal{A}) \tag{4.17}$$

then an activity in $\mathcal{A}'$ *must start first or an activity in* $\mathcal{A}''$ *must end last.*

Proof. Similar to proof of Theorem 2. □

In contrast to the Sequence Consistency Theorem, we can no longer assume that $u \neq v$ because it is now possible that an activity that starts first also ends last.

Comparison of Condition (4.17) to the general Interval Capacity Constraint (4.3) shows that the condition only considers time intervals defined by a set $\mathcal{A}$ of activities and the total work of $\mathcal{A}$, as opposed to interval work. In the disjunctive case we were able to show that it was sufficient to consider activity intervals and that there was nothing to be gained from using interval work instead of set based work on the right side. However, it turns out that this is not the case for cumulative scheduling, so that the condition can actually be strengthened. The reason for presenting the condition in the above form is that this extension of the disjunctive case allows to generalise algorithms originally designed for sequencing. We will discuss a sharper form in Section 4.6.3.

The theorem can be used to derive consistency tests in analogy to the sequencing tests by using suitable values for $\mathcal{A}'$ and $\mathcal{A}''$, as shown in Table 4.1. Note that the meaning of conclusions such as $\mathcal{A}_i \rightarrow i$ or $i \rightarrow \mathcal{A}_i$ is that i must end after (start before) all activities in $\mathcal{A}_i$; in contrast to the disjunctive case this, however, does not imply that it must also start after (end before) $\mathcal{A}_i$.

Useful domain reductions can be deduced for the cumulative version of the input-or-output test with $i = j$. For $\mathcal{A}' = \mathcal{A}'' = \{i\}$, i.e., for testing the hypothetical constraint $H : i \not\rightarrow \mathcal{A}_i \wedge \mathcal{A}_i \not\rightarrow i$, Theorem 7 yields the following consistency test:

$$R_k \cdot \max_{u \in \mathcal{A}_i, v \in \mathcal{A}_i} (LC_v - ES_u) < W(\mathcal{A}) \quad \Longrightarrow \quad i \rightarrow \mathcal{A}_i \vee \mathcal{A}_i \rightarrow i \qquad (4.18)$$

Clearly, the excess amount of work that cannot be processed in the interval defined by $\min_{u \in \mathcal{A}_i} ES_u$ and $\max_{v \in \mathcal{A}_i} LC_v$ is the difference of the total work required by $\mathcal{A}$ and the capacity available within the interval. Since only activity i can move partially or completely out of the interval, we can conclude that the amount of processing time of i to be moved outside to the left and/or right, denoted by $\mathrm{rest}(\mathcal{A}, i)$, is:

$$\mathrm{rest}(\mathcal{A}, i) := \lceil (W(\mathcal{A}) - R_k \cdot \max_{u \in \mathcal{A}_i, v \in \mathcal{A}_i} (LC_v - ES_u)) / r_{ik} \rceil.$$

This observation allows to deduce domain reductions if the minimum amount of processing time that is always outside of the interval, regardless of the chosen start time, is less than the required amount:

$$p_i - \max_{u \in \mathcal{A}_i, v \in \mathcal{A}_i} (LC_v - ES_u) < \mathrm{rest}(\mathcal{A}, i). \qquad (4.19)$$

If Condition (4.19) holds, then the part of i that must be outside of the interval must either be completely on the left or be completely on the right side of the interval. This leads to the following domain reduction rule that can be applied if Conditions (4.18) and (4.19) hold:

$$\Delta_i := \Delta_i \backslash \,] \min_{u \in \mathcal{A}_i} ES_u - \mathrm{rest}(\mathcal{A}, i), \ \max_{v \in \mathcal{A}_i} LC_v + \mathrm{rest}(\mathcal{A}, i) - p_i [. \qquad (4.20)$$

This rule can actually be sharpened as follows: If the left or right bound reduction may be applied for $\mathcal{A}_i$ then it can also be applied for all subsets $\mathcal{A}' \subseteq \mathcal{A}_i$; this is not shown here. The sharpened form of the rule is equivalent to domain reduction

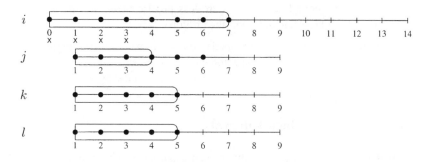

Figure 4.10: Four activities requiring 1 unit of a resource with capacity 2

rule (4.11). We refer to the conditions and this domain reduction rule as the cumulative input-or-output test.

Figure 4.10 illustrates the test. It shows an example (Nuijten 1994) with four activities to be processed by the same resource k with capacity $R_k = 2$. Inspection shows that if activity i is started before time 4, then it is impossible to schedule all of the other activities j, k, l within their time window. This is detected by the input-or-output test in the following way: Because $2 \cdot (9 - 1) < 18$ we conclude that $i \rightarrow \{j, k, l\} \vee \{j, k, l\} \rightarrow i$. The amount of processing time of i that must take place outside of the interval $[1, 9[$ is $\operatorname{rest}(\{i, j, k, l\}, i) = \lceil (18 - 2 \cdot (9 - 1))/1 \rceil = 2$. Because $7 - 8 < 2$, Condition (4.19) is satisfied and we apply the domain reduction rule $\Delta_i := \Delta_i \setminus \,]1 - 2, 9 + 2 - 7[= [4, 7]$, as shown in Figure 4.10.

It is interesting to consider a slight modification of the example: For $p_i = 6$ the reduction rule yields $\Delta_i := \Delta_i \setminus \,]0, 4[= \{0, 4, \dots, 7\}$; the value 0 is thus left in Δ_i and the domain bounds remain untouched.

The test presented here is similar to the three cumulative tests described by Nuijten (1994), who also describes a corresponding extension of his disjunctive consistency checking algorithm. The time complexity of the resulting algorithm is $O(|\{r_{ik}\}| \cdot |\mathcal{V}_k|^3)$, where $|\{r_{ik}\}|$ is the number of distinct resource capacity requirements. Another $O(|\mathcal{V}_k|^3)$ consistency checking algorithm for activity intervals has been described by Caseau and Laburthe (1996b).

Baptiste and Le Pape (2000) have recently proposed an $O(|\mathcal{V}_k|^2)$ algorithm for checking activity interval consistency that is based on the idea of transforming a cumulative resource and cumulative, non-preemptable activities to a disjunctive resource and corresponding disjunctive activities with preemption allowed; they then apply an algorithm that implements the input/output consistency test for disjunctive preemptive scheduling (Le Pape and Baptiste 1996b) and reduce the domains of the original, cumulative activities based on the domain reductions deduced for their disjunctive counterparts. While the computational complexity of the algorithm is lower, the time bound adjustments are less precise than with the algorithms of Nuijten (1994) and Caseau and Laburthe (1996b).

As mentioned before, the tests described in this Section could be strengthened by using interval work instead of simple work and by considering additional time intervals other than activity intervals. This is explained in the following section.

4.6.3   Minimum Slack Intervals

Figure 4.11 shows an example, similar to an example used by Baptiste et al. (1999), with five activities that require one unit of a resource with capacity 2. We can conclude that activity i must start after time 6. This can be deduced by first imposing the hypothetical constraint $H : C_i \leq 10$ or equivalently $S_i \leq 6$, and then testing the general Interval Capacity Constraint (4.3) for the interval $[1, 9[$. If i is constrained

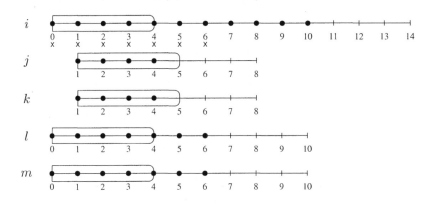

Figure 4.11: Five activities requiring one unit of a resource with capacity 2

to finish at time 10 or before, then the total amount of interval work to be processed within $[1, 9[$ is $2 \cdot 4 + 3 \cdot 3 = 17$ units, whereas only $2 \cdot (9 - 1) = 16$ units are available. We can thus conclude $\neg H$ and remove values less than or equal to 6 from the start time domain Δ_i. We emphasise that H can only be refuted by testing the interval $[1, 9[$, while the Interval Capacity Constraint is satisfied for all other intervals, including all activity intervals.

The example leads us back to the initial question, posed in Section 4.3, for what time intervals the capacity constraint should be tested. This question has recently been answered by Schwindt (1998b) and, independently, by Baptiste et al. (1999). By studying the possible extrema of the slack function (4.2) for a given set of activities $\mathcal{V}_k$, the set of intervals $[t_1, t_2[$ can be characterised for which the slack function can take a local or global minimum and may thus violate an Interval Capacity Constraint (4.3). Schwindt and Baptiste et al. have shown that the number of such minimum slack intervals is of order of magnitude $O(|\mathcal{V}_k|^2)$ and have given a characterisation of the intervals (the one in Schwindt (1998b) is slightly tighter). Thus, as we know from the initial example, the set of minimum-slack intervals is larger than the set of activity intervals but still of order of magnitude $O(|\mathcal{V}_k|^2)$. Since an intuitive description of the minimum slack intervals is hard to give, and because the proof is lengthy, we do not describe the set of minimum-slack intervals in more detail.

Baptiste et al. have developed an $O(|\mathcal{V}_k|^2)$ algorithm for computing the value of the slack function for all potential minimum-slack intervals, and an $O(|\mathcal{V}_k|^2 \log |\mathcal{V}_k|)$ algorithm has been described by Schwindt, who has used the interval capacity constraint for computing lower bounds for the problem $PS|temp|C_{max}$ by using a destructive improvement approach.

In order to reduce activity domains, Baptiste et al. suggest to use hypothetical constraints of the type $S_i \leq t_x$, similar to the example above, where t_x depends on the right bound of a minimum slack interval; there is an obvious symmetrical test.[7] The time complexity of an algorithm that computes all domain reductions which can be obtained on the minimum-slack intervals is $O(|\mathcal{V}_k|^3)$; this follows from the fact that the slack for all potential minimum-slack intervals can be computed with effort $O(|\mathcal{V}_k|^2)$, that there are $|\mathcal{V}_k|$ activities to be tested and that the candidate values for t_x and t_y depend on the minimum slack interval and the activity under consideration.

The development of a quadratic algorithm to compute all domain reductions is an open issue.

4.6.4 Fully and Partially Elastic Relaxations

This section describes two relaxations of the scheduling problem that have been suggested by Baptiste et al. (1999). The relaxations describe necessary conditions for the existence of a feasible schedule. They are based upon the idea of trying to answer the question whether there exists an integer function $es_k(t, i)$, (for *elastic schedule*), that describes the number of work units assigned to all activities over time so that for every activity the total number of units assigned equals the required work. The capacity assignment defined by $es_k(t, i)$ is elastic in the sense that it allows that the amount of resources assigned to activity i may vary while i is in process, as long the total amount of work corresponding to i is covered.

---

[7]Baptiste et al. (1999, Proposition 13) actually use the right bound of a minimum slack interval for t_x. However, we would like to point out that the resulting conclusion can be strenthened if, for a distinct activity i and a minimum slack interval $[t_1, t_2[$ the value $t_x = t_2 + \max\{0, t_1 - ES_i\}$ is used instead of $t_x = t_2$; this can easily be integrated in the proposed algorithm. Simply speaking, the value of t_x should be chosen in such a way that the minimum processing time of activity i within the interval $[t_1, t_2[$ that is obtained when i is right-shifted equals the minimum processing time when i is left-shifted.

In the example above, we thus obtain $t_x = 9 + \max\{0, 1 - 0\} = 10$; it can easily be seen that the domain reduction obtained for the hypothesis $t_x = 9$ is weaker.

The fully elastic relaxation is the decision problem of deciding whether a function $es_k(t, i)$ exists such that the following constraints hold:

$$es_k(t, i) = \quad 0, \qquad \text{for all } i \in \mathcal{V}_k \text{ and } t \notin \Delta_i \tag{4.21}$$

$$\sum_t es_k(t, i) = \quad p_i r_{ik}, \quad \text{for all } i \in \mathcal{V}_k \tag{4.22}$$

$$\sum_{i \in \mathcal{V}_k} es_k(t, i) \leq \quad R_k, \qquad \text{for all } t. \tag{4.23}$$

A tighter relaxation can be obtained by adding the two following constraints.

$$\sum_{t' < t} es_k(t', i) \leq \quad R_k \cdot (t - \min \Delta_i), \quad \text{for all } i \text{ and } t \in \Delta_i \tag{4.24}$$

$$\sum_{t \leq t'} es_k(t', i) \leq \quad R_k \cdot (\max \Delta_i - t), \quad \text{for all } i \text{ and } t \in \Delta_i. \tag{4.25}$$

The resulting decision problem is called partially elastic relaxation; the way in which assigned work may float within the activity time window is more restricted than in the fully elastic case.

The partially and fully elastic relaxations can be used to deduce activity domain reductions in the usual way. If, after adding hypothetical constraint H, it can be shown that no function $es_k(t, i)$ exists that satisfies Constraints (4.21) to (4.25), then $\neg H$ must hold. Baptiste et al. describe an $O(|\mathcal{V}_k|^2)$ domain reduction algorithm based upon the fully elastic relaxation and an $O(\log |\{r_{ik}\}| \cdot |\mathcal{V}_k|^2)$ algorithm using the partially elastic relaxation, where $|\{r_{ik}\}|$ is the number of distinct resource capacity requirements.

The partially elastic relaxation is strictly weaker than the general interval consistency constraint (Baptiste et al. 1999).

4.7 Multi-Mode Consistency Tests

Given an instance of the multi-mode project scheduling problem $MPS|temp|C_{max}$ we can obtain an associated instance of the problem $PS|temp|C_{max}$ by replacing the input data that depends on the mode assignments, i.e., processing times, time lags, and resource requirements, with the corresponding minimal values over all modes (Heilmann 1998). As the resulting associated problem is a single-mode problem we can apply the consistency tests to it that have been described in the preceding sections. If the associated problem is a relaxation of the original problem then any domain reduction obtained for the associated problem must also apply for the original problem instance. The concept of the associated problem instance is formally expressed in the following definition.

Definition 1 (Mode-Minimal Problem Instance). *Given an instance* $\mathcal{P}$ *of the problem MPS|temp|C_{max} described by*

$$\mathcal{P} = (\mathcal{V}, \mathcal{E}, (p_{iM_i}), (d_{iM_i jM_j}), (r_{iM_i k}), R^\rho, R^\nu, \Delta_S, \Delta_M)$$

the associated mode-minimal problem instance $\widetilde{\mathcal{P}}$ *is the instance of the problem PS|temp|C_{max} that is described by*

$$\widetilde{\mathcal{P}} = (\mathcal{V}, \mathcal{E}, \widetilde{p}, (\widetilde{d}_{ij}), (\widetilde{r}_{ik}), R^\rho, \Delta_S),$$

where

$$
\begin{aligned}
\widetilde{p}_i &:= \min_{\mu \in \Delta_{M_i}} p_{i\mu}, & \forall i \in \mathcal{V}, \\
\widetilde{d}_{ij} &:= \min_{\mu \in \Delta_{M_i}, \nu \in \Delta_{M_j}} d_{i\mu j\nu}, & \forall (i,j) \in \mathcal{E}, \\
\widetilde{r}_{ik} &:= \min_{\mu \in \Delta_{M_i}} r_{i\mu k}, & \forall i \in \mathcal{V}, \forall k \in \mathcal{R}^\rho.
\end{aligned}
$$

Given an instance $\mathcal{P}$ of the problem *MPS|temp|C_{max}*, the consistency tests for the temporal constraints and the interval consistency tests may then be applied to the corresponding minimal problem instance $\widetilde{\mathcal{P}}$. Since $\widetilde{\mathcal{P}}$ is a relaxation of $\mathcal{P}$, any domain reduction obtained for $\widetilde{\mathcal{P}}$ must also apply for $\mathcal{P}$. As $\widetilde{\mathcal{P}}$ is a single-mode problem, any consistency test applied to it can, of course, only lead to reductions of the activity start time domains.

We therefore introduce three additional simple consistency tests for reducing the activity mode domains Δ_{M_i} based on the consideration of temporal constraints, renewable resource constraints, and non-renewable resource constraints. The tests are presented in the form of condition and conclusion. We do not comment on the obvious computational complexity of the tests.

If a temporal constraint (i,j) can never hold in case a particular mode assignment $\mu \in \Delta_{M_i}$ is chosen for activity i, regardless of the mode of j, then we may remove μ from Δ_{M_i}:

$$
\begin{aligned}
(i,j) \in \mathcal{E}, \mu \in \Delta_{M_i} : \\
ES_i + \min_{\nu \in \Delta_{M_j}} d_{i\mu j\nu} > LS_j \quad \Longrightarrow \quad \Delta_{M_i} := \Delta_{M_i} \setminus \{\mu\}.
\end{aligned}
\tag{4.26}
$$

Additionally, any mode assignment $\mu \in \Delta_{M_i}$ that leads to a violation of a unit interval capacity constraint for a renewable resource may be removed from Δ_{M_i}:

$$
\begin{aligned}
i \in \mathcal{V}_k, \mu \in \Delta_{M_i}, t \in [LS_i, EC_i[: \\
slack_\Delta^\rho(\mathcal{V}_k \setminus \{i\}, k, t, t+1) < r_{i\mu k} \quad \Longrightarrow \quad \Delta_{M_i} := \Delta_{M_i} \setminus \{\mu\}.
\end{aligned}
\tag{4.27}
$$

A similar test may be applied for the constraints for non-renewable resources. In analogy to Definition (4.2), a slack function for non-renewable resources may be defined as follows.

Algorithm 2 Mode Shaving

> **repeat**
> $\Delta^{old} := \Delta$
>   **for all** activities $i \in \mathcal{V}$ **do**
>   **for all** modes $\mu \in \Delta_{M_i}$ **do**
> $\Delta' := \Delta$
> $\Delta'_{M_i} := \{\mu\}$
>   **if** a current domain in $CP(\Delta')$ is empty **then**
> $\Delta_{M_i} := \Delta_{M_i} \setminus \{\mu\}$
>   **end if**
>   **end for**
>   **end for**
> **until** $\Delta = \Delta^{old}$

$$slack_\Delta^\nu(\mathcal{V}, k) := R_k^\nu - \sum_{i \in \mathcal{V}_k} \min_{\mu \in \Delta_{M_i}} r_{i\mu k}$$

Using this function we can state the following consistency test that removes any mode assignment $\mu \in \Delta_{M_i}$ that leads to a violation of a non-renewable resource constraint:

$$i \in \mathcal{V}_k, \mu \in \Delta_{M_i} :$$
$$slack_\Delta^\nu(\mathcal{V}_k \setminus \{i\}, k) < r_{i\mu k} \quad \Longrightarrow \quad \Delta_{M_i} := \Delta_{M_i} \setminus \{\mu\}. \tag{4.28}$$

The three mode consistency tests 4.26 to 4.28 are subsumed in the *mode shaving* test, which repeatedly tries to show that a mode assignment $\mu \in \Delta_{M_i}$ leads to a contradiction by applying constraint propagation until a fixed point is reached or a domain becomes empty. The idea of the test is similar to the shaving test for reducing start time domains described in Section 4.5.8. The test is shown in Algorithm 2. The operator CP may apply any number of consistency tests but, of course, must not recursively apply the mode shaving test itself.

4.8   Summary

We have introduced simple consistency tests for temporal constraints and have presented a general, unifying framework for understanding interval capacity consistency tests. Within this framework, we have surveyed and extended previous results that have been obtained in the areas of Operations Research and Artificial Intelligence. We have related the concept of energetic reasoning to sequence consistency tests known under the names of immediate selection or edge finding.

The interval consistency tests described in this chapter have been applied frequently and with great success for solving disjunctive scheduling problems. Fewer and so far less conclusive results have been reported for the application of the tests for cumulative scheduling. Several tests that we have described are available in general purpose scheduling software libraries such as ILOG Scheduler (Le Pape 1994b, 1995, Nuijten and Le Pape 1998), CHIP (Aggoun and Beldiceanu 1993), or CLAIRE Schedule (Le Pape and Baptiste 1996a).

Chapter 5

A Branch-and-Bound Algorithm

This chapter describes a time-oriented, constraint propagation based approach to resource-constrained project scheduling with generalised precedence constraints. We present a branch-and-bound algorithm for the general problem $PS|temp|C_{max}$ that enumerates possible activity start times based on the idea that, at a given node of the search tree, an activity must either start as early as possible or be delayed. A central feature of the algorithm is the application of constraint propagation techniques that actively exploit the temporal and resource constraints during the search in order to narrow down the set of possible activity start times and thus reduce the search space. Further reduction of the search effort is achieved by enforcing some necessary conditions that must be met by active schedules.

One of the main advantages of the time-oriented branching scheme is its conceptual simplicity which allows to modify and extend the approach for related practical scheduling problems that are often complicated by additional constraints. Furthermore, the constraint propagation techniques that we use are not custom-tailored for the problem $PS|temp|C_{max}$ but are of an elementary nature and have a wide applicability.

Extensive computational experiments with systematically generated test cases for the problem $PS|temp|C_{max}$ with one hundred up to five hundred activities per problem instance show that the algorithm solves more problems to optimality and feasibility than other exact solution procedures which have recently been proposed, and that the truncated version of the algorithm is also a very good heuristic.

In addition to the general problem $PS|temp|C_{max}$ the algorithm is evaluated for the special case of the problem $PS|prec|C_{max}$ which contains only simple precedence constraints. Computational experiments with large benchmark test sets, ranging in size from thirty to one hundred and twenty activities per problem instance, show that the algorithm scales well and is competitive with other exact solution approaches for this special problem.

The structure of this chapter is as follows. Section 5.1 reviews the most relevant previous solution approaches. Section 5.2 summarizes which of the consistency tests introduced in Chapter 4 are used within the branch-and-bound algorithm. The algorithm itself is then presented in Section 5.3, and Section 5.4 finally describes the computational experiments.

5.1   Previous Solution Approaches

Already the problem $PS|prec|C_{max}$ is NP-hard. Most exact solution methods are therefore based on branch-and-bound search. Beginning with the work of Johnson (1967), a great number of branch-and-bound algorithms for solving the problem $PS|prec|C_{max}$ have been developed, and we refer the reader to the recent survey papers of Brucker et al. (1999), Herroelen et al. (1998), Kolisch and Padman (2001), and Elmaghraby (1995) for a description and classification of the various approaches. Currently, the most effective exact algorithms seem to be the ones of Demeulemeester and Herroelen (1997b), Sprecher (2000), Mingozzi et al. (1998), Brucker et al. (1998) and the procedures of Klein and Scholl (2000, 1999b), which can solve a generalised version of the problem $PS|prec|C_{max}$ with arbitrary minimal time lags.

While the classic resource-constrained project scheduling problem $PS|prec|C_{max}$ has been intensively studied, algorithms for solving the problem $PS|temp|C_{max}$ have only recently received growing attention in the literature as can be seen in the surveys by Herroelen et al. (1998) and Brucker et al. (1999). This may to some extent have been caused by the fact that the problem $PS|prec|C_{max}$ itself is intractable. As an extension, the problem $PS|temp|C_{max}$ is, of course, also NP-hard, and even the question whether a problem instance has a feasible solution is NP-hard (Bartusch et al. 1988).

Different heuristics for resource-constrained project scheduling with generalised precedence constraints have been proposed, and we refer the reader to Zhan (1994), Neumann and Zhan (1995), Brinkmann and Neumann (1996), Schwindt (1998b), Franck and Neumann (1998), Franck and Selle (1998), and Neumann and Zimmermann (1999) for a discussion.

Exact branch-and-bound algorithms for the problem $PS|temp|C_{max}$ have been developed by Bartusch et al. (1988), De Reyck and Herroelen (1998) (see also De Reyck et al. 1999), Schwindt (1998a,b), and Fest et al. (1999). The common idea behind these algorithms is to relax the resource constraints and compute an optimal time-feasible schedule. The resulting schedule will usually violate resource constraints and is therefore scanned for resource conflicts, i.e., times when more resources are consumed than are available. The procedures then branch over the possible alternatives for resolving these conflicts. A resource conflict is resolved by adding new constraints that delay some of the activities causing the conflict (conflict set). Subject to the constraints added so far, an optimal time-feasible schedule is then re-computed and again tested for further resource conflicts. In the algorithms of Bartusch et al. (1988) and De Reyck and Herroelen (1998) activities from a conflict set are delayed by introducing additional classic precedence constraints. The procedure of Schwindt (1998b) delays activities by adding special precedence constraints between pairs of disjoint sets of conflicting activities; all activities in the second set are delayed until the completion time of a first activity in the first set. The algorithm of Fest et al. (1999) resolves conflicts by dynamically increasing release dates for certain activities.

The time-oriented branch-and-bound algorithm that we describe here is different in the sense that it simultaneously considers temporal and resource constraints. Instead of enumerating alternatives for resolving resource conflicts that occur in a relaxed problem, the procedure enumerates possible activity start times based on the following simple idea: at a given node of the search tree, an activity must either start as early as possible or be delayed. A central feature of the algorithm is the application of constraint propagation techniques that actively exploit the temporal and resource constraints during the search in order to narrow down the set of possible activity start times and thus reduce the search space. Further reduction of the search effort is achieved by enforcing some necessary conditions that must be met by active schedules.

Time-oriented branching schemes that branch over activity start times have previously been applied for solving several special cases of the problem $PS|temp|C_{max}$. The first time-oriented branching schemes for the problem $PS|prec|C_{max}$ have been described by Elmaghraby (1977) and Talbot and Patterson (1978); the common idea behind these algorithms is to branch over all possible start time assignments of the next activity to be scheduled, and the number of child nodes generated at a given node of the search tree thus depends on the selected activity. Carlier and Latapie (1991) have proposed a binary search scheme in which branching consists of selecting an activity and splitting its interval of possible start times into two intervals of equal size. Martin and Shmoys (1996) have developed a time oriented algorithm for the job shop scheduling problem. Caseau and Laburthe (1996b) have independently designed a branch-and-bound algorithm for a multi-mode project scheduling problem that can be classified as $MPS|prec|C_{max}$ in the scheme of Brucker et al. (1999). For the single mode case the algorithm uses the same branching strategy as the procedure of Martin and Shmoys, which schedules an activity at its earliest start time or delays it upon backtracking until the earliest completion time of some other activity, resulting in a binary search tree. The branching scheme described here also makes use of this elementary approach. The branching strategy described by Caseau and Laburthe has also been used in modified form in the studies of Baptiste et al. (1999) and Baptiste and Le Pape (2000). Heipcke and Colombani (1997) have developed an algorithm for a version of the problem $PS|prec|C_{max}$ in which resource supply and demand may vary over time; the branching scheme of their algorithm is also binary; an activity is scheduled at its earliest start time or delayed upon backtracking by a single unit of time. An unusual feature of their algorithm is that activities are in general not scheduled in order of increasing start times.

5.2   Constraint Propagation

5.2.1   Consistency Tests

The branch-and-bound algorithm that will be described in the next section relies to a great extent on efficient constraint propagation techniques. At each node of the search tree, a fixed point is computed by applying at least the two most basic consistency tests introduced in Chapter 4 within the constraint propagation algorithm:

- Precedence Consistency Test 1;

- Unit-Interval Consistency Test 8.

As we will see, the application of these two tests is an essential part of the branch-and-bound algorithm.

Additionally, the following consistency tests for pair-wise disjunctive activities as defined by Lemma 1 are applied:

- Lag-Based Disjunctive Consistency Test 2;

- Input/Output Consistency Test 3 for pairs of disjunctive activities;

- General Input/Output Consistency Test 3 for disjunctive sub-problems, which are selected as described in Section 4.4.2.

5.2.2   Some Properties of the Earliest Start Times

The Precedence Consistency Test 1 and the Unit Interval Consistency Test 8 that are applied within the fixed point constraint propagation algorithm affect the earliest activity start times as follows. Let $pc_j(\Delta)$ be the minimal start time of an activity $j \in \mathcal{V}$ if only the precedence constraints (i, j) between activities i in the set $\mathcal{V}^s(\Delta) := \{i \in \mathcal{V} \mid |\Delta_i| = 1\}$ of scheduled activities and j are considered:

$$pc_j(\Delta) := \max_{i \in \mathcal{V}^s(\Delta)} \{S_i + d_{ij} \mid (i, j) \in \mathcal{E}\}. \tag{5.1}$$

Here, we have used the convention that the maximum of the empty set is 0. Let further $rc_j(\Delta)$ be the minimal start time of j if additionally resource constraints are considered:

$$rc_j(\Delta) := \min_{t \geq pc_j(\Delta)} \{t \mid \quad \forall k \in \mathcal{R}, \forall t' \in [t, \ldots, t + p_j[: \\ slack_\Delta(\mathcal{V}_k \setminus \{j\}, t', t' + 1) \geq r_{jk}\}.$$

Then, obviously,

$$ES_j(\Delta) \geq rc_j(\Delta) \geq pc_j(\Delta).$$

A schedule S can be naturally identified with a set of current domains, where each domain Δ_i contains the corresponding start time, i.e., $\Delta_i := \{S_i\}$. This justifies the notation $rc_j(S)$ and $pc_j(S)$. Clearly, S can only be active if for all activities either a precedence constraint or insufficient resource capacity prevents a left-shift. Thus, in any active schedule S, the identity

$$S_j = rc_j(S) \qquad (5.2)$$

holds for all $j \in \mathcal{V}$.

Since we may without loss of generality assume that an activity has at most $|\mathcal{V}| - 1$ predecessors, the calculation of pc_j requires effort $O(|\mathcal{V}|)$. The calculation of rc_j is based upon pc_j and a traversal of the support points of the remaining capacity profile, as introduced in Section 4.6.1, and requires a worst case effort $O(|\mathcal{R}| \, |\mathcal{V}|)$. The average effort for typical problems is much lower because the number of predecessors of an activity is usually significantly smaller than $O(|\mathcal{V}|)$ and in general only a small part of the capacity profile must be traversed.

5.3 The Branch-and-Bound Algorithm

The main component of the branch-and-bound algorithm described in this section is a time-oriented, binary branching scheme. We will show that this branching scheme generates at least all active schedules, so that traversing the search tree will result in an optimal solution. Inversely, the branching scheme tries to avoid constructing non-active schedules, which cuts down the search space considerably. A detailed description of the branching scheme is given in Section 5.3.1.

Section 5.3.2 deals with the "bounding" part of the algorithm. Generally, nodes of the search tree can be fathomed through the comparison of upper and lower bounds for the optimal makespan, which are computed in the nodes of the search tree. As a peculiarity, however, our algorithm does *not* explicitly compute lower bounds. Indeed, the bound-oriented fathoming of nodes is a useful by-product of constraint propagation techniques, that have to be applied anyway in the "branching" part of the algorithm.

Additionally, the search space is reduced by adding constraints that must be satisfied by all active schedules that can be developed from a given node, and through the application of a simple left-shift dominance test. This is discussed in Section 5.3.3.

5.3.1 The Branching Scheme

The branching structure that we describe here is based on a simple time-oriented schedule generation scheme, which results in a binary search tree. Each node α

of the search tree is associated a set $\Delta(\alpha) = \{\Delta_i(\alpha) \mid i \in \mathcal{V}\}$ of current do-
mains, which uniquely determine the sets $\mathcal{V}^s(\Delta(\alpha)) := \{i \in \mathcal{V} \mid |\Delta_i(\alpha)| = 1\}$
and $\mathcal{V}^f(\Delta(\alpha)) := \{i \in \mathcal{V} \mid |\Delta_i(\alpha)| > 1\}$ of scheduled and non-scheduled activi-
ties, respectively. (In order to simplify the notation we will write $\mathcal{V}^s(\alpha)$ instead of
$\mathcal{V}^s(\Delta(\alpha))$, etc., whenever possible.) Generating a specific schedule is equivalent to
reducing the current domains until all activities are appropriately scheduled. One
method of domain reduction that will be extensively used is the application of constraint propagation. Since in general, however, constraint propagation alone does not
schedule all activities, some activities additionally will have to be scheduled by an
explicit assignment of their start time variables.

At every node α of the search tree an unscheduled activity $j \in \mathcal{V}^f(\alpha)$ is chosen
and two child nodes are generated. Denoting the left child node with $l(\alpha)$ and the
right child node with $r(\alpha)$, the branching scheme relies on the following simple node
generation rule.

$l(\alpha)$:   Start j at its earliest start time by setting $S_j(l(\alpha)) := ES_j(\alpha)$.

$r(\alpha)$:   Increase the earliest start of j by choosing $ES_j(r(\alpha)) > ES_j(\alpha)$.

A complete specification of the branching scheme now requires the answer to two
questions. The first question deals with the problem of which activity $j \in \mathcal{V}^f(\alpha)$ to
choose in node α. The second question is how the earliest start time of j should be
increased in $r(\alpha)$. We will first describe the choice of an activity j and then derive
an earliest start time adjustment for the right child node. We will then summarize
the branching scheme and show its completeness, i.e., prove that it can generate any
active schedule.

Selection of Activities

At node α, an activity can be selected for branching if it is free and *non-delayed*. For
the time being, it is not necessary to describe this attribute more closely. We only
assume that the set of non-delayed activities $\mathcal{V}^{f'}(\alpha)$ is a non-empty subset of the set
of free activities. An activity j is then selected according to the following rule:

Choose $j \in \mathcal{V}^{f'}(\alpha)$, such that $ES_j = t(\alpha)$ where $t(\alpha)$ is the schedule
time:

$$t(\alpha) := \min_{i \in \mathcal{V}^{f'}(\alpha)} ES_i(\alpha). \qquad (5.3)$$

Ties are first broken by selecting an activity which satisfies some secondary criterion,
then randomly. In general, we use the minimal *time slack*, i.e. $|\Delta_i|$, as secondary
criterion; this means that we use the well known first fail principle which consists
of first instantiating the variable with the fewest remaining possible values. We will
denote with $act(\alpha)$ the activity chosen in α.

After the description of the selection rule, we are left with the problem of how to identify the set of non-delayed activities. Of course, we can always set $\mathcal{V}^{f'}(\alpha) := \mathcal{V}^f(\alpha)$. This, however, is not sensible, since choosing an arbitrary free activity will often lead to a non-active schedule. We will therefore show how to specify the set of delayed activities, so as to capture the notion of active schedules more closely.

It will prove useful to partition the set of free activities into a set of activities which still have to satisfy a maximal time lag and a set of activities which do not have to. Let $\mathcal{E} = \mathcal{E}^{min} \cup \mathcal{E}^{max}$, where $\mathcal{E}^{min} := \{(i,j) \in \mathcal{E} \mid d_{ij} > 0\}$ and $\mathcal{E}^{max} := \{(i,j) \in \mathcal{E} \mid d_{ij} \leq 0\}$ are the relations specifying the minimal and maximal time lags between pairs of activities. We then define the set

$$\mathcal{V}^{tc}(\alpha) := \{j \in \mathcal{V}^f(\alpha) \mid \exists i \in \mathcal{V}^f(\alpha) : (i,j) \in \mathcal{E}^{max}\}$$

of *timemax-constrained* activities and the set $\mathcal{V}^{tu}(\alpha) := \mathcal{V}^f(\alpha) \setminus \mathcal{V}^{tc}(\alpha)$ of *timemax-unconstrained* activities.

We can now describe the set of free and non-delayed activities:

$$\mathcal{V}^{f'}(\alpha) := \mathcal{V}^{tc}(\alpha) \cup \{j \in \mathcal{V}^f(\alpha) \mid ES_j(\alpha) = rc_j(\alpha)\}$$

This means that a free activity is a candidate for branching if it either has an "incoming" backward arc, or if its earliest start time equals its current earliest resource feasible start time $rc_i(\alpha)$. Note that the latter condition may in particular not be given if the constraint propagation algorithm has adjusted $ES_j(\alpha)$ to some value greater than $rc_j(\alpha)$, or if an activity has been delayed (by an amount of time to be defined below). The definition of the set of free and selectable activities $\mathcal{V}^{f'}$ can therefore be interpreted as follows: a delayed activity i without an incoming backward arc remains un-selectable until we know that the resource capacity "provided" by delaying i has been used by some other activity. The following lemma justifies our choice of the set $\mathcal{V}^{f'}$.

Lemma 2 (Existence of Earliest Start Time Schedules). *Let α be a node of the search tree. If there is an unscheduled activity then $\mathcal{V}^{f'}(\alpha)$ is not empty, or α cannot lead to an active schedule.*

Proof. Let S be an active schedule which is domain feasible in α, and let us assume that $\mathcal{V}^{tc}(\alpha) = \emptyset$. We then have to prove that there exists an activity $j \in \mathcal{V}^f(\alpha)$ satisfying $ES_j(\alpha) = rc_j(\alpha)$. Since $S_j \geq ES_j(\alpha) \geq rc_j(\alpha)$, we only have to show that for some $j \in \mathcal{V}^f(\alpha)$ the identity $S_j = rc_j(\alpha)$ holds.

Suppose that $S_j > rc_j(\alpha)$ for all $j \in \mathcal{V}^f(\alpha)$. Observe that the set of timemax-unconstrained activities $\mathcal{V}^{tu}(\alpha)$ is not empty, since $\mathcal{V}^f(\alpha)$ is not empty. It is therefore possible to choose an activity $j \in \mathcal{V}^{tu}(\alpha)$ with minimal start time in S:

$$S_j = \min_{i \in \mathcal{V}^{tu}(\alpha)} S_i. \tag{5.4}$$

Using the obvious identity $\mathcal{V}^s(S) = \mathcal{V}$, Equation (5.1) tells us that

$$pc_j(S) = \max_{i \in \mathcal{V}}\{S_i + d_{ij} \mid (i,j) \in \mathcal{E}\},$$

If there exists a precedence constraint $(i,j) \in \mathcal{E}^{min}$, then $i \in \mathcal{V}^s(\alpha)$, since otherwise $S_i + d_{ij} \leq S_j$ and $d_{ij} > 0$ immediately imply $S_i < S_j$, which is a contradiction to Equation (5.4). If $(i,j) \in \mathcal{E}^{max}$, then $i \in \mathcal{V}^s(\alpha)$ follows directly from $j \in \mathcal{V}^{tu}(\alpha)$. So for all $(i,j) \in \mathcal{E}$, we have $i \in \mathcal{V}^s(\alpha)$ and the last equation can be simplified as follows:

$$pc_j(S) = \max_{i \in \mathcal{V}^s(\alpha)}\{S_i + d_{ij} \mid (i,j) \in \mathcal{E}\}.$$

Domain feasibility now allows us to deduce the identity $S_i = S_i(\alpha)$ for all $i \in \mathcal{V}^s(\alpha)$, which leads to

$$pc_j(S) = \max_{i \in \mathcal{V}^s(\alpha)}\{S_i(\alpha) + d_{ij} \mid (i,j) \in \mathcal{E}\} = pc_j(\alpha). \tag{5.5}$$

As S is active we know from Equation (5.2) that $S_j = rc_j(S)$, so that we can conclude $rc_j(S) > rc_j(\alpha)$. More formally

$$\min_{t \geq pc_j(S)}\{t \mid \forall k \in \mathcal{R}, \forall t' \in [t,\ldots,t + p_j[: slack_S(\mathcal{V}_k, t', t' + 1) \geq r_{jk}\}$$
$$> \min_{t \geq pc_j(\alpha)}\{t \mid \forall k \in \mathcal{R}, \forall t' \in [t,\ldots,t + p_j[: slack_\alpha(\mathcal{V}_k, t', t' + 1) \geq r_{jk}\}.$$

Because $pc_j(S) = pc_j(\alpha)$, this means that there must be some resource $k \in \mathcal{R}$, such that for $t = S_j - 1$ the following conditions hold:

$$slack_\alpha(\mathcal{V}_k - \{j\}, t, t + 1) \geq r_{jk},$$
$$slack_S(\mathcal{V}_k - \{j\}, t, t + 1) < r_{jk}.$$

If the slack of period t in S is smaller than the slack of this period at node α, then the interval processing time $p_v(t, t + 1)$ of at least one activity $v \in \mathcal{V}^f(\alpha) = \mathcal{V}^{tu}(\alpha)$ must assume the value 0 in α and 1 in S. According to the definition of interval processing times in (4.1), $p_v(t, t + 1) = 1$ implies that $t + 1 - S_v > 0$. We thus obtain $S_v \leq t < S_j$, which is a contradiction to Condition (5.4). So, in fact, there must exist $j \in \mathcal{V}^f(\alpha)$ with $S_j = rc_j(\alpha)$.   □

Delaying Duration

Let us now turn to the question of how to increase the earliest start time of a selected activity $j = act(\alpha)$ if we branch to the right. A first simple alternative is to delay the activity by a single time unit. However, we can do better by observing that the resulting schedule S can only be active if either (1) a precedence constraint or (2) low slack prohibits a left-shift of the selected activity. Since the activity will be delayed by at least one time unit, the first case can be ruled out if all precedence constraints $(i,j) \in \mathcal{E}$ are already resolved (see pages 20 and 34) in node α. The second case requires that the slack of all activities except j is insufficient to the left of $S_j(\alpha)$. Intuitively, this can only be the case if $S_j(\alpha)$ matches the completion time of some activity that shares resources with j. This leads to the following lemma, in which $\mathcal{R}_i := \{k \in \mathcal{R} \mid r_{ik} > 0\}$ denotes the set of resources required by activity i.

Lemma 3 (Delaying Duration). *Let α be the current node of the search tree and all $(i, j) \in \mathcal{E}$ be resolved for $j = act(\alpha)$. The set of all activities that share resources with j and finish after $t(\alpha)$ is denoted with $\mathcal{V}' := \{i \in \mathcal{V} \setminus \{j\} \mid \mathcal{R}_i \cap \mathcal{R}_j \neq \emptyset \wedge EC_i(\alpha) > t(\alpha)\}$. Let further*

$$t^+(\alpha) := \begin{cases} \min_{i \in \mathcal{V}'} EC_i(\alpha) & \text{if } \mathcal{V}' \neq \emptyset, \\ t(\alpha) + 1 & \text{otherwise.} \end{cases}$$

Then $S_j \geq t^+(\alpha)$ in any active schedule S developed from $r(\alpha)$.

Proof. We need only consider the case where $\mathcal{V}' \neq \emptyset$. If j is delayed in $r(\alpha)$ and S is active then, according to equation (5.2), $rc_j(S) = S_j > t(\alpha)$. If $rc_j(S) > t(\alpha)$ then, obviously, either

$$rc_j(S) \geq pc_j(S) > t(\alpha) \tag{5.6}$$

or

$$rc_j(S) > t(\alpha) \geq pc_j(S). \tag{5.7}$$

If, for the given j, all $(i, j) \in \mathcal{E}$ are resolved, then $LS_i + d_{ij} \leq ES_j$ for all $(i, j) \in \mathcal{E}$. Thus $pc_j(S) \leq t(\alpha)$ and condition (5.6) cannot hold. Now consider condition (5.7). We will show that any time $t = rc_j(S)$ satisfying this condition must correspond to the completion time of some activity. If condition (5.7) holds then there must be some time t and some resource $k \in \mathcal{R}$ for which:

$$slack_S(\mathcal{V}_k \setminus \{j\}, t-1, t) < r_{jk} \wedge slack_S(\mathcal{V}_k \setminus \{j\}, t, t+1) \geq r_{jk}.$$

This immediately implies that there must be some activity in $\mathcal{V}_k \setminus \{j\}$ that is processed in the interval $[t-1, t[$ but not in $[t, t+1[$, i.e. an activity which finishes at time t.

We have thus derived that if j is delayed from $ES_j(\alpha)$ and the resulting schedule is active, then $S_j = rc_j(S)$ must equal some completion time $t > t(\alpha)$. Therefore we can conclude that $ES_j(r(\alpha))$ must be greater than or equal to an earliest completion time greater than $t(\alpha)$. Of course, we need only consider activities that share a common resource with j. $\square$

It is worth mentioning that the precedence constraints $(i, j) \in \mathcal{E}$ are always resolved if j has only incoming arcs with positive weight, i.e. if $j \in \mathcal{V}^{tu}(\alpha)$.

At the root ρ   Let ρ be the root of the search tree, and let $\Delta_i' := [0, UB - p_i]$ for all $i \in \mathcal{V}$. Then:

$$\Delta(\rho) := CP(\Delta').$$

In node α   Let α be a node of the search tree. Let $\Delta(\alpha) = \{\Delta_i(\alpha) \mid i \in \mathcal{V}\}$ be the set of current domains in α and $j := act(\alpha)$ the activity chosen in α.

Branching to the left $l(\alpha)$
Let $\Delta'(\alpha) := \{\Delta_1(\alpha), \ldots, \Delta_j'(\alpha), \ldots, \Delta_n(\alpha)\}$, where

$$\Delta_j'(\alpha) := \{t(\alpha)\}.$$

Then: $\Delta(l(\alpha)) := CP(\Delta'(\alpha))$.

Branching to the right $r(\alpha)$
Let $\Delta''(\alpha) := \{\Delta_1(\alpha), \ldots, \Delta_j''(\alpha), \ldots, \Delta_n(\alpha)\}$, where

$$\Delta_j''(\alpha) := \begin{cases} \Delta_j(\alpha) \cap [t(\alpha) + 1, \infty[& \text{if there is an unresolved } (i, j) \in \mathcal{E}^{max} \\ \Delta_j(\alpha) \cap [t^+(\alpha), \infty[& \text{otherwise.} \end{cases}$$

Then: $\Delta(r(\alpha)) := CP(\Delta''(\alpha))$.

Figure 5.1: The branching scheme

Summary of the Branching Scheme

We are now able to define the branching scheme recursively; this is done in Figure 5.1. Recall that we only have to specify $\Delta(\alpha)$, since this determines all other sets and values.

The search tree is traversed in depth-first order until a leaf node is generated. This happens whenever $\mathcal{V}^{f'}(\alpha) = \emptyset$. This leaf node represents a solution, if $\mathcal{V}^s(\alpha) = \mathcal{V}$. Backtracking occurs when a leaf node is reached or when an inconsistency has been detected, i.e. when $\Delta_i(\alpha)$ has become empty for some activity $i \in \mathcal{V}$.

The minimum possible depth of the tree is zero and is obtained if all activities are scheduled through constraint propagation at the root node. The maximum depth of the search tree that is possible in the worst case is reached when branching to the very right side of the tree in the following way. Starting at the root node, we can initially at most delay $|\mathcal{V}| - 1$ activities and must then schedule the remaining activity or backtracking would be initiated. Next we can, at most, branch $|\mathcal{V}| - 2$ times to the right before branching a single time to the left. By continuing in this way, we may reach a theoretical worst case depth of $1/2|\mathcal{V}|(|\mathcal{V}| + 1)$.

The following theorem states that our time-oriented branching scheme is complete, i.e., that an optimal schedule is generated. As we have already discussed in Section 2.1.4, it is sufficient to prove that all active schedules can be generated.

Theorem 8 (Completeness of Time-Oriented Branching). *The time-oriented branching scheme generates all active schedules, i.e., if S is an active schedule, then the search tree contains a leaf node α in which all activities are scheduled and $S_i = S_i(\alpha)$ for all $i \in V$.*

Proof. Let S be an active schedule. We will first prove the following assertion: if S is domain feasible in α, then S is domain feasible in either $l(\alpha)$ or $r(\alpha)$.

Lemma 2 ensures that $V^{f'}(\alpha)$ is not empty, so that there exists an activity $j \in V^{f'}$ that is selected in α. Now, if $S_j = ES_j(\alpha)$, then S is domain feasible with respect to $\Delta'(\alpha)$ as defined in Figure 5.1. Constraint propagation only removes values from current domains Δ_i not belonging to any schedule that is domain feasible with respect to Δ. This implies that S must be domain feasible with respect to $\Delta(l(\alpha)) = CP(\Delta'(\alpha))$. If $S_j > ES_j(\alpha)$, then a similar argumentation in combination with Lemma 3 shows that S must be domain feasible with respect to $\Delta(r(\alpha))$.

We can conclude, that there exists a path $\rho, \alpha_1, \alpha_2, \ldots$, along which S is domain feasible. Let $|\Delta| := \sum_{i \in V} |\Delta_i|$. Given the finiteness of the current domains, $\infty > |\Delta(\rho)| > |\Delta(\alpha_1)| > |\Delta(\alpha_2)| > \ldots \geq n$ must hold. This implies, that S is domain feasible in some node α_m satisfying $|\Delta(\alpha_m)| = n$, i.e. $V^s(\alpha_m) = V$. This completes the proof. □

5.3.2 Upper and Lower Bounds

The makespan of an initial or improved schedule is, of course, used as upper bound UB.

If Δ is a set of current domains then constraint propagation implies a lower bound of all domain feasible schedules in the following way. Let us assume that $UB' \leq UB$ is a hypothetical upper bound. Setting $\Delta' := \{\Delta_i \cap [0, UB' - p_i[\mid i \in V\}$ we can then apply constraint propagation and examine $CP(\Delta')$. If $CP(\Delta')$ yields an inconsistency, i.e. an empty domain for some activity, then there cannot be a domain feasible solution with completion time less than UB', so we can deduce that UB' in fact is a lower bound. The approach of computing lower bounds by repeatedly refuting hypothetical upper bounds has been called destructive improvement by Klein and Scholl (1999a) who have successfully applied it to the problem $PS|prec|C_{max}$.

It is possible to compute the best constraint propagation based lower bound through a bi-section search in the interval $[0, \ldots, UB]$. However, we only have to answer the following "yes/no" question: Is the lower bound less than the current best upper bound or not? This question is answered by applying constraint propagation to the set Δ, which is already a fixed component of the branching scheme, so that an *explicit* computation of lower bounds is not implemented in our algorithm.

5.3.3   Some Properties of Active Schedules

This section describes some additional conditions and a simple left-shift test that aim at further reducing the search space by ruling out non-active schedules. We make use of an effect caused by the activity selection rule: The choice of an activity $j \in \mathcal{V}^{f'}(\alpha)$ with minimal earliest start time, which, according to Equation (5.3), determines the schedule time $t(\alpha)$, ensures that any time point smaller than $t(\alpha)$ does not have to be considered any more.

Clearly, the selection rule implies that in any schedule S developed from α the condition $S_j \geq t(\alpha)$ must hold for all $j \in \mathcal{V}^{f'}(\alpha)$. But there might be free and delayed activities $j \in \mathcal{V}^f(\alpha) \setminus \mathcal{V}^{f'}(\alpha)$ for which $ES_j(\alpha) < t(\alpha)$ and which could therefore possibly be scheduled at a time earlier than $t(\alpha)$, either by the propagation algorithm or through an explicit start time assignment, once they have become selectable again. However, the following lemma states that this cannot happen if the resulting schedule is active.

Lemma 4 (Start of Delayed Activities). *Let α be a node of the search tree and let S be an active schedule that is domain feasible in α. Then:*

$$S_j > t(\alpha), \quad \text{for all } j \in \mathcal{V}^f(\alpha) \setminus \mathcal{V}^{f'}(\alpha).$$

Proof. The proof is quite similar to the proof of Lemma 2, so we will only briefly discuss the main differences.

Suppose there is an activity $j \in \mathcal{V}^f(\alpha) \setminus \mathcal{V}^{f'}(\alpha)$ that starts not later than $t(\alpha)$. Then the set

$$\mathcal{A} := \{ i \in \mathcal{V}^f(\alpha) \setminus \mathcal{V}^{f'}(\alpha) \mid S_i \leq t(\alpha) \}$$

is not empty, and we can always choose $j \in \mathcal{A}$ so that its start time is minimal among all activities in $\mathcal{A}$. A similar line of argumentation as in Lemma 2 shows that $pc_j(S) = pc_j(\alpha)$.

The fact that $S_j \geq ES_j(\alpha) \geq rc_j(\alpha)$ then allows us to conclude that $S_j > rc_j(\alpha)$: otherwise, if $S_j = rc_j(\alpha)$ then $ES_j(\alpha) = rc_j(\alpha)$ and consequently $j \in \mathcal{V}^{f'}(\alpha)$, which yields a contradiction.

Hence $S_j = rc_j(S) > rc_j(\alpha) \geq pc_j(\alpha) = pc_j(S)$ holds. This means that there must be an activity $i \in \mathcal{V}^f(\alpha)$ that finishes at time S_j and consumes resources required by j, which implies that $S_i < S_j$. Since $S_i \geq t(\alpha)$ for all $i \in \mathcal{V}^{f'}(\alpha)$ we can conclude that $i \in \mathcal{V}^f(\alpha) \setminus \mathcal{V}^{f'}(\alpha)$. But then $i \in \mathcal{A}$, which contradicts the fact that S_j is minimal among all $j \in \mathcal{A}$. $\square$

We can directly use Lemma 4 to reduce the search space in the following way. At node α we additionally set

$$ES_i(\alpha) := t(\alpha) + 1, \quad \text{for all } i \in \mathcal{V}^f(\alpha) \setminus \mathcal{V}^{f'}(\alpha) : ES_i \leq t(\alpha),$$

before applying constraint propagation. The start time adjustment can be further improved by applying a similar argument as in Lemma 3. Observe that the adjustment of the earliest start time will lead to an empty domain for all delayed activities i for which $LS_i \leq t(\alpha)$, i.e., for those activities which have been "needlessly" delayed. Because the adjustment of a single start time requires constant effort, the total adjustment effort is $O(|\mathcal{V}|)$.

Lemma 4 and the fact that $S_i \geq t(\alpha)$ for all $i \in \mathcal{V}^f(\alpha)$ also imply the following result.

Corollary 9 (Constant Slack to the Left of $t(\alpha)$). *Let α be a node of the search tree; then the slack in any period $t < t(\alpha)$ does not change in descendant nodes of α that lead to an active schedule.*

This allows us to apply a simple left-shift dominance test. If, for any free, timemax-unconstrained activity $j \in \mathcal{V}^{tu}(\alpha)$ with $p_j > 0$, the condition $rc_j(\alpha) + p_j \leq t(\alpha)$ holds, i.e., if j can resource and precedence-feasibly be scheduled so that it finishes not later than at time $t(\alpha)$, then node α cannot lead to an active schedule. While it is possible to formulate more powerful left-shift conditions that consider sets of activities rather than just a single activity (Schwindt 1998b), the advantage of the test described here is that it can be easily evaluated. The effort for the left-shift dominance test for all free, timemax-unconstrained activities is $O(|\mathcal{V}|^2)$ since rc_j must be calculated for every activity in $\mathcal{V}^{tu}(\alpha)$.

The fact that the slack to the left of $t(\alpha)$ remains constant can be exploited further. Let j be an activity scheduled at node α at time $t(\alpha)$. If $rc_j(\alpha) < t(\alpha)$, then sufficient slack and the temporal constraints involving the currently scheduled activities admit a left-shift of j. Hence, a resulting schedule S can only be active if a temporal constraint involving a currently *unscheduled* activity prevents this left-shift. This means that the following condition must hold in order for S to be active:

$$\exists (i,j) \in \mathcal{E}^{max} : (i \in \mathcal{V}^f(\alpha) \wedge S_i + d_{ij} = S_j).$$

We add a corresponding constraint that takes part in the propagation mechanism. The consistency test for this constraint works in the following way. If no temporal constraint can satisfy this condition, then the node is fathomed. Otherwise, if only one single temporal constraint (i,j) can satisfy the condition, then the domain of activity i can be adjusted.

The effort required to test whether the constraint may be added is dominated by the calculation of rc_j. The constraint is a disjunction over the temporal constraints with $O(|\mathcal{V}|)$ possible predecessors and can be defined in time $O(\mathcal{V})$. Since a constraint of this type can be added whenever an activity is scheduled, there may be $O(|\mathcal{V}|)$ of these constraints. The constraints may thus cause $O(|\mathcal{V}|^2 d)$ enqueueing and dequeueing operations in the constraint propagation algorithm. The corresponding consistency test can be performed with effort $O(|\mathcal{V}|)$. The overall worst case propagation effort caused by this constraint and test is therefore $O(|\mathcal{V}|^3 d)$. Again, if the number of predecessors of an activity is small as in typical project scheduling problems, then the average effort is lower.

5.4   Computational Experiments

5.4.1   Implementation of the Algorithm

The branch-and-bound algorithm has been implemented in C++ using the constraint programming libraries ILOG SOLVER and ILOG SCHEDULER which support the implementation of tree search algorithms that apply constraint propagation at the nodes of the tree (Le Pape 1994b). The basic propagation algorithm used in SOLVER is a variant of the AC-5 arc consistency algorithm of Van Hentenryck et al. (1992).

The most important features of the SOLVER library are (1) fundamental data types such as integer domain variables, (2) generic constraints upon these variables together with corresponding domain reduction rules, e.g., linear constraints on integer domain variables, (3) the propagation algorithm, (4) classes for defining a search (branching) scheme, and (5) support for reversible actions that are automatically undone upon backtracking, for instance the definition and propagation of constraints. Based upon the generic data types and algorithms found in SOLVER, the SCHEDULER library provides an object model and algorithms that facilitate the development of scheduling applications. For instance, SCHEDULER includes classes for representing activities and resources as well as associated constraints such as precedence or resource constraints.

Besides the support for implementing backtracking algorithms and the generic propagation mechanism, we have used the following features of the libraries. The decision variables S_i are represented as integer domain variables. The temporal constraints and the corresponding Consistency Test 1 are realised through the built-in linear constraints provided by SOLVER. The resource constraints and the Unit-Interval Consistency Test 8 are provided by SCHEDULER. For the administration of the temporal and resource constraints we have used the activity and resource classes of SCHEDULER. Consistency Test 3 for pairs of activities is implemented as a generic disjunctive SOLVER constraint; a general version of the test for sets of more than two activities is provided by SCHEDULER.

The logic of the branch-and-bound algorithm, the other consistency tests and the additional node fathoming rules described in Section 5.3 have been hand coded. By using the SOLVER search tree classes, the amount of code required for the branching and backtracking part has been kept low.

All results reported for our algorithm in the following tables have been obtained on a Pentium Pro/200 PC with NT 4.0 as operating system.

5.4.2   Bidirectional Planning

When trying to solve a given problem instance, we apply our algorithm in forward and backward direction (*bidirectional planning*). A problem can be solved in backward fashion by simply reversing the project network and applying the algorithm to the resulting mirror-network (for a discussion of backward and bidirectional planning for a related scheduling problem see Klein 2000a).

While no scheduling direction is uniformly superior for all test problems, some instances are easier to solve in one direction than in the other. Intuitively, a branch-and-bound algorithm works best if the difficult part of the problem, or bottleneck, is handled at beginning of the search, since otherwise a solution for the difficult subproblem has to be rediscovered many times in different branches of the search tree. This means that if the bottleneck is towards the beginning of the project then forward planning is advantageous; otherwise, if the bottleneck is at the end then backward planning works best.

Because it is hard to predict the location of the bottleneck to chose a favourable planning direction, we simply proceed as follows. We allocate half of the run-time to solve the problem in forward direction; if the problem remains open after this time then we apply the algorithm to the mirror problem, now using the makespan of the best schedule found so far, if any, as initial upper bound.

5.4.3 Characteristics of the Test Sets

We have tested the algorithm on several large sets of benchmark problems that were systematically generated with the problem generators ProGen (Kolisch et al. 1995) and ProGen/max (Schwindt 1996), which allow to specify several control parameters that characterise a resulting problem instance. The test sets are collected in the project scheduling problem library PSPLIB (Kolisch and Sprecher 1996, Kolisch et al. 1999). All test sets have also been used in other recent studies so that it is possible to compare the effectiveness and efficiency of different algorithms. For a discussion of the relative advantages of the systematic, generator based approach and of other approaches for generating or collecting project scheduling benchmark instances we refer to Schirmer (1999, Chapter 3).

Previous studies (see e.g. Kolisch et al. 1995, Schwindt 1998b) have concluded that the difficulty of a problem instance is most strongly influenced by (1) the project network, (2) the structure of the resource demand and (3) the level of resource supply. These characteristics are measured by the following variables that are used as problem generator parameters:

- The *network complexity* $C \geq 1$ used by ProGen indicates the average number of immediate successors of an activity and is a measure of the complexity of the precedence constraints. The network complexity has the disadvantage of not being normalized and it has been empirically shown to have little influence on the difficulty of instances of the problem $PS|prec|C_{max}$ (Kolisch et al. 1995).

  The newer problem generator ProGen/max uses a control variable called the *network restrictiveness* $RT \in [0, 1]$. The restrictiveness of a network is a measure of the number of strict orderings of the nodes or activities that are compatible with the partial order induced by the precedence constraints. A

parallel network has a restriveness of zero, and a series network has a restrictiveness of 1. The higher the restrictiveness, the fewer linear orderings of the
activities are feasible and the smaller the solution space becomes, leading to
easier problem instances. As the calculation of the exact restrictiveness of a
project network is NP-hard ,Thesen (1977) has proposed an approximation
for the restrictiveness.

- The *resource factor* $RF \in [0, 1]$ (Pascoe 1966) indicates the average percentage of resources required to process an activity. Formally, the resource factor
  with respect to resource $k \in \mathcal{R}$ is

$$RF_k := \frac{|\{i \in \mathcal{V} \mid r_{ik} > 0\}|}{|\mathcal{V}|}.$$

  RF is the average over all RF_k, for $k \in \mathcal{R}$. It takes a value of 1 if every activity requires every resource. The higher the resource factor, the more difficult a
  problem instance becomes.

- The *resource strength* $RS \in [0, 1]$ (Kolisch et al. 1995) describes the average tightness of the resource constraints. Formally, the resource strength for
  resource $k \in \mathcal{R}$ is

$$RS_k := \frac{R_k - R_k^{\min}}{R_k^{\max} - R_k},$$

  where $R_k^{\min} := \max_{i \in \mathcal{V}} r_{ik}$ is the minimal resource capacity required for
  performing the project; $R_k^{\max}$ is the smallest capacity of resource k for which
  the earliest start schedule for the resource relaxation of the problem becomes
  resource feasible with respect to k. RS is the average over all RS_k, for $k \in \mathcal{R}$.

  A resource strength of 0 indicates maximal tightness, which results from the
  minimal feasible resource availability, i.e., a supply equal to the maximum
  requirement of any single activity. For a resource strength of 1, the earliest
  start schedule does not contain any resource conflicts and the problem becomes
  easy.

The complexity measures described above are used to control the problem instance
generators that were employed to create the test sets used in this study. Additionally,
the generation of instances of the problem $PS|temp|C_{max}$ can also be influenced by
specifying the desired number of cycle structures in the precedence constraints and
detailed characteristics of these cycle structures, e.g. their tightness (Schwindt 1996).

Baptiste et al. (1999) have proposed another complexity measure, the *disjunction
ratio*, which is the ratio between a lower bound on the number of activity pairs that
cannot be processed in parallel and the overall number of activity pairs. A simple
lower bound is obtained by considering all activity pairs, for which either the transitive time lags or the resource constraints forbid a parallel execution. Baptiste et al.
(1999) conclude that for problem instances with a high disjunction ratio disjunctive

Test	Size	Fixed parameters				Variable parameters			
set		$\|\mathcal{V}\|$	$\|\mathcal{R}\|$	p_i	r_{ik}	Cycles	RT	RF	RS
A	1080^a	100	5	$\{5\ldots15\}$	$\{1\ldots5\}$	$[2,5]$	0.35	0.50	0.2
						$[6,9]$	0.50	0.75	0.5
							0.65	1.00	0.7
B	120^b	500	5	$\{1\ldots10\}$	$\{1\ldots10\}$	$[2,21]$	0.25	0.50	0.25
							0.50	0.75	0.50
								1.00	

[a]Only 1059 of the 1080 problem instances have a feasible solution.
[b]Only 119 of the 120 problem instances have a feasible solution.

Table 5.1: Characteristics of the test sets for the problem $PS|temp|C_{max}$

constraint propagation techniques are most appropriate, while cumulative constraint propagation techniques are most likely to be successful for highly cumulative instances with a low disjunction ratio.

5.4.4 Experiments for the Problem $PS|temp|C_{max}$

Test Data

We have tested the algorithm on two large sets of benchmark problems that were systematically generated by Schwindt (1998b) using the problem generator Pro-Gen/Max (Schwindt 1996). The test sets are collected in the project scheduling problem library PSPLIB (Kolisch et al. 1999). The major characteristics of the test sets are shown in Table 5.1. A detailed description of the characteristics is given by Schwindt (1998b).

Test Set A contains 1080 problems with 100 activities, not including the fictitious start and end activities. Each activity requires up to 5 resources; the processing times p_i and the resource requirements r_{ik} are randomly chosen from the sets $\{5\ldots15\}$ and $\{1\ldots5\}$, respectively. For each combination of values for the control parameters "*Cycles*", RT, RF, and RS, that are shown on the right side of table, ten instances have been generated, leading to a total of 1080 instances. Only 1059 problem instances have a feasible solution.

Test Set B consists of 120 problem instances with 500 activities; 119 of these problems have a feasible solution.

Version of the algorithm				$t_{\max}$	Feasible	Optimal	Infeasibility proven	$Dev._{LB}$
No.	B^a	D^b	A^c	BP^d	(sec)	(%)	(%)	(%)	(%)
1	$-$	$-$	$-$	$-$	3	91.1	55.9	0.0	5.7
2	$+$	$-$	$-$	$-$	3	95.6	61.7	0.0	5.6
3	$+$	$+$	$-$	$-$	3	96.3	63.3	1.9	5.5
4	$+$	$+$	$+$	$-$	3	96.7	64.2	1.9	5.5
5	$+$	$+$	$+$	$+$	3	97.8	66.2	1.9	5.2
6	$-$	$-$	$-$	$+$	3	96.0	61.1	0.0	5.8
7	$+$	$-$	$-$	$+$	3	97.4	63.5	0.0	5.3
8	$+$	$+$	$-$	$+$	3	97.7	65.7	1.9	5.2
9	$-$	$-$	$-$	$-$	30	91.1	56.0	0.0	5.7
10	$+$	$-$	$-$	$-$	30	96.8	63.1	0.0	5.6
11	$+$	$+$	$-$	$-$	30	97.2	65.6	1.9	5.5
12	$+$	$+$	$+$	$-$	30	97.5	67.0	1.9	5.2
13	$+$	$+$	$+$	$+$	30	98.1^e	70.4	1.9	4.8
14	$-$	$-$	$-$	$+$	30	96.0	61.2	0.0	5.8
15	$+$	$-$	$-$	$+$	30	98.0	65.1	0.0	5.1
16	$+$	$+$	$-$	$+$	30	98.1^e	67.9	1.9	5.0

[a]Branching: + indicates that $\mathcal{V}^{f'}$ and $t^+(\alpha)$ are defined as in Section 5.3.1; otherwise $\mathcal{V}^{f'} := \mathcal{V}^f$ and $t^+(\alpha) := t(\alpha) + 1$.

[b]Disjunctive consistency tests: + indicates use of Consistency Tests 2 and 3 for activity pairs.

[c]Active schedules: + indicates use of the tests and conditions described in Section 5.3.3.

[d]Bidirectional planning.

[e]Corresponding to 100% of the problems that have a feasible solution.

Table 5.2: Impact of different modules of the algorithm for 1080 problems with 100 activities

Impact of Different Modules of the Algorithm

Table 5.2 shows the impact of the different modules of our algorithm for the test set of 1080 problems with 100 activities. For a given algorithm version, which is characterised by the presence or absence of the modules, and a given run time limit t_{max}, the table shows the percentage of problems for which (1) a feasible solution could be found, (2) an optimal solution was found and verified, (3) infeasibility was proven, and (4) the average deviation $Dev._{LB}$ from the lower bounds calculated in the study of Schwindt (1998b). Except for the $Dev._{LB}$ values, all percentages are given with respect to the total number of 1080 problems. For comparison purposes, the percentages for the average deviation from the lower bound are given with respect to the number of problems solved to feasibility, including the number of instances solved to optimality[1].

The first five columns of the table characterise different versions of the algorithm; in addition to a reference number they show whether a particular module has been used (+) or omitted (–) in a version. To keep the size of the table within reasonable limits we have grouped related features of the algorithm into modules and present data for several interesting module combinations.

Rows 1 and 9 of the table show the results obtained for the minimal version of our algorithm in which only the precedence and the unit interval consistency tests are applied within the constraint propagation algorithm. Observe that these test are always required as they are the only means by which the algorithm will obey the temporal and resource constraints. In the minimal version, we use a very basic activity selection rule where any free activity is selectable, i.e., we set $\mathcal{V}^{f'} := \mathcal{V}^f$, and the simple delaying strategy of always postponing an activity by a single time unit, i.e., we set $t^+(\alpha) := t(\alpha) + 1$. The advanced activity selection and delaying rules described in Sections 5.3.1 and 5.3.1 are referred to as the branching module which is shown as column B. The minimal version does not use the disjunctive Consistency Tests 3 and 2 (column D), it does not apply the tests and conditions for active schedules described in Section 5.3.3 (column A), and it does not use bidirectional planning (column BP). Row 1 of the table shows that, within a time limit of 3 seconds, the minimal algorithm solves 91.1% of the problems to feasibility and 55.9% to optimality; it cannot prove the infeasibility of any of the 21 infeasible problems, and the average deviation from the lower bound is 5.7%. As Row 9 shows, these results are hardly improved within the tenfold run time.

The minimal version is then improved by activating the advanced branching module; the results are shown in Row 2 (10). Rows 3 (11) and 4 (12) show the effect of adding the disjunctive Consistency Tests 3 and 2 for activity pairs and the active schedule dominance rules described in Section 5.3.3. When the disjunctive tests are

---

[1]The deviation of a problem instance with (possibly optimal) upper bound UB_i and lower bound LB_i is $(UB_i - LB_i)/LB_i$. This means that problems that were solved to optimality but where the lower bound is not tight have a positive deviation and that the lowest possible $Dev._{LB}$ value is therefore greater than zero. The average deviations are approximately 0.1 percentage points smaller if the deviation of an instance solved to optimality is always set to zero.

used infeasibility can be proven at the root node for 20 of the 21 infeasible instances. Row 5 (13) shows the impact of applying the full algorithm bidirectionally, i.e., to the original problem and to the mirror problem. The table shows that the more advanced versions of the algorithm solve more problems to feasibility and optimality than their simpler counterparts while at the same time achieving a smaller average deviation from the lower bound.

Row 6 (14) shows the results for the minimal version of the algorithm with bidirectional planning. For the smaller time limit, the improvement with respect to Version 1 is comparable to the effect obtained by the advanced branching module shown in Row 2. However, Row 14 shows that in contrast to the other modules bidirectional planning alone does hardly lead to further improvements within the higher run time. By comparing Rows 7 and 8 (15 and 16) to Rows 2 and 3 (10 and 11) we can see that the combination of bidirectional planning and the other modules has a positive effect. It is interesting to note that in contrast to the minimal version with or without bidirectional planning the higher run time always leads to improved results and that all modules contribute to the improvements.

Comparison to Other Branch-and-Bound Algorithms

Table 5.3 compares the results obtained with our algorithm for the test set of 1080 problems with 100 activities to those of the three most recent other exact solution approaches by — in historical order — De Reyck and Herroelen (1998), Schwindt (1998a, and personal communication), and Fest et al. (1999, and personal communication), who have all used the same test set. De Reyck et al. (1999) describe a newer version of the procedure of De Reyck and Herroelen; the improvements mainly concern a different conflict detection and resolution mechanism (the conflicts are resolved in a different, more effective, sequence) as well as more efficient coding, which has led to slightly improved results (personal communication De Reyck 1999); however, as test data for this new version for Schwindt's benchmark problem set is not available, Table 5.3 shows the results published in De Reyck and Herroelen (1998). For run time limits t_{max} of 3, 30, 100, and 1000 seconds, including a scaling factor to account for different hardware, the table shows the percentage of problems for which (1) a feasible solution could be found, (2) an optimal solution was found and verified, (3) infeasibility was proven, and (4) the average deviation $Dev._{LB}$ from the lower bounds calculated in the study of Schwindt (1998b). Dashes indicate that the corresponding information is not available.

For comparison purposes the $Dev._{LB}$ values for our algorithm and for the algorithms of Fest et al. (1999) and Schwindt (1998b) were all calculated in the way described above using the lower bounds of Schwindt[2]. As the deviations reported by De Reyck

---

[2]In contrast to the values shown for our algorithm and the procedure of Schwindt, the values shown for the algorithm of Fest et al. have been calculated by setting the deviation of a problem instance solved to optimality to zero, leading to a slightly more favourable average value. However, in our experience the resulting difference is usually less than 0.1 percentage points and thus negligible.

Procedure	t_{max}	Feasible	Optimal	Infeasibility proven	Dev.$_{LB}$
	(sec)	(%)	(%)	(%)	(%)
Time-oriented B&B	3	97.8	66.2	1.9	5.2
	30	98.1[a]	70.4	1.9	4.8
	100	98.1[a]	71.7	1.9	4.6
	1000	98.1[a]	74.5	1.9	4.3
Fest, Möhring, Stork & Uetz	3	92.2	58.1	1.9	10.9
	30	98.1[a]	69.4	1.9	7.7
	100	98.1[a]	71.1	1.9	7.0
	1000	98.1[a]	73.3	1.9	6.1
Schwindt	3	98.1[a]	58.0	1.9	7.5
	30	98.1[a]	62.5	1.9	7.0
	100	98.1[a]	63.4	1.9	6.9
	1000	—	—	—	—
De Reyck & Herroelen	3[b]	97.3	54.8	1.4	—[c]
	30[b]	97.5	56.4	1.4	—[c]
	100[b]	—	—	—	—
	1000[b]	—	—	—	—

[a]Corresponding to 100% of the problems that have a feasible solution.

[b]Corresponding to 60/200 of the real computation time.

[c]Published values are based on different lower bounds than values for the other procedures.

Table 5.3: Results of exact algorithms for 1080 problems with 100 activities

and Herroelen (1998) are based on different, possibly weaker bounds, the corresponding fields are left empty.

The results of De Reyck and Herroelen have been obtained on a Pentium/60 PC; the run time limits used in their study were 1, 10, and 100 seconds. Schwindt has used a Pentium/200 PC and Fest et al. have used a Sun Ultra with 200 MHz clock pulse. As mentioned above, our results have been obtained on a Pentium Pro/200 PC. For comparison purposes the run time limits for all procedures but the one of De Reyck and Herroelen were set to 3, 30, 100, and 1000 seconds, thus reflecting the clock pulse ratio.

For time limits less than 100 seconds, the time-oriented algorithm applies the disjunctive consistency test 3 for activity pairs only. For the large time limit of 1000 seconds, the test is applied in its full form for all disjunctive sub-problems that are selected as described in Section 4.4.

The table shows that the time-oriented branch-and-bound algorithm solves more problems to optimality than the other procedures. With respect to this criterion, the results obtained within 3 seconds are already better than the results obtained with the procedures of Schwindt (1998a) or De Reyck and Herroelen (1998) within the maximum allowed time. Within a limit of 30 seconds, a feasible solution for all 1059 problems that can be feasibly solved is found; only Schwindt's algorithm, which applies a cycle structure based decomposition heuristic at the root node for finding initial upper bounds, finds a feasible solution for all problems within 3 seconds and does better on this criterion.

The interpretation of the average deviation from the lower bound ($Dev._{LB}$) can be problematic since this value depends on the individual problems that are solved to feasibility as well as on the lower bounds used for calculating $Dev._{LB}$. Strictly speaking, two $Dev._{LB}$ values can only be compared if they are both based on the same bounds and on the same subset of problems that were solved feasibly; in our experience, the problems for which it is difficult to find a feasible solution tend to increase $Dev._{LB}$. The $Dev._{LB}$ values shown for the first three algorithms are all based on Schwindt's lower bounds, and the values shown for time limits of 30 seconds or more are based upon all instances that have a feasible solution. Table 5.3 shows that the average lower bound deviation of the solutions found by the time-oriented algorithm is significantly lower than that of the procedures of Fest et al. (1999) and Schwindt (1998a).

Because our algorithm does not use explicit lower bounds, we were interested in the possible improvement that could be achieved by adding such bounds. To partially answer this question we have used the lower bounds of Schwindt and have examined those test problems for which our algorithm could find a solution matching a lower bound without being able to prove optimality within the time limit. We found that for one of the 1080 test problems our algorithm finds a solution matching a lower bound but cannot prove optimality within 3 seconds. Within 30 seconds, this solution is proven to be optimal, and for another problem a solution matching a lower bound is found without proof of optimality; this problem remains open after 100 seconds. This means that the results of our algorithm could only be marginally improved by using these lower bounds. Data concerning the tightness of the lower bounds can be found in Table 5.4.

Comparison to Heuristics

Table 5.4 compares our algorithm to the best heuristic results reported for the same problem set, this time using only the 1059 solvable instances. In addition to the columns shown in the previous tables, column "t_{avg}" shows the average required run time, and column "$C_{max} = LB$" contains the percentage of problems for which a solution with a value matching a lower bound was found. The results for our algorithm are identical to those shown in the corresponding rows in Tables 5.2 and 5.3, except that all percentages in the columns "feasible", "optimal", and "$C_{max} = LB$" are now given with respect to the 1059 solvable problems. Again, all values re-

Procedure	t_{max} (sec)	t_{avg} (sec)	Feasible (%)	Optimal (%)	$C_{max} = LB$ (%)	$Dev._{LB}$ (%)
Time-oriented B&B	3	1.3	99.7	67.5	64.6	5.2
	30	9.4	100.0	71.8	66.0	4.8
	100	29.7	100.0	73.1	66.1	4.6
Franck & Neumann						
Direct	—	0.5	99.4	—	56.8	7.7
Contraction	—	1.3	100.0	—	42.5	9.4
Franck & Selle						
GA_{prec}	—	16.0^a	100.0	—	59.9	5.3
GA_{vary}	—	16.0^a	81.1	—	61.0	2.0
Tabu Search	—	16.6^a	100.0	—	56.0	5.8
Simulated Annealing	—	10.4^a	100.0	—	59.5	5.7

[a]Corresponding to 266/200 of the real computation time.

Table 5.4: Comparison of heuristics for 1059 of the 1080 problems with 100 activities

garding lower bounds shown in the table are based on the bounds of Schwindt. As mentioned above, the time-oriented algorithm has been tested on a Pentium Pro/200 PC; the algorithms of Franck and Neumann (1998) have been run on a Pentium/200 PC, and Franck and Selle (1998) have used a Pentium/266 PC. As before, we have scaled the run times according to the clock pulse.

The results of Franck and Neumann (1998) have been obtained by applying a combination of serial and parallel list scheduling algorithms using several different priority rules; the algorithms include limited backtracking capabilities. The basic idea behind the direct and the contraction method is to give preferential treatment to activities which are on cycle structures induced by the temporal constraints. The two approaches differ in the specific way in which they handle cycle structures; the contraction heuristic initially solves subproblems defined by the activities and corresponding precedence constraints on the same cycle structure and then integrates these solutions in a complete schedule. The results of Franck and Neumann greatly improve upon the results reported by Schwindt (1998b) for the older priority rule based heuristics of Zhan (1994) (see also Neumann and Zhan 1995) and Brinkmann (1992) (see also Brinkmann and Neumann 1996), which can solve approximately 98% of the problems with an average deviation from the lower bound of roughly 80%. This indicates the progress that has been made in this area in the past years.

Franck and Selle (1998) have improved these results by embedding a variant of the direct method in four meta-heuristics, specifically in two genetic algorithms (GA)

based on two different solution encodings and in a tabu search and simulated annealing framework. The meta-heuristics all manipulate the order in which activities are
scheduled by the list scheduling algorithm, which thus serves for evaluating (neigh-
bouring) solutions. The table shows that, at the cost of an increased average run
time, the meta-heuristics solve more problems to optimality than the priority rule
based methods and achieve a significantly smaller average deviation from the lower
bound. The low average deviation from the lower bound shown for the second genetic algorithm is probably caused by the fact that this procedure reaches the smallest
number of feasible solutions; this conjecture is supported by the observation that the
81.1% of the problems with lowest individual deviation that are found by our algorithm within a maximum time of 3 seconds have an average deviation of 0.9%.

Other heuristics have been developed by Schwindt (1998b) based upon truncated
versions of his branch-and-bound algorithm. However, since the newer version of
his exact algorithm (Schwindt 1998a), whose results are cited in Table 5.3, improves
upon the results of these heuristics, we do not present them in Table 5.4. Of course,
the results of any exact method shown in Table 5.3 may also be compared to the data
in Table 5.4.

When comparing the time-oriented algorithm to the priority rule based heuristics
of Franck and Neumann we can observe that for average run times in the order of
magnitude of one second the algorithm finds more solutions matching a lower bound
while achieving a very small average deviation. However, the contraction method
is faster at finding feasible solutions for all problems. It can also be seen that for
average times in the order of magnitude of 10 seconds the time-oriented algorithm
performs better with respect to all criteria shown in the table than any of the meta-
heuristics that can solve all problems.

Influence of Problem Characteristics

Table 5.5 shows the influence of the resource strength RS, the resource factor RF,
the network restrictiveness RT, and the number of cycle structures on the difficulty
of the 1080 problem instances with 100 activities. The table shows the percentage
of problems with a given characteristic that could be solved to optimality and the
average deviation from the lower bounds of Schwindt (1998b). For example, line
three shows that 99.7% of the problems with a resource strength of 0.7 could be
solved to optimality with an average deviation from the lower bounds of 0.1%.

The table shows that the resource strength has the strongest influence on the difficulty of the problems. The hardest problems occur when a low resource strength is
combined with a high resource factor. The influence of the given variation of the
network restrictiveness and the number of cycles in the network appears to be weak.

Parameter	Value	Optimal[a] (%)	Dev.$_{LB}$[a] (%)
RS	0.20	28.6	12.7
	0.50	92.2	0.7
	0.70	99.7	0.1
RF	0.50	82.8	1.9
	0.75	72.8	4.8
	1.00	65.0	6.9
RT[b]	]0.0, 0.3]	72.8	6.3
	]0.3, 0.4]	71.3	5.2
	]0.4, 0.5]	77.7	3.1
	]0.5, 0.6]	74.4	4.2
	]0.6, 1.0]	74.1	3.4
Cycles	[2, 5]	74.6	4.2
	[6, 9]	72.4	4.8

[a]Within a time limit of 100 seconds.

[b]Problems were generated with the target restrictiveness values shown in Table 5.1, but the actual values may vary from the target values.

Table 5.5: Influence of problem characteristics for the problem $PS|temp|C_{max}$ for test set A

Procedure	t_{max} (sec)	t_{avg} (sec)	Feasible (%)	Optimal (%)	$C_{max} = LB$ (%)	$Dev._{LB}$ (%)
Time-oriented B&B	200	98	97.5	71.4	61.3	0.5
	1000	306	99.2	77.3	61.3	0.5
Fest, Möhring,						
Stork & Uetz	200	—	100.0	58.8	—	5.2
	1000	—	100.0	58.8	—	3.8
Franck & Neumann						
Direct	—	56	84.9	—	40.3	1.2
Contraction	—	18	100.0	—	5.0	5.1
Neumann & Zimmermann						
Filtered Beam Search	—	14	80	—	62	0.1
Decomposition	200	51	100	—	6	5.0

Table 5.6: Results for 119 of 120 large problems with 500 activities

Results for Large Problems

To demonstrate the scalability of our algorithm, Table 5.6 presents results for the second test set of 120 problem instances with 500 activities. For comparison, the table also shows the results reported by Fest et al. (1999), the only other exact procedure for which results have been published for this test set. The table also contains the results obtained by Franck and Neumann (1998) for their priority rule based heuristics, and by Neumann and Zimmermann (1999) for the two branch-and-bound based heuristics that they found effective for this test set in terms of the criteria reported in Table 5.6. The latter heuristics are based on the algorithm of Schwindt (1998b). Similar to the priority rule based contraction method, the decomposition heuristic initially solves subproblems corresponding to the cycle structures. All percentages except for those in the $Dev._{LB}$ column are based only on the 119 problem instances that have a feasible solution. Again, the lower bounds used for calculating the average lower bound deviation have been found in the study of Schwindt (1998b). The results of Neumann and Zimmermann as well as those of Franck and Neumann have been obtained on Pentium/200 PCs.

The results in Table 5.6 show that our algorithm scales quite well. Within 200 seconds, the algorithm solves 71.4% of the problems to optimality and leaves only 3 of the 119 feasible problems unsolved; the infeasibility of the remaining problem is proven at the root node. For a time limit of 1000 seconds, 118 of the 119 problems that have a feasible solution are solved to feasibility and 92 instances or 77.3% to optimality; the time-oriented algorithm also achieves a very small average deviation

Test	Size	Fixed parameters				Variable parameters		
set		$|\mathcal{V}|$	$|\mathcal{R}|$	p_i	r_{ik}	C	RF	RS
j30	480	30	4	$\{1\ldots10\}$	$\{1\ldots10\}$	1.5	0.25	0.2
j60	480	60	4	$\{1\ldots10\}$	$\{1\ldots10\}$	1.8	0.50	0.5
j90	480	90	4	$\{1\ldots10\}$	$\{1\ldots10\}$	2.1	0.75	0.7
							1.00	1.0
j120	600	120	4	$\{1\ldots10\}$	$\{1\ldots10\}$	1.5	0.25	0.1
						1.8	0.50	0.2
						2.1	0.75	0.3
							1.00	0.4
								0.5

Table 5.7: Characteristics of the test sets for the problem $PS|prec|C_{max}$

from the lower bound. The table shows that those procedures which can also solve the remaining problem(s) left open by the time-oriented algorithm can only do so at the price of a significantly lower solution quality, as indicated by the $Dev._{LB}$ values. The number of problems solved to optimality within the maximum allowed time is 18.5 percentage points, corresponding to 22 problems, higher than for the algorithm of Fest et al.

5.4.5 Experiments for the Problem $PS|prec|C_{max}$

Test Data

We have tested the algorithm on four standard sets of benchmark instances of the problem $PS|prec|C_{max}$ that were systematically generated with the problem generator ProGen (Kolisch et al. 1995).

Table 5.7 shows the detailed characteristics of the test sets. The number of activities, $|\mathcal{V}|$, does not include the fictitious start and end activities. All processing times and resource requirements were randomly drawn from the set $\{1,\ldots,10\}$. The first three test sets with 30, 60, and 90 activities per problem contain ten instances for each combination of the three control parameter values shown in the three right-most columns and four top-most rows of the table, leading to a total number of 480 instances. The last test set, which contains problems with 120 activities, has been generated with different, more difficult resource strength values; again, the set contains 10 problem instances for each combination of the variable parameters shown in the last 5 rows of the table, resulting in a total number of 600 problems.

Procedure	t_{max}	t_{avg}	Optimal	$Dev._{opt}$	
				avg.	max
	(sec)	(sec)	(%)	(%)	(%)
Time-oriented B&B					
	1	0.3	80.2	0.57	10.9
	10	1.6	88.3	0.19	8.9
	60	6.0	92.7	0.10	6.0
	300	19.4	95.4	0.05	6.0
	1800	66.4	97.3	0.03	4.5

Table 5.8: Results for 480 problems with 30 activities (test set j30)

Results

Table 5.8 shows the results obtained with the time-oriented branch-and-bound algorithm for the smallest test set with 30 activities per problem. For a given run time limit t_{max} the table shows the average run time t_{avg}, the percentage of problems solved to optimality within the time limit, and the remaining average and maximum deviation from the optimal solution (all optimal solutions for this test set are known). For example, the table shows that within a time limit of 300 seconds 95.4 % or 458 problem instances can be solved to optimality within an average run time of 19.4 seconds and a remaining average deviation from the optimal solution of 0.05 %. Within the maximum allowed run time of 1800 seconds, 97.3 % of the problems are solved. We found that the difficulty of the problem instances for the time-oriented algorithm strongly depends on the resource strength. While all instances with a resource strength greater than 0.2 can be solved within less than 10 seconds, the problems with a resource strength of 0.2 are considerably more difficult.

We must mention that the currently most effective algorithms for this problem set, which have been developed by Klein and Scholl (1999b), Demeulemeester and Herroelen (1997b), Sprecher (2000) and Mingozzi et al. (1998), perform better on this problem set and can solve more instances within shorter time. For example, Klein (2000b) reports that the scatter search algorithm of Klein and Scholl can solve all problems within a maximum time of 361 seconds on a Pentium/166 computer.

Table 5.9 shows the results of our algorithm for the larger test set with 60 activities per problem instance and compares them to the results of the procedures of Brucker et al. (1998), Sprecher (2000), and Klein and Scholl (1999b), which have been tested on the same problem set. The table shows the algorithms in inverse historical order. For a given time limit, the table presents the average run time, the percentage of problems solved to optimality, and the average and maximum deviations from several lower bounds as well as the average deviation from the best known solutions collected in the corresponding benchmark file of the project scheduling problem library PSPLIB. Dashes indicate that the corresponding information was not available. When comparing the results of different algorithms, the different computer platforms, which are described in the table footnotes, must be taken into account; observe that we have *not* scaled the run time values.

The development of tight lower bounds for the problem $PS|prec|C_{max}$ is an area of active research (see e.g. Klein and Scholl 1999a, Brucker and Knust 1999, Möhring et al. 1998, Heilmann and Schwindt 1997). In Table 5.9 and in the following tables we show the deviations of our algorithm with respect to the best lower bounds that are currently available in the corresponding PSPLIB benchmark files. A comparison of the performance of different algorithms with respect to deviations from lower bounds is, of course, only meaningful if the deviations are based on the same bounds. Table 5.9 and Table 5.10 below therefore also include deviations from the lower bounds of Brucker et al. (1998), which have been used in the other studies. For easy reproducibility we also give the deviations with respect to the precedence based lower bound LB_0 which corresponds to the optimal solution of the resource relaxation of the problem.

Table 5.9 shows that the time-oriented algorithm is competitive with the other procedures and that, for small run times, it achieves the highest percentage of optimally solved problems. For large run times, the algorithm of Klein and Scholl seems to perform slightly better than our algorithm.

Table 5.10 compares the results of the time-oriented algorithm for the test set j90 to those of the procedure of Sprecher (2000), which is the only algorithm for which results on this test set have been published. The format of the table is the same as in Table 5.9.

Table 5.11 shows the results of our algorithm for the largest test set with 120 activities per problem instance. Recall that this problem set has been generated with more difficult resource strength values than the three smaller sets. As we will see in Table 5.12 below, this appears to be the main reason for the strong decrease in the percentage of problems solved to optimality when compared to the smaller test sets. We can also observe that the average deviations from the lower bounds are roughly three times as high as for the smaller and easier test sets with 60 and 90 activities per instance. As before, the percentage of problems solved to optimality grows only slowly when the run time is increased.

Data on the performance of other exact procedures for this problem set has not been published. We have compared our results with respect to the average deviation from the precedence based lower bound LB_0 to that of several state of the art heuristics reported by Kolisch and Hartmann (1999), who have analysed the performance of eight heuristics within a maximum number of 1000 and 5000 iterations; an iteration corresponds to the application of a serial or parallel schedule generation scheme. The minimal deviation obtained by the best heuristic within 1000 iterations is 39.4 %. Within the maximum number of iterations, only the best of the eight heuristics, the genetic algorithm of Hartmann (1998), achieves a lower deviation (36.7 %) than our algorithm within the maximum allowed time.

Procedure	t_{max}	t_{avg}	Opt.	$Dev._{LB}{}^{a}$		$Dev._{LB}{}^{b}$		$Dev._{LB_0}$	$Dev._{UB}{}^{c}$
				avg.	max	avg.	max	avg.	avg.
	(sec)	(sec)	(%)	(%)	(%)	(%)	(%)	(%)	(%)
T-O B&B[d]	1	0.4	73.5	4.3	34.0	5.8	39.8	13.7	1.9
	10	2.7	75.4	3.6	25.8	5.1	34.9	12.8	1.3
	60	14.7	76.2	3.4	24.4	4.8	34.2	12.5	1.1
	300	69.2	78.5	3.2	23.3	4.6	32.9	12.3	0.9
	1800	386.0	80.0	3.0	22.6	4.5	30.3	12.0	0.8
Klein and Scholl[e]	10	3.7	69.6	—	—	5.3	32.5	—	—
	60	17.8	73.3	—	—	4.8	31.3	—	—
	300	77.7	76.0	—	—	4.6	29.7	—	—
	1800	396.7	80.2	—	—	4.3	29.7	—	—
	3600	736.1	81.9	—	—	4.2	29.0	—	—
Sprecher[f]	300	88.1	72.7	—	—	5.7	45.8	13.6	—
	1800	472.7	75.8	—	—	5.3	40.7	13.0	—
Brucker et al.[g]	3600	—	67.9	—	—	4.8	30.8	—	—

[a]Based on the best known lower bounds collected in the PSPLIB.
[b]Based on the lower bounds of Brucker et al. (1998).
[c]Based on the best known solutions collected in the PSPLIB.
[d]Impl. in C++, results obtained on Pentium Pro/200 with Windows NT.
[e]Impl. in C++, results obtained on Pentium/166 with Windows 95.
[f]Impl. in C++, results obtained on Pentium/166 with Linux.
[g]Impl. in C, results obtained on SUN/Sparc 20/801 (80 MHz) with Solaris 2.5.

Table 5.9: Results of exact algorithms for 480 problems with 60 activities (test set j60)

Procedure	t_{max}	t_{avg}	Opt.	$Dev._{LB}{}^{a}$		$Dev._{LB}{}^{b}$		$Dev._{LB_0}$	$Dev._{UB}{}^{c}$
				avg.	max	avg.	max	avg.	avg.
	(sec)	(sec)	(%)	(%)	(%)	(%)	(%)	(%)	(%)
T-O B&B^{d}	1^{e}	0.6	71.2	4.7	35.5	6.2	43.4	13.4	2.2
	10	3.0	74.2	4.0	28.8	5.4	37.0	12.4	1.5
	60	15.9	75.0	3.8	26.5	5.2	37.0	12.2	1.4
	300	76.1	76.0	3.7	26.4	5.1	36.1	12.1	1.3
Sprecher^{f}	300	120.3	61.5	—	—	8.3	58.7	15.7	—

[a]Based on the best known lower bounds collected in the PSPLIB.
[b]Based on the lower bounds of Brucker et al. (1998).
[c]Based on the best known solutions collected in the PSPLIB.
[d]Impl. in C++, results obtained on Pentium Pro/200 with Windows NT.
[e]Based only on forward planning.
[f]Impl. in C++, results obtained on Pentium/166 with Linux.

Table 5.10: Results of exact algorithms for 480 problems with 90 activities (test set j90)

Procedure	t_{max}	t_{avg}	Optimal	$Dev._{LB}{}^{a}$		$Dev._{LB_0}$	$Dev._{UB}{}^{b}$
				avg.	max	avg.	avg.
	(sec)	(sec)	(%)	(%)	(%)	(%)	(%)
Time-oriented B&B	10	7.4	31.0	9.9	40.6	38.0	3.6
	60	41.9	32.2	9.5	40.6	37.5	3.3
	300	205.3	33.3	9.2	40.6	37.1	3.0

[a]Based on the best known solutions collected in the PSPLIB benchmark file.
[b]Based on the best known lower bounds collected in the PSPLIB benchmark file.

Table 5.11: Results for 600 problems with 120 activities (test set j120)

Param.	Value	Optimal[a]				Dev.$_{LB}$[b]			
		j30 (%)	j60 (%)	j90 (%)	j120 (%)	j30 (%)	j60 (%)	j90 (%)	j120 (%)
RS	0.1	—	—	—	2.5	—	—	—	19.9
	0.2	81.7	30.8	20.0	9.2	0.2	11.6	14.0	13.4
	0.3	—	—	—	25.0	—	—	—	8.3
	0.4	—	—	—	49.2	—	—	—	3.9
	0.5	100.0	83.3	84.2	80.8	0.0	1.2	0.8	0.8
	0.7	100.0	100.0	100.0	—	0.0	0.0	0.0	—
	1.0	100.0	100.0	100.0	—	0.0	0.0	0.0	—
RF	0.25	100.0	100.0	95.0	84.2	0.0	0.1	0.5	3.3
	0.50	100.0	80.8	73.3	38.3	0.0	3.1	4.6	14.5
	0.75	93.3	71.7	67.5	25.0	0.0	4.7	5.2	15.4
	1.00	88.3	61.7	68.3	19.2	0.2	4.9	4.5	13.1
C	1.5	95.0	80.0	78.8	46.3	0.1	4.0	4.2	13.2
	1.8	94.4	78.8	74.4	44.4	0.1	4.4	5.0	14.7
	2.1	96.7	76.9	75.0	34.4	0.0	4.4	5.6	18.3

[a]Within a time limit of 300 seconds.
[b]Based on the best known lower bounds collected in the PSPLIB.

Table 5.12: Influence of problem characteristics for the problem $PS|prec|C_{max}$

Table 5.12 analyses the influence of the resource strength RS, the resource factor RF, and the network complexity C on the difficulty of the problem instances. For the four test sets, the table gives the percentage of problems with a particular characteristic that could be solved to optimality and the average deviation from the best known lower bounds collected in the corresponding PSPLIB benchmark files. For example, line five of the table shows that 80.8 % of the problem instances with 120 activities that were generated with a resource strength of 0.5 could be solved to optimality, and the remaining average deviation from the lower bound for these problems was 0.8 %. The data shown in Table 5.12 confirms the results of earlier studies, see e.g. Kolisch (1995), regarding the influence of the problem characteristics.

The table shows that the hardest problems are those with a low resource strength. For a resource strength of 0.2, the percentage of problems that could be solved to optimality sharply decreases with growing problem size; for the lowest resource strength value of 0.1, only three of the problems with 120 activities could be solved to optimality. Problems with $RS \geq 0.7$ appear to be easy independent of problem size, and the benchmark lower bounds for these instances are always tight. For $RS = 0.5$, we can observe that the percentage of problems that can be solved remains roughly constant when the problem size grows from 60 to 120 activities, although the time limit is not increased.

The influence of the resource factor is also clearly visible: problems become harder as the average number of resource types required by an activity increases. For example, for the minimal resource factor of 0.25, which means that on average each activity requires only a single resource type, the algorithm can solve 84.2 % of the problems with 120 activities. As the resource factor grows, the value drops to 19.2%.

The influence of the network complexity is not as significant as that of the other two control parameters. While the results for test set j120 indicate that the problems become more difficult with increasing network complexity, the data for the smaller test sets is inconclusive.

As to be expected after examining Table 5.12, the hardest problems occur when a low resource strength is combined with a high resource factor. For example, roughly speaking, the 30.8 % of the problems with 60 activities and a resource strength of 0.2 that can be solved to optimality include all those instances for which the resource factor takes a value of 0.25 and a few instances with a resource factor of 0.5. Intuitively, a low resource strength causes many activity pairs to be disjunctive and thus leads to cliques of pairwise disjunctive activities of considerable size. Additionally, if the average number of resource types required by an activity is high, then, simply speaking, there are many "links" between the cliques induced by each resource type. This combined effect leads to large and difficult disjunctive sub-problems.

We also analysed in how many cases our algorithm could find values matching a best known lower bound without being able to prove optimality within the maximum allowed run time. We found that this occurs for none of the instances in the test sets j60 and j90 and for only a single instance of the test set j120. This means that even the best known lower bounds, if calculated at the root of the search tree, would only marginally improve the results of our algorithm. Also, it seems questionable if a re-calculation of bounds during the search would pay off in terms of overall computation time. For example, Klein (1999) has found that for his branch-and-bound algorithm the pruning power of the bounds described by Klein and Scholl (1999a) does often not outweigh the associated computational effort and does in general not lead to a reduction of computation times.

Dominance Criterion Based on Partial Schedules

We also experimented with a dominance rule based on storing and comparing partial schedules, which is similar to the well known cutset rule described by Demeule-meester and Herroelen (1992). While the use of this rule led to some improvements, the overall effect for the larger test sets was rather small; for example, when using this rule, only a single additional instance of the test set j60 could be solved within the maximum time limit of 1800 seconds. Because the performance of the rule within our algorithm was disappointing and because the rule cannot easily be adapted for the general case of arbitrary minimal and maximal time lags, we did not further consider it in our study.

5.5 Summary

This chapter has presented a branch-and-bound algorithm for a very general scheduling model, the resource-constrained project scheduling problem with generalised precedence relations, with the objective of minimising the project makespan. The algorithm uses a binary, time-oriented branching scheme that relies on efficient constraint propagation techniques for reducing the search space. The power of constraint propagation lies in the systematic and computationally efficient application of basic consistency tests. The search effort is reduced further by adding some necessary conditions that must be satisfied by active schedules and through a simple left-shift test. The algorithm can also easily be applied for optimising other regular measures of performance.

Given the conventional wisdom that the efficiency of branch-and-bound procedures depends largely on good lower bounds, it is quite interesting to note that our algorithm does not use any *explicit* lower bounds. Instead, lower bounding is implicitly achieved through the constraint propagation process.

Computational experiments on several large test sets of systematically generated benchmark problems taken from the literature have demonstrated the effectiveness of the approach.

On a data set of over thousand instances of the problem $PS|temp|C_{max}$ with one hundred activities each, the algorithm finds feasible solutions for all problems and it solves more problems to optimality than other methods, while at the same time achieving a significantly smaller deviation from a lower bound for those instances for which optimality cannot be proven. The results obtained for another test set consisting of problems with five hundred activities show that the algorithm also scales very well. In addition, the truncated version of the algorithm compares favourably to the best heuristic procedures for the problem.

The algorithm also performs well for the special project scheduling problem with ordinary precedence constraints, i.e., the problem $PS|prec|C_{max}$. Computational experiments with four large, systematically generated sets of benchmark problems, ranging in size from 30 to 120 activities per problem instance, indicate again that the algorithm scales well and, especially for larger instances, is competitive to other exact procedures for this problem. The results for the largest test set show that the time truncated version of the algorithm may be a useful heuristic for solving large project scheduling problems. Surprisingly, many exact algorithms for the problem $PS|prec|C_{max}$ have mainly been evaluated on the smallest of the four test sets. The good performance of the time-oriented algorithm on the larger test sets is also interesting because the algorithm does not include features such as partial schedule based dominance pruning or explicit lower bound computation; while these features often make exact algorithms perform well on the small test set, they have the disadvantage that they are usually not easy to extend or to adapt for generalised or modified versions of the problem $PS|prec|C_{max}$.

We have found that, for the problem $PS|temp|C_{max}$ and for the larger test sets of the problem $PS|prec|C_{max}$, even the use of the currently best known lower bound values available in the benchmark files of the project scheduling library PSPLIB would only marginally improve the results of the algorithm with respect to the number of optimally solved problems.

The computational analysis has shown that the difficulty of the problem instances for the algorithm depends primarily on the problem characteristics, in particular on the combination of resource supply and demand as measured by the resource strength and resource factor, and that the problem size is not the most important factor. As the hardest problems are characterised by a high share of disjunctive activities, we expect that further improvements may be achieved by concentrating on the disjunctive aspects of the problem.

Chapter 6

Multi-Mode Extension of the Branch-and-Bound Algorithm

This chapter addresses project scheduling with generalised precedence constraints and multiple execution modes per activity, reflecting time-resource and resource-resource tradeoffs. It shows how the branch-and-bound algorithm developed for the single-mode problem $PS|temp|C_{max}$ in the previous chapter can be extended for the multi-mode problem $MPS|temp|C_{max}$.

After a brief review of the literature on multi-mode project scheduling in Section 6.1, Section 6.2 explains how constraint propagation may be used, and Section 6.3 then introduces the extended branching scheme.

6.1 Previous Work

Despite its general nature, the problem $MPS|temp|C_{max}$ has only very recently been studied from an algorithmic point of view, and very few solution approaches have been reported in the literature. Traditionally, algorithms for multi-mode project scheduling on the one hand and project scheduling with generalised precedence constraints on the other hand have been developed separately. Multi-mode project scheduling has almost exclusively been studied for the problem $MPS|prec|C_{max}$ with classic precedence constraints; generalised precedence constraints have mainly been considered within the single-mode problem $PS|temp|C_{max}$. It appears that the difficulty of the combined problem has lead researchers to focus on only one of two the aspects at a time.

Exact algorithms for the problem $MPS|prec|C_{max}$ have been developed by Talbot (1982), Patterson et al. (1989), Sprecher (1994), Nudtasomboon and Randhawa (1997), Sprecher et al. (1997), and Sprecher and Drexl (1998). Pesch (1999) describes lower bounds. A comparison of exact algorithms is given by Hartmann and Drexl (1998). An exact algorithm for a generalisation of the problem $MPS|prec|C_{max}$ with arbitrary minimal time lags has been proposed by Hove and Deckro (1998) and Van-Hove et al. (1999).

Heuristic solution procedures have, among others, been described by Talbot (1982), Drexl (1991), Drexl and Grünewald (1993), Slowinski et al. (1994), Boctor (1993, 1996a,b), Kolisch (1995), Kolisch and Drexl (1997), Hartmann (1998), and Ahn and Erengüç (1998). An overview of the various approaches is given in the recent survey papers of Brucker et al. (1999), Herroelen et al. (1998), and Kolisch and Padman (2001).

As discussed in Chapter 2, multi-mode project scheduling problems can be divided into two sub-problems. The mode assignment problem consists of assigning a mode to every activity. Given a mode assignment, the scheduling sub-problem is to find a start time assignment for all activities. Algorithms for the problem $MPS|prec|C_{max}$, and, in analogy, for the problem $MPS|temp|C_{max}$, can be classified as *decomposition* or *integration* approaches, depending on whether the mode assignment sub-problem and the scheduling sub-problem are addressed sequentially or simultaneously.

The first heuristic algorithm for the problem $MPS|temp|C_{max}$ has been described by De Reyck and Herroelen (1999). It is based on a decomposition approach and contains a mode assignment phase and a subsequent scheduling phase with fixed mode assignments. A mode assignment is found using tabu search; during the search, a given mode vector is evaluated by solving the corresponding scheduling sub-problem of the type $PS|temp|C_{max}$. A schedule is computed with a truncated version of the branch-and-bound algorithm of De Reyck and Herroelen (1998). Upon termination of the tabu search, a final schedule is computed for the best mode assignment found by again applying the truncated branch-and-bound algorithm, this time using a larger time limit.

Another tabu search procedure based on a decomposition approach has been proposed by Franck (1999). Heilmann (1999) has presented a priority rule heuristic with limited backtracking that is based upon his exact algorithm described below.

The only exact procedure for the problem $MPS|temp|C_{max}$ that has been described so far is the one of Heilmann (1998, 1999). The algorithm is based on an integration approach, i.e., it simultaneously makes decisions concerning mode assignments and the resolution of resource conflicts. The idea is to consider the current mode-minimal problem instance[1], to relax the resource constraints and compute an optimal time-feasible schedule. The resulting schedule, which will usually violate resource constraints, is then tested for resource conflicts. Branching consists of (1) assigning a mode to an activity or (2) adding special precedence constraints to resolve a resource conflict. As in the algorithm of Schwindt (1998a,b), conflicts are resolved by introducing special precedence constraints between pairs of disjoint sets of activities; all activities in the second set are delayed until the completion of some activity in the

---

[1] See Definition 1 on page 63.

first set. The decision whether to branch over a mode assignment or a resource conflict is made based on a heuristic that tries to select the most difficult decision, which on average has the strongest influence on a lower bound of the objective function value.

6.2 Constraint Propagation

Constraint propagation proceeds mostly in the same way as in the single-mode case, the main differences being that all consistency tests are applied to the mode-minimal problem instance introduced in Definition 1 on page 63 and that the additional mode reduction tests described in Section 4.7 are used.

At every node of the search tree, a fixed point is computed by applying at least the two most basic consistency tests, i.e., the Precedence Consistency Test 1 and the Unit-interval Consistency Test 8. As before, the application of these two tests is an essential part of the branch-and-bound algorithm. The values $pc_j(\Delta)$ and $rc_j(\Delta)$ are calculated for the mode-minimal problem instance in the way defined in Section 5.2.

6.3 Extended Branching Scheme

The branching scheme of the multi-mode algorithm is an extension of the single-mode branching structure developed in the previous chapter. It combines the time-oriented branching scheme with simultaneous mode decisions.

Each node α of the search tree is associated a set $\Delta(\alpha) := \{\Delta_S(\alpha), \Delta_M(\alpha)\} := \{\Delta_{S_i}(\alpha), \Delta_{M_i}(\alpha) \mid i \in \mathcal{V}\}$ of start time and mode assignment variable domains. An activity is *unscheduled* if its mode or its start time have not yet been assigned. Inversely, an activity is scheduled if its start time *and* mode are bound. The set of domain sets $\Delta(\alpha)$ uniquely determines the set $\mathcal{V}^s(\Delta(\alpha)) := \{i \in \mathcal{V} \mid |\Delta_{S_i}| = 1 \wedge |\Delta_{M_i}| = 1\}$ of scheduled activities and the set $\mathcal{V}^f(\Delta(\alpha)) := \mathcal{V} \setminus \mathcal{V}^s(\Delta(\alpha))$ of unscheduled or free activities. To simplify the notation, we will again write $\mathcal{V}^s(\alpha)$ instead of $\mathcal{V}^s(\Delta(\alpha))$, etc., whenever no confusion is possible. Generating a schedule is equivalent to reducing the start time and mode domains until exactly one entry remains in every domain. As before, domains will be reduced by constraint propagation and by explicit branching.

The key idea of the branching scheme is to interleave a binary branching over a mode assignment or restriction with the binary time-oriented branching developed for the single-mode case. The branching decisions are interleaved in such a way that the assigned activity start times are non-decreasing, as in the single-mode algorithm. The non-decreasing start-times will again allow to apply simple dominance rules that rule out non-active schedules.

At every node α of the search tree, an unscheduled activity $j \in \mathcal{V}^f(\alpha)$ is selected and two child nodes are generated according to the following rule:

If M_j is unbound, then select a mode $\lambda \in \Delta_{M_j}(\alpha)$ and create a left child node $l'(\alpha)$ and a right child node $r'(\alpha)$ as follows:

$l'(\alpha)$:   Assign mode λ by setting $M_j(l'(\alpha)) := \lambda$.

$r'(\alpha)$:   Forbid mode λ by setting $M_j(r'(\alpha)) := M_j(\alpha) \setminus \{\lambda\}$.

Otherwise, if M_j is bound, then branch over the start times of j by creating a left child node $l(\alpha)$ and a right child node $r(\alpha)$ as follows:

$l(\alpha)$:   Start j at its earliest start time by setting $S_j(l(\alpha)) := ES_j(\alpha)$.

$r(\alpha)$:   Increase the earliest start of j by choosing $ES_j(r(\alpha)) > ES_j(\alpha)$.

The rules for the time-oriented branching step leading to the child nodes $l(\alpha)$ and $r(\alpha)$ are identical to the single-mode algorithm. If all modes are bound, the branching scheme reduces to the single-mode scheme.

To completely specify the branching scheme we must now answer three questions. Firstly, we must describe how to choose activity $j \in \mathcal{V}^f(\alpha)$, and secondly how to select the corresponding mode λ if applicable. Thirdly we must specify how to increase the earliest start time of j in $r(\alpha)$. We will first address the selection of an activity and a corresponding mode.

Selection of Activities and Modes

The propagation process by which the earliest start of activity i, $ES_i(\alpha)$, is calculated only makes use of the mode-minimal problem instance, and in particular of the mode-minimal duration and resource requirements of activity i. Because these values may increase if the mode of i is chosen, the actual earliest start time that can be realised for some mode assignment may be greater than $ES_i(\alpha)$. In order to determine the realisable earliest start time of an activity considered for branching we will often tentatively assign a mode to this activity and evaluate the effect of the assignment by applying constraint propagation. The modified domain set in which a mode $\mu \in \Delta_{M_i}(\alpha)$ has been assigned to activity i is is denoted with $\Delta(\alpha)^{M_i=\mu}$ and is defined as follows:

$$\Delta(\alpha)^{M_i=\mu} := \{\Delta_{S_1}(\alpha), \ldots, \Delta_{S_n}(\alpha), \\ \Delta_{M_1}(\alpha), \ldots, \Delta_{M_{i-1}}(\alpha), \{\mu\}, \Delta_{M_{i+1}}(\alpha), \ldots, \Delta_{M_n}(\alpha)\}.$$

$$(6.1)$$

We can now introduce the *realisable earliest start time* $ES_i'(\alpha) \geq ES_i(\alpha)$ of an activity i, which is defined as the minimal start time of i that can be realised if a mode for i is chosen and this mode assignment is propagated by applying a fixed point constraint propagation algorithm *CP*.

$$ES_i'(\alpha) := \min_{\mu \in \Delta_{M_i}(\alpha)} ES_i(CP(\Delta(\alpha)^{M_i=\mu})).$$

$$(6.2)$$

If the mode of i is bound, we obtain, of course, $ES_i'(\alpha) = ES_i(\alpha)$.

We are now ready to address the activity and mode selection rule. As in the single-mode case, the idea behind the rule is to only branch in such way that the creation of non-active schedules is avoided where possible. At node α of the search tree, we choose an activity j from the set $\mathcal{V}^{f'}(\alpha)$ of free and non-delayed activities, which will be defined in a way very similar to the single-mode case. For the time being, we only assume that $\mathcal{V}^{f'}(\alpha)$ it is a non-empty subset of the set of free activities. The activity and mode selection rule can be stated as follows:

> Choose $j \in \mathcal{V}^{f'}(\alpha)$ such that $ES_j'(\alpha) = t(\alpha)$, where the schedule time $t(\alpha)$ is the minimal realisable earliest start time, i.e.,
>
> $$t(\alpha) := \min_{i \in \mathcal{V}^{f'}(\alpha)} ES_i'(\alpha).$$
>
> If M_j is not bound, then choose a mode λ for which $ES_j'(\alpha)$ is realised:
>
> $$\lambda = \arg\min_{\mu \in \Delta_{M_i}(\alpha)} ES_i(CP(\Delta(\alpha)^{M_i=\mu})). \tag{6.3}$$

Ties are broken by first selecting an activity with minimal time slack, i.e., an activity for which $|\Delta_{S_i}(\alpha)|$ is minimal. Ties concerning the mode selection are broken by first choosing the mode with minimal processing time p_{jM_j}.

We are now left with the task of specifying the set of free and non-delayed activities. In a similar fashion as in the single-mode algorithm, it will prove useful to partition the set of free activities into (1) a set of activities that, depending on the mode assignment, *may* still have to satisfy a maximal time lag, and (2) a set of activities which do not, no matter what modes are chosen.

Let $\mathcal{E} = \mathcal{E}^{min}(\alpha) \cup \mathcal{E}^{max}(\alpha)$, where $\mathcal{E}^{min}(\alpha) := \{(i,j) \in \mathcal{E} \mid \tilde{d}_{ij}(\alpha) > 0\}$ and $\mathcal{E}^{max}(\alpha) := \{(i,j) \in \mathcal{E} \mid \tilde{d}_{ij}(\alpha) \leq 0\}$ are the relations specifying the minimal and maximal time lags between pairs of activities. In contrast to the single-mode case, the sets $\mathcal{E}^{min}(\alpha)$ and $\mathcal{E}^{max}(\alpha)$ depend on the time lags $\tilde{d}_{ij}(\alpha)$ of the minimal problem instance, i.e., on the mode domains and thus on the search tree node.

We then define the set

$$\widehat{\mathcal{V}}^{tc}(\alpha) := \{(j,\mu) \mid \ j \in \mathcal{V}^f(\alpha) \ \wedge \ \mu \in \Delta_{M_i}(\alpha) \ \wedge$$
$$\exists i \in \mathcal{V}^f(\alpha) : (i,j) \in \mathcal{E}^{max}(CP(\Delta(\alpha)^{M_j=\mu}))\}$$

of *timemax-constrained* activity-mode combinations and the set $\mathcal{V}^{tu}(\alpha) := \mathcal{V}^f(\alpha) \setminus \mathcal{V}^{tc}(\alpha)$ of *timemax-unconstrained* activity-mode pairs.

The set of free and non-delayed activity-mode pairs can then be described in analogy to the single-mode algorithm:

$$\widehat{\mathcal{V}}^{f'}(\alpha) := \ \widehat{\mathcal{V}}^{tc}(\alpha) \cup$$
$$\{(j,\mu) \mid \ j \in \mathcal{V}^f(\alpha) \ \wedge \ \mu \in \Delta_{M_i}(\alpha) :$$
$$ES_j(CP(\Delta(\alpha)^{M_i=\mu})) = rc_j(CP(\Delta(\alpha)^{M_i=\mu}))\}.$$

The interpretation of the set $\widehat{\mathcal{V}}^{f'}$ is very similar to the single-mode case: An activity-mode pair (j, μ) with a free activity j is a candidate for branching if j, under the assumption that it is performed in mode μ, may have an incoming backward arc, or if the earliest start time of j in mode μ equals its current earliest resource feasible start time $rc_j(CP(\Delta(\alpha)^{M_i=\mu}))$. In the same way as in the single-mode algorithm, this means that a delayed activity that is not constrained by a maximal time lag remains un-selectable until the resource capacity made available by delaying j has been used by some other activity. The choice of the set $\widehat{\mathcal{V}}^{f'}$ is justified by a generalised version of Lemma 2.

Delaying Duration

The delaying duration, i.e., the rule how to increase the earliest start time of an activity j selected at node α in the child node $r(\alpha)$ is the same as explained for the single mode case in Section 5.3.1.

Recall that in order for the resulting schedule S to be active, either (1) a precedence constraint or (2) low slack must prohibit a left-shift of the selected activity j. Since the activity will be delayed by at least one time unit, the first case can be ruled out if all precedence constraints $(i, j) \in \mathcal{E}$ are already resolved (see page 20) in node α.; otherwise, we can only delay j by a single time unit. The second case requires that the slack of all activities except j is insufficient to the left of $S_j(\alpha)$, which can only be the case if $S_j(\alpha)$ matches the completion time of some activity that shares resources with j. Since the earliest possible completion time EC_i is based upon constraint propagation for the mode-minimal problem instance, the multi-mode aspect, is taken into account when using Lemma 3 for the multi-mode case.

Chapter 7

Applications in Airport Operations Management

In the past decades, the volume of worldwide civil air transport has been steadily increasing with an average growth rate of more than five percent. Passenger and freight traffic have roughly doubled since the mid 1980s. The growth is generally expected to continue at the same rate: The International Air Transport Association currently predicts an annual average growth rate for total scheduled international traffic of 5.6% for passengers and of 6.7% for freight for the next five years (IATA 2000b,c).

The growth has been accompanied by a wave of deregulation and liberalisation in the airline industry in Europe, in the United States, and in many other parts of the world. Airlines left free to provide service with few regulations have significantly changed their services and schedules, for example by introducing airline hubs. At the same time, privatisation and commercialisation are changing the mode of operation of many airports (ADV 1997, Endler and Peters 1998).

From the point of view of an airport or ground service provider it has become increasingly important to utilise the available resources in the best possible way in order to cope with these trends. To handle the growing traffic volume, it is essential that a good resource utilisation is achieved. This holds true for the staff and equipment concerned with ground handling on the ramp and in the terminal, as well as for infrastructure and building resources, such as runways or terminal gates, which typically can only be extended in the long run, if at all, and with very large financial effort.

The high resource utilisation required to satisfy the growing demand for ground services leads to complex planning and scheduling problems that can no longer be adequately addressed with traditional, manual planning methods. The scheduling of resources on the operational level is additionally complicated by frequent, unpredictable changes in the flight schedule, such as delays, re-routings, or aircraft changes.

The complexity and size of the problems call for computerised decision support tools. This chapter analyses two important areas within the total airport operations system, in which the project scheduling models and solution techniques described in the previous chapters can be applied:

1. The scheduling of ground handling activities required for serving aircrafts while at an airport gives rise to a resource-constrained multi-project scheduling problem with time windows. The ground handling scheduling problem is briefly described in Section 7.1.

2. Gate scheduling deals with the problem of assigning flights to terminal gates or parking positions and scheduling the start or end times of the assignments. Section 7.2 shows in depth how this decision problem can be modelled as a special multi-mode resource-constrained project scheduling problem and develops a solution approach based on the techniques described in the previous chapters.

For a general introduction to airport operations and airport engineering that describes the role of the two areas mentioned above within the total airport system, we refer to the books by Ashford et al. (1997) and Ashford and Wright (1992).

7.1   Scheduling of Ground Handling Operations

In airport ground handling, a large number of activities required for serving an aircraft while on the ground have to be scheduled. These activities include, for example, (1) technical services, such as fuelling, wheel and tire checks, ground power supply, de-icing, cooling and heating, routine maintenance, or cleaning of cockpit windows, (2) loading and unloading of cargo and baggage, (3) passenger and flight crew disembarkment and embarkment, and (4) catering and cleaning services. The activities have to respect certain precedence constraints and must be processed within given time windows that depend on the aircraft arrival and departure times. The turn-round or transit processing of an individual aircraft can be seen as a resource-constrained project scheduling problem with generalised precedence constraints, and the overall scheduling problem for the complete airport or its terminal areas is a corresponding multi-project scheduling problem.

Airlines try to reduce aircraft ground times at airports for two reasons: firstly, to keep up the flight schedule in case of operational irregularities, and secondly to increase the fleet utilisation. Short turn-round or transit times are also advantageous for the airport or ground service provider, as the use of heavy investment, such as terminal gates or costly ramp equipment, is maximised if ground times are kept as short as possible.

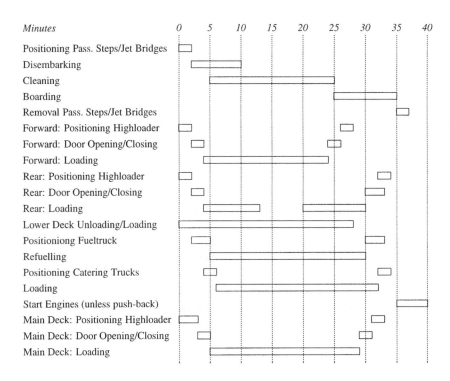

Figure 7.1: Minimum transit time of a B747 aircraft

Scheduled arrival and departure times are therefore derived from a set of minimum transit or turn-round times which reflect the technical possibilities with standard equipment and normally productive manpower. The times are obtained by analysis, including the timing of individual activities and critical path calculations, and through actual demonstrations. The minimum times define the performance that may be needed in case of delay on arrival.

Figure 7.1, taken from an airport handling manual (IATA 2000a), shows an example of how the minimum transit time of a B747 aircraft is determined. The Gantt-chart-style figure shows a subset of the required activities with their start and completion times when started as early as possible (left-shifted). There are obvious (generalised) precedence relations between certain activities.

For modern containerised aircraft, the critical path of a transit or turn-round processing usually consists of passenger disembarkment, cabin cleaning, and embarkment. In few cases, before very long flights, fuelling operations may determine the critical path (IATA 2000a).

The scheduled ground times are usually approximately ten to fifteen minutes higher than the minimum times in order to allow for delayed arrivals while still achieving on-time departure. This, the fact that not all activities are critical even when the ground times are minimal, and the fact that the actual required processing times for some activities depend on the actual (vs. expected) load data and may thus vary from the processing times used for deriving the minimum ground time, leads to degrees of freedom that may be exploited when scheduling the ground handling activities. Additionally, there are usually a number of aircraft which, for various reasons, stay at the airport for considerably longer than the minimum necessary ground time.

The task of scheduling the ground handling activities may be modelled as single- or multi-mode project scheduling problem with time windows with cumulative and/or disjunctive resources. A possible fine-grained approach is to model all available staff and equipment as individual disjunctive resources and to represent the assignment of an activity to a resource as mode selection in a multi-mode model. This allows to introduce individual availability times, e.g., shift times, as well as sequence dependent setup times between activities. The setup times can reflect the necessary travelling durations between aircraft positions, which may be an important consideration if these times are significant and vary considerably.

The performance measure will usually consider multiple attributes. One of the main goals frequently simply is to find a feasible schedule, if one exists, or to find a schedule that comes as close as possible to feasibility. Other useful criteria are, for example, a levelling of the resource usage or requirements and an even distribution of the staff workload.

Some of the modelling aspects mentioned above will also appear in the application described in the following section.

7.2   Gate Scheduling

7.2.1   Introduction

Gate scheduling is concerned with finding an assignment of flights to terminal or ramp positions, called gates, and an assignment of the start and completion times of the processing of a flight at its position. It is a key activity in airport operations. With the increase of civil air-traffic and the corresponding growth of airports in the past decades, the complexity of the task has increased significantly. At large international airports, several hundreds of flights must be handled per day. The task is further complicated by frequent changes of the underlying flight schedule on the day of operations, such as delays or aircraft changes.

The main input for gate scheduling is a flight schedule with flight arrival and departure times and additional detailed flight information, including pair-wise links between successive flights served by the same aircraft, the type of aircraft, the number of passengers, the cargo volume, and the origin or destination of a flight, classified e.g. as domestic or international. The information in the flight schedule defines the time frame for processing a flight and the subset of gates to which it can or should be assigned, taking into account, e.g., aircraft-gate size compatibility, access to governmental inspection facilities for international flights, etc.

Gates are scarce and expensive resources. Increasing the resource supply involves a time-consuming and costly re-design of terminal buildings or the ramp and is usually not feasible in the short run. It is therefore of great economic importance for an airport or terminal operator to use the available gates in the best possible way.

The gate assignment also influences the quality of passenger service in manifold ways. A problem well known to many passengers is that arriving flights sometimes have to wait on the ramp before travelling to their final position, because the assigned gate is still occupied by another flight. Such a situation is often caused by a poor gate assignment or by failure to adapt an initial assignment to updates of the flight schedule. When changing a gate schedule, however, it must be taken into account that gate assignments are published some time before the actual arrival or departure of a flight, for instance for planning purposes in other operational units, on passenger information displays and on boarding passes. Passengers already waiting at a gate may have to be re-directed if the gate of a departing flight is changed on short notice. Another example of the influence of the gate assignment on passenger service is the required passenger walking distance, which depends on the chosen gates.

The gate assignment also affects other ground services. A good assignment may reduce the number of aircraft tows required and may lead to reduced setup times for several ground service activities on the ramp as well as in the terminal.

The problem of finding a suitable gate assignment usually has to be addressed on three levels. Firstly, during the preparation of seasonal flight schedule revisions, the ability to accommodate the proposed flights must be examined. Secondly, given a current flight schedule, daily plans have to be prepared before the actual day of operation. Thirdly, on the day of operation, the gate schedule must be frequently altered to accommodate updates or disruptions in the flight schedule; this is referred to as *reactive* scheduling.

The new optimisation model and algorithm for gate scheduling described in this section differ from previous approaches reported in the literature in several ways.

While at the airport, an aircraft goes through the three stages of (1) arrival processing, (2) optional intermediate parking, depending on the length of the ground time, and (3) departure processing. In contrast to previous models, these stages are considered as separate entities that can potentially be assigned to different positions if necessary or advantageous. The aircraft may then have to travel between the assigned arrival, parking, and departure positions; as this usually requires the use of tow tractors, we will generally refer to it as *towing*. In addition to assigning the three stages to positions, the start and completion times of processing at a position, which can vary within certain time windows, have to be assigned.

The model can consider an arbitrary time horizon, typically set to a day. This stands in contrast to approaches that split the overall problem into isolated, short time slots, that correspond to waves of arriving and departing flights, a simplification that can be justified at some hub airports where many passengers change between connecting flights and where there is little relation between the flights in two successive arrival-transfer-departure waves.

Previous optimisation based approaches have usually modelled the problem by representing the arrival, parking, and departure stages as a single entity to be assigned to the same position, and they only consider a single flight wave. The objective function most frequently used is the minimisation of walking distances for arriving, transferring, and departing passengers. The problem then becomes similar to a quadratic assignment problem (Lawler 1963). However, for many airports, this modelling approach leads to an over-simplification that does not adequately reflect the original decision problem.

The key idea behind the model presented here is to look at the problem as a modified multi-mode resource-constrained project scheduling problem with a multi-criteria objective function. The most important goals are the maximisation of a total flight-gate preference value and the minimisation of the number of tows.

The basic optimisation algorithm is a truncated branch-and-bound procedure that branches over (1) gate (mode) assignments and (2) the disjunctive constraints used to model the capacity restrictions of the disjunctive resources (gates). The algorithm uses constraint propagation techniques to reduce the search space. To cope with large practical problems with in the order of magnitude of thousand activities per day, the problem is decomposed into loosely coupled sub-problems using a new generic problem partitioning technique. The sub-problems are used within a *layered* branch-and-bound approach: The search tree is conceptually split into layers that correspond to the sub-problems. In each layer, only decision variables of the current sub-problem are selected for branching; limited backtracking is performed within the current layer before proceeding to the next layer. Initial solutions obtained in this way are iteratively improved using a large neighbourhood search (LNS) technique (Kilby et al. 2000) that relaxes some of the decisions and uses the branch-and-bound algorithm to reform the relaxed part of the solution at a lower cost. LNS can also serve to adapt an existing schedule to changes in the input data in a smooth way.

The model and algorithm have been evaluated using small manually designed test cases as well as two weeks of real-life flight schedule data from a large international airport. A comparison of the computational results with a rule based approach, as often used in commercial systems, shows that the algorithm greatly improves the solution quality.

Beyond their application for the gate scheduling problem at hand, the problem partitioning technique and the layered branch-and-bound approach are of general interest, since they address a common task and can easily be generalised.

The remainder of this chapter is structured as follows. After a review of the relevant literature in Section 7.2.2, Section 7.2.3 describes the problem in detail and develops the optimisation model. Section 7.2.5 presents the basic branch-and-bound algorithm. Section 7.2.7 shows how the problem can be partitioned into sub-problems, and Section 7.2.8 describes how these sub-problems are used within the layered branch-and-bound approach. The iterative improvement of solutions is discussed in Section 7.2.9. Section 7.2.10 finally reports on computational experiments.

7.2.2 Literature Review

Gate assignment strategies have been studied for a long time, and the first quantitative approaches have already been described in the late 1960's (Baron 1969). One of the first studies that demonstrated the effect of gate assignment strategies on passenger walking distances was undertaken by Braaksma (1977). As an example, the mean walking distance per passenger at Terminal 2 of Toronto International Airport could be reduced by more than ten percent as a result of a change in gate assignment policy. The minimisation of total walking distance within the terminal for arriving, transferring, and terminating passengers has remained one of the most frequently considered objectives in the literature.

Passenger walking distance minimisation is an important issue not only in the operation of airport terminals but also in the design of a terminal. Several efforts to integrate a method to minimise intra-terminal travel into the *terminal design* process have been reported, and as an example we refer to the discussions by Wirasinghe and Bandara (1990) and Bandara and Wirasinghe (1992).

The main part of the literature on gate assignment deals with *terminal operations*. The various contributions can be roughly classified according to the underlying technology as (1) optimisation based and (2) rule based or expert system approaches.

Previous studies that have developed optimisation models and algorithms have focused on the assignment aspect of the gate scheduling problem; the resulting problem is usually referred to as gate assignment problem (GAP). The basic constraints of the GAP are that a gate can only accommodate a single aircraft and that two flights must therefore not be assigned to the same gate if they overlap in time. Arrival processing, intermediate parking, and departure processing are considered as a single entity to be planned and must be assigned to the same gate.

Gate assignment optimisation models can be classified as *single* or *multiple time slot* models. Single time slot models consider the assignment of a batch of flights that arrive within a given time period, or slot, to gates; in these models, only one flight can be assigned to each gate. The GAP can be modelled in analogy to the quadratic assignment problem, which is a location problem where the cost of placing a facility (flight) at a location (gate) depends on the placement of other facilities and the transport volume between two facilities (Lawler 1963).

Babic et al. (1984) have formulated the single-slot GAP as integer linear program with the objective of minimising the total walking distance for arriving and departing passengers. Mangoubi and Mathaisel (1985) have proposed an integer program for the problem with an extended objective function that additionally takes transfer passengers into account. Their single-slot model, which is similar to a quadratic assignment problem, is solved using an LP-relaxation and a heuristic. Another approach has been described by Bihr (1990), who proposes to model the single-slot problem as a linear assignment problem for fixed arrivals in a hub operation. Chang (1994) describes a single-slot GAP that considers the effect of an assignment on baggage transport distances in addition to passenger walking distances. Xu and Bailey (2001) have recently proposed a tabu search algorithm for a single slot GAP with the objective function of minimising the overall passenger connecting times or distances; the problem is formulated as a quadratic assignment problem and reformulated as a mixed 0-1 integer linear program.

Haghani and Chen (1998) formulate a multiple time slot GAP with walking distance and baggage transport distance minimisation as an integer program. One of their main contributions is a model that extends the single-slot GAP with time constraints; this is achieved by introducing time-indexed binary variables that indicate the assignment of a particular flight to some gate in a given time slot. Haghani and Chen (1998) propose a branch-and-bound algorithm as well as a heuristic to solve the problem. The size, or width, of the time slots must be carefully selected as it influences the problem size as well as the possible gate utilisation; the authors conclude that the slot width should be roughly equal to the minimum time that an aircraft can occupy a gate.

"Traditional approaches utilising classical operations research techniques have difficulty with uncertain information and multiple performance criteria, and do not adapt well to the needs of real-time operations support" (Gosling 1990). As a result, the use of rule based or expert systems for the operational control of terminal and ramp activities has been investigated from the mid 1980's on. Hamzawi (1986) has developed a rule based system for simulating the assignment of gates to flights and for evaluating the effects of particular rules on the gate utilisation. Gosling (1990) describes a prototype expert system for gate assignment that has been evaluated in a case study at Denver Stapleton Airport, a major hub airport. Srihari and Muthukrishnan (1991) use a similar approach for solving the GAP and also describe how to apply sensitivity analysis. Cheng (1997) describes the integration of mathematical programming techniques into a knowledge-based gate assignment system.

Both optimisation based and rule based approaches have been combined with simulation analysis to study the effect of assignment policies and rules (see e.g. Baron 1969, Hamzawi 1986).

7.2.3   Problem Description

This section formally describes the gate scheduling problem. After explaining the problem in detail by looking at a small example gate schedule, the system of constraints is formally presented and the objective function is introduced.

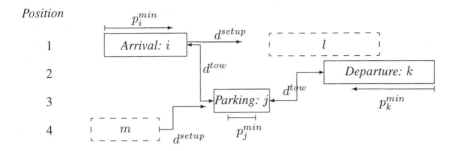

Figure 7.2: Example from a gate schedule

An Example

Figure 7.2 shows an example from a gate schedule represented as a Gantt-Chart. The figure shows four positions or gates on the vertical axis and three activities i, j, and k that are represented as solid rectangles and correspond to the arrival processing, parking, and departure processing of an aircraft. The example shows the special case where these three activities are assigned to different gates; although it is generally desirable to assign the three activities to one and the same gate, the special case illustrates the problem better. We will use the example to introduce the system of constraints of the gate scheduling problem.

Let us first consider the activity i corresponding to the arrival processing, or arrival, for short. The start time S_i of the arrival depends on the flight schedule and is fixed. Beginning at this time, the aircraft must be assigned to a gate for at least p_i^{min} units of time, which is the fixed minimum time required for processing the arrival, including passenger disembarkment, baggage unloading, etc. The minimum processing time is visualised in Figure 7.2 as an arrow of length p_i^{min} starting at the arrival time S_i. After time $S_i + p_i^{min}$, the aircraft may either stay at the gate or may be towed to another position for parking. The completion time C_i at which the aircraft leaves the arrival gate is a decision variable. Of course, $S_i + p_i^{min} \leq C_i$ must hold. In the example, the aircraft remains at the arrival gate for more than the minimum required time and then moves to the parking gate.

In an analogous way, the departure activity k has a fixed completion time C_k at which the aircraft must leave the gate. The fixed minimum required departure processing time p_k^{min} is visualised as a backward arrow of length p_k^{min}, beginning at time C_k. The start of the departure processing, S_k is a decision variable. Again, $S_k + p_k^{min} \leq C_k$ must hold.

While at the airport, an aircraft must be continuously assigned to some position or be moving between two successively assigned positions. In the example, the aircraft moves from the assigned arrival gate 1 to gate 3 for intermediate parking. The start time S_j of the parking at gate 3, which is a decision variable, must be equal to the completion time C_i of the arrival processing plus the required travel, or tow, time d^{tow} between the arrival and parking gates. To avoid degenerate solutions in which an aircraft is towed to a parking position, and immediately afterwards towed to another gate for departure processing, we impose a minimum processing time $p_j^{min} > 0$ for parking. The parking completion time C_j is a decision variable. As before, $S_j + p_j^{min} \leq C_j$ must hold. At time C_j, the aircraft is towed to the departure gate; in the example, $C_j + d^{tow} = S_k$ must hold. Because the tow time depends on the gates and on the aircraft, it will later be indexed accordingly.

A gate can only accept one aircraft at a time, and between two successive assignments a sequence dependent setup time d^{setup} that depends on the associated two aircraft must pass. In Figure 7.2, the setup time between the arrival activity i and some other, following activity l, that is also assigned to position 1, is shown as an arrow of length d^{setup}, beginning at time C_i. Setup times mainly serve to model the time required for the push-back of an aircraft from a gate using a tow tractor and the time required for the following aircraft to move to the free gate. The setup duration depends on the gates and on the affected aircraft and will later be indexed accordingly.

An assignment of an aircraft to a particular gate does not only restrict the use of this gate for other aircraft, but may also influence possible assignments at other adjacent gates due to wingtip proximity problems or blocked access. Additionally, the ramp layout often includes overlapping positions, that may, for instance, either accommodate one large aircraft or two small ones. The restrictions between adjacent gates are sometimes intuitively called *shadowing*. Figure 7.2 shows an example of shadowing between the parking activity assigned to gate 3 and another activity m shown as dashed rectangle at position 4. Intuitively, the aircraft at gate 3 casts its shadow on the adjacent gate 4 and restricts the use of position 4 during the assignment of the parking activity as well as for a certain amount of setup time before and afterwards. The restrictions between pairs of (adjacent) gates generally depend on the gates and the aircraft type or size.

This completes the discussion of the example gate schedule, that has shown the special and most general case where the arrival, parking and departure of an aircraft are assigned to three different gates. Other assignments involving only one or two gates are often possible and preferable because ground service setup times as well as tows and the associated ramp traffic are avoided. In addition to the case shown in the example where an aircraft goes through the three stages of arrival, parking, and departure, a flight schedule may also contain arrivals without a linked departure, and vice versa; for example, such a situation can occur when an arriving aircraft has to stay at the airport for maintenance or returns from maintenance, respectively.

Constraints

The gate scheduling problem can be modelled in analogy to a multi-mode resource-constrained project scheduling problem; the choice of a processing mode corresponds to a gate assignment. The model developed in the following is summarised in Figure 7.3; the notation used is analogous to the standard project scheduling notation.

For every pair of *linked* arrival and departure flights, i.e., successive transit or turn-round flights served by the same aircraft, we introduce three activities corresponding to the arrival processing, parking, and departure processing. The activities are referred to simply as arrival, parking, and departure; the arrival is linked to the parking, which in turn is linked to the departure. The set of all links (i, j) between two activities i and j is denoted with $\mathcal{E}^{tow}$ (every link implies a potential towing operation). For an arriving flight that is not linked to a departure, and for a departing flight without a corresponding arrival, we introduce a single activity. The set of all arrivals is denoted with $\mathcal{V}^a$; $\mathcal{V}^p$ is the set of all parking activities, $\mathcal{V}^d$ is the set of departures, and the set of all activities is $\mathcal{V} := \mathcal{V}^a \cup \mathcal{V}^p \cup \mathcal{V}^d$.

An activity i has a given minimal processing time p_i^{min}, a start time S_i, and a completion time C_i. By choosing sufficiently small time units, we can assume without loss of generality that the processing times and the start and completion times are natural numbers. The start and completion times are decision variables. However, in case of arrival activities, the start time must equal the flight arrival time t_i^a given in the flight schedule, and departure activities must complete at the scheduled flight departure time t_i^d; for parking activities, both the start and completion time are variable. In contrast to classical project scheduling models, only a minimal processing time is given, and the actual processing time $p_i := C_i - S_i$ is not fixed in advance but follows from the selected start and completion times. The minimal required processing time leads to Constraint (7.1) in Figure 7.3. The domains of the start and completion times are restricted by Constraints (7.4) – (7.6).

The set of all gates, or modes, is denoted with $\mathcal{M}$. An activity i must be assigned a processing mode M_i from its associated set of possible mode assignments $\mathcal{M}_i \subseteq \mathcal{M}$, which is given. The chosen processing mode M_i corresponds to a gate assignment, and the set $\mathcal{M}_i$ corresponds to the set of gates to which the aircraft may be feasibly assigned. To cope with situations where the constraints do not allow to assign all aircraft to a real gate — for example if the number of flights to be scheduled exceeds the number of available gates — we introduce a fictitious gate 0, or dummy gate, with unlimited capacity. By default, every mode set $\mathcal{M}_i$ contains this dummy gate; assignments to the dummy gate will be penalised in the objective function. Constraint (7.7) restricts the mode variables. The set of all possible modes is denoted with $\mathcal{M}$, and $\mathcal{M}_i \subseteq \mathcal{M}$.

The completion and start times of two successive (linked) activities i and j for the same aircraft may differ only by the time required for towing the aircraft between the assigned gates. This tow time naturally depends on the distance between the

Find a schedule (S, C, M) **w.r.t.**

Minimal processing time

$$S_i + p_i^{min} \leq C_i, \qquad \forall i \in \mathcal{V}. \tag{7.1}$$

Continuous processing

$$C_i + d_{iM_i jM_j}^{tow} = S_j, \qquad \forall (i,j) \in \mathcal{E}^{tow}. \tag{7.2}$$

Disjunctive activities and setup times

$$\left. \begin{array}{l} C_i + d_{iM_i jM_j}^{setup} \leq S_j \\ \vee \\ C_j + d_{jM_j iM_i}^{setup} \leq S_i, \end{array} \right\} \forall i,j \in \mathcal{V} : \left\{ \begin{array}{l} M_i = M_j \neq 0 \\ \vee \\ \exists (i, M_i, j, M_j) \in \mathcal{E}^{shadow}. \end{array} \right. \tag{7.3}$$

Start and completion time

$$S_i = t_i^a, \qquad \forall i \in \mathcal{V}^a, \tag{7.4}$$

$$C_i = t_i^d, \qquad \forall i \in \mathcal{V}^d, \tag{7.5}$$

$$S_i, C_i \in \mathbb{N}_0, \qquad \forall i \in \mathcal{V}. \tag{7.6}$$

Mode selection

$$M_i \in \mathcal{M}_i, \qquad \forall i \in \mathcal{V}. \tag{7.7}$$

Figure 7.3: Constraints of the gate scheduling problem

gates, and also on the aircraft type associated with the activity. It is denoted with $d_{iM_i jM_j}^{tow} \in \mathbb{N}_0$; due to the large number of activities and possible modes in practical problem instances, it will be implemented as some function f of the activities and chosen modes, i.e., $d_{iM_i jM_j}^{tow} := f(i, M_i, j, M_j)$, rather than as table or array lookup, as suggested by the index notation. The tow time takes the value zero if and only if two activities are assigned to the same gate, i.e., $d_{iM_i jM_j}^{tow} = 0$ if $M_i = M_j$, for all $i, j \in \mathcal{V}$, and it is strictly positive otherwise. Using the tow time, the continuous processing requirement can be formulated as Constraint (7.2).

Gates are disjunctive resources that can only process one activity (aircraft) at a time; the only exception is the dummy gate 0, which can hold an infinite number of aircraft. Between the processing of two activities i and j, a setup time $d_{iM_i jM_j}^{setup} \in \mathbb{N}_0$ must pass. The setup time can reflect the time required to push back the first aircraft back from the gate and for moving the second aircraft to the gate, as well as the duration required for setting up equipment such as aircraft bridges. It depends on the gates and aircraft types associated with the activities and is therefore indexed with the activities and their corresponding mode variables. Setup times are only required between the processing of two different aircraft; if i and j are successive activities served by the same aircraft, i.e., if $(i, j) \in \mathcal{E}^{tow}$ then $d_{iM_ijM_j}^{setup} = 0$. In analogy to the tow times, the setup times will be implemented as some function f of the activities (aircraft types) and modes (gates), i.e., $d_{iM_ijM_j}^{setup} := f(i, M_i, j, M_j)$.

The basic disjunctive resource constraint that forbids the simultaneous assignment of two aircraft to the same gate can now be formulated as follows:

$$
\left.
\begin{aligned}
C_i + d_{iM_ijM_j}^{setup} &\leq S_j \\
\vee \\
C_j + d_{jM_jiM_i}^{setup} &\leq S_i,
\end{aligned}
\right\}
\quad \forall i, j \in \mathcal{V} : M_i = M_j \neq 0.
$$

This corresponds to the first case covered by Constraint (7.3).

Additionally, Constraint (7.3) also covers shadowing restrictions between gates. A shadowing restriction between a pair of gates μ and ν can be conceptually represented as a tuple (i, μ, j, ν) that has the following interpretation: If mode $\mu \in \mathcal{M}_i$ is assigned to activity i, then activity j must not be "simultaneously" processed in mode $\nu \in \mathcal{M}_j$. The set of all shadowing restrictions is denoted with $\mathcal{E}^{shadow}$.[1] In the same way and for the same reasons as for activities assigned to the same gate, setup durations must also be taken into account for activities at adjacent gates affected by a shadowing restriction. This leads to the following disjunctive constraint:

$$
\left.
\begin{aligned}
C_i + d_{iM_ijM_j}^{setup} &\leq S_j \\
\vee \\
C_j + d_{jM_jiM_i}^{setup} &\leq S_i,
\end{aligned}
\right\}
\quad \forall i, j \in \mathcal{V} : \exists (i, M_i, j, M_j) \in \mathcal{E}^{shadow}.
$$

This corresponds to the second case covered by Constraint (7.3). In summary, Constraint (7.3) must hold for two activities i and j either (1) if the same mode is assigned to i and j or (2) if the modes are chosen in such a way that a shadowing restriction applies. In both cases, the activities and their setup durations must not overlap in time. Of course, the constraints only need to be explicitly defined for those pairs of activities for which the start and completion time domains allow for such an overlap and where the mode domains intersect or may trigger a shadowing restriction, as the constraint is always satisfied otherwise. Formally, the set $\mathcal{D}$ of disjunctive activity pairs for which Constraint (7.3) must be explicitly defined can be described as follows:

$$
\begin{aligned}
\mathcal{D} := \{ \quad &\{i, j\} \in \mathcal{V} \times \mathcal{V} \mid \\
& LC_i + \max_{\mu \in \mathcal{M}_i, \nu \in \mathcal{M}_j} d_{i\mu j\nu}^{setup} > ES_j \quad \wedge \\
& LC_j + \max_{\mu \in \mathcal{M}_i, \nu \in \mathcal{M}_j} d_{j\nu i\mu}^{setup} > ES_i \\
& \wedge \\
& (\mathcal{M}_i \cap \mathcal{M}_j \setminus \{0\} \neq \emptyset \\
& \vee \\
& \exists (i, \mu, j, \nu) \in \mathcal{E}^{shadow} : \mu \in \mathcal{M}_i \wedge \nu \in \mathcal{M}_j) \}.
\end{aligned}
\tag{7.8}
$$

---

[1] It is not reasonable to define a shadowing restriction for the fictitious gate (mode) 0.

It is worth mentioning that the disjunctive constraints do not apply for activities assigned to the fictitious gate, i.e., which are processed in mode zero. Because Constraint (7.3) is the only resource constraint in the model, the number of activities that can be simultaneously assigned to the fictitious gate is unlimited.

Finding a solution to the gate scheduling problem is equivalent to finding an assignment of the start and completion time and mode variables that is compatible with the Constraints (7.1) – (7.7). A gate schedule is thus defined by the tuple (S, C, M) of start time, completion time, and mode vectors.

The problem is similar in structure to a multi-mode project scheduling problem with unary, or disjunctive, resources. As a peculiarity, only minimal required processing times are given. In addition to start time decision variables, the completion times therefore also become decision variables. Constraints (7.2) are the temporal constraints of the problem. They are of equality type; they could also be represented in a way similar to the problem $MPS|temp|C_{max}$ by using two precedence constraints with appropriate minimal and maximal time lags. Constraints (7.3) are the resource constraints and additionally serve to model shadowing restrictions. Constraints (7.4) – (7.7) are domain constraints.

The ground time of an aircraft, which is defined as the duration between its arrival and departure, is sometimes so short that the arrival, parking, and departure activity must always be assigned to the same gate (*block* processing). If this is detected in a preprocessing step which serves to define the minimal processing times, then the minimal processing times for activities that require block processing can be set accordingly: If i, j, and k are the arrival, parking, and departure activities, then set $p_i^{min} := t_k^d - t_i^a, p_j^{min} := 0$ and $p_k^{min} := 0$. Because the tow time d^{tow} between different gates is strictly positive, Constraints (7.1), (7.2), and (7.4) – (7.6) then imply that $M_i = M_j = M_k$ must hold.

Objective Function

The objective function is a linear combination of several goals. In extensive discussions with a terminal operator, it has been concluded that the most important goals are (1) the maximisation of a total assignment preference score, (2) the minimisation of the number of required towing operations, and (3) the minimisation of the deviation from a given reference gate schedule. In order to further differentiate between gate schedules that are of equal quality with respect to these goals it is reasonable to add other goals of lower importance. In the following we will concentrate on the three top goals.

Using goal weights α_i, which are non-negative real numbers, the objective function $z(S, C, M)$ is formulated as follows:

$$z(S, C, M) := \min \alpha_1 z_1 + \alpha_2 z_2 + \alpha_3 z_3.$$

We will see below that the values of three goals z_1, z_2, and z_3 depend only on the mode vector M but not on the start and completion time vectors S and C, so that we can write $z(M)$ instead of $z(S, C, M)$.

The first goal z_1 is the maximisation of the total gate preference score. We associate a preference value $u_{i\mu}$ with every activity-mode combination, i.e., for all $i \in \mathcal{V}$ and $\mu \in \mathcal{M}$. Each activity is further associated a weight, or priority, $w_i \in [0, 1]$. An assignment to the fictitious gate 0 is penalised with a large negative value; otherwise, the preference values are normalized numbers, i.e., $u_{i\mu} \in [0, 1]$, for all $i \in \mathcal{V}$ and all $\mu \in \mathcal{M} \setminus \{0\}$; the preference $u_{i\mu}$ is always 0 if $\mu \notin \mathcal{M}_i$ and usually greater than zero otherwise. The goal of maximising the total mode assignment preference score can be formulated as follows:

$$z_1 := -\sum_{i \in \mathcal{V}} w_i u_{iM_i}.$$

It is evident that the preferences and weights have a large influence on the optimal gate schedule. Choosing suitable values for the assignment preference and weight parameters u_{iM_i} and w_i is a difficult problem in itself, but is beyond the scope of this study. The task is delegated to a rule-based system that defines the values based on the detailed characteristics of the associated flights, for example, origin, destination(s), number of passengers, type of aircraft, airline, and many more.

The movement of an aircraft from a terminal position to another position generally requires the use of an aircraft tow tractor, because the aircraft needs to be pushed back from the terminal building. Tow tractors are scarce and expensive resources. Furthermore, aircraft movements may restrict access to other gates, that are being passed, and add to ramp traffic congestion. It is therefore of great importance to minimise the number of movements. This is captured in the second goal:

$$z_2 := |\{(i, j) \in \mathcal{E}^{tow} : M_i \neq M_j\}|.$$

The third goal is to minimise the deviation from a given reference gate schedule, which will be denoted with (S', C', M'). This goal is important for two main reasons. Firstly, in the preparation of daily plans before the actual day of operations, is desirable to obtain a maximum similarity between the gate schedules for different days of the week. For example, it is considered advantageous if the eight o'clock flight to a particular destination always departs at the same gate, as this tends to ease other operational planning tasks. Secondly, in reactive re-scheduling, which is made necessary by flight schedule disruptions, conflicts or infeasibilities in the gate schedule should be resolved in such a way that the changes to the schedule are kept minimal. Here, the rationale behind minimising the number of changes is that the gate schedule is published for passengers and for other operational systems within the airport and that gate changes may cause considerable effort in these areas. The goal can be formally expressed as follows:

$$z_3 := \sum_{i \in \mathcal{V}: M_i \neq M_i'} w_i.$$

It is interesting to note that this goal addresses one of the typical weaknesses of optimisation based systems, namely that small changes in the input data may easily lead to large changes in the output data.

7.2.4 Constraint Propagation

The gate scheduling problem is solved using a branch-and-bound approach. At each node of the search tree a fixed point is computed by applying constraint propagation. The basic propagation algorithm is a variant of the AC-5 arc consistency algorithm described by Van Hentenryck et al. (1992). Within the constraint propagation algorithm, we use the following consistency tests introduced in Chapter 4, which are all based on the mode minimal problem instance introduced in Definition 1 on page 63:

- A variant of the precedence consistency test 1 for the minimal processing time constraints (7.1), for the continuous processing constraints (7.2)[2], and for the disjunctive precedence constraints (7.3) once it can be deduced or has been explicitly decided which part of a disjunction must hold.

- The disjunctive pair test, which enforces constraints (7.3).

- A mode shaving test as described in Algorithm 2 on page 64.

7.2.5 A Branch-and-Bound Algorithm

The branch-and-bound algorithm described in this section builds gate schedules by iteratively assigning modes to activities and by resolving resource conflicts. As we have seen in the previous section, the objective function value depends only on the mode vector, but not on the start and completion times. We will therefore search for a solution in which at least an assignment for all mode variables has been selected and in which the start and completion time domains are generally reduced from their initial values; however, the time domains may still contain more than one entry, i.e., start and completion variables may still be unbound. The remaining degree of freedom can be exploited in a sub-sequent optimisation step, not covered here, that chooses start and completion times in a way that allows to schedule all required towing operations. This can for instance be achieved by solving a vehicle routing and scheduling problem with time windows for the tow crews, where the time windows for the start and end of a towing operation are defined by the start and completion time domains of the corresponding arrival and parking, or parking and departure activities.

At each node of the search tree, we first apply constraint propagation and then branch in one of two alternative ways by either

---

[2]Recall that a continuous processing constraint can be replaced by two precedence constraints with minimal and maximal time lags.

1. assigning a mode to an activity or forbidding the mode assignment, or

2. resolving a resource conflict by selecting which part of the disjunction in Constraint (7.3) must hold.

In the following we shall first explain the details of the binary branching scheme and then show how simple lower bounds can be developed.

Branching Scheme

Each node α of the search tree has an associated set of current domains $\Delta(\alpha)$:

$$
\begin{aligned}
\Delta(\alpha) &:= \{\Delta_S(\alpha), \Delta_C(\alpha), \Delta_M(\alpha)\} \\
&:= \{\Delta_{S_i}(\alpha), \Delta_{C_i}(\alpha), \Delta_{M_i}(\alpha) \mid i \in \mathcal{V}\}.
\end{aligned}
$$

$\Delta(\alpha)$ uniquely determines the sets of scheduled and free activities. The set $\mathcal{V}^s$ of scheduled or assigned activities contains all activities whose mode domain contains exactly one entry, i.e.,

$$\mathcal{V}^s(\alpha) := \{i \in \mathcal{V} \mid |\Delta_{M_i}(\alpha)| = 1\}.$$

$\mathcal{V}^f(\alpha) := \mathcal{V} \setminus \mathcal{V}^s(\alpha)$ is the set of *free* or unassigned activities. We thus consider an activity as scheduled as soon as it is assigned a mode (gate), even though its start and completion time domains may still vary.

Disjunctive Branching   If there is a pair of scheduled activities $i, j \in \mathcal{V}^s(\alpha)$ for which Constraint (7.3) must be explicitly defined, i.e., for which $\{i, j\} \in \mathcal{D}$, as introduced in Definition (7.8), and where both cases $i \to j$ and $j \to i$ of Constraint (7.3) may still hold, then we branch by creating two child nodes $l'(\alpha)$ and $r'(\alpha)$ that correspond to the two possible orientations of the disjunction:

$$
\begin{aligned}
l'(\alpha) : \quad &\text{add the constraint } C_i + d^{setup}_{iM_ijM_j} \leq S_j, \\
r'(\alpha) : \quad &\text{add the constraint } C_j + d^{setup}_{jM_jiM_i} \leq S_i.
\end{aligned}
$$

If multiple activity pairs are eligible for branching then we first choose the pair with the smallest time domains, i.e., the pair $\{i, j\}$ for which $|\Delta_{S_i}| + |\Delta_{C_i}| + |\Delta_{S_j}| + |\Delta_{C_j}|$ is minimal. We then choose activity i and j so that $ES_i \leq ES_j$ and first branch to the left child node $l'(\alpha)$. All ties are broken arbitrarily.

The reason why the branching over disjunctions between pairs $\{i, j\} \in \mathcal{D}$ is delayed until modes have been chosen for both i and j is that any previous reductions of the mode domains Δ_{M_i} and Δ_{M_j} and constraint propagation may allow to deduce which part of a disjunction must hold without the need for explicit branching.

It is easy to see that explicit branching will only be required for activity pairs where at least one of the activities is a parking activity: All other pairs involve only arrival and departure activities, i.e., activities for which either the start or completion time is fixed through Constraint (7.4) and (7.5); the order in which the two activities must execute can thus be immediately deduced.

Mode Branching   If there is no pair $\{i, j\} \in \mathcal{D}$ that is eligible for disjunctive branching, then we branch over a mode assignment in the following way.

At node α we select the next unassigned activity from $\mathcal{V}^f(\alpha)$ for mode branching according to a variable selection rule that we will explain below; we denote the chosen activity with $act(\alpha)$. A value selection rule that will also be introduced below then chooses a mode $m(i, \alpha) \in \Delta_{M_i}(\alpha)$ which is assigned to i in one of the child nodes. Let $i = act(\alpha)$ be the activity chosen at α. When branching from node α, two child nodes $l(\alpha)$ and $r(\alpha)$ are created by either assigning $m(i, \alpha)$ to i or prohibiting this assignment:

$$
\begin{aligned}
l(\alpha): & \quad \Delta_{M_i} := \{m(i, \alpha)\}, \\
r(\alpha): & \quad \Delta_{M_i} := \Delta_{M_i} \setminus \{m(i, \alpha)\}.
\end{aligned}
$$

Activities and modes are chosen according to a *maximal regret* criterion, which is based on lower bounds of the objective function. The rationale behind the well known maximal regret principle is to first make those assignments which otherwise, if not made, will cause the greatest loss as indicated by the increase of the lower bound. For every activity, we consider (1) the currently "best" mode assignment, i.e., the one for which the resulting lower bound value is minimal, and (2) the currently second best assignment. The regret of not assigning the currently best mode to an activity is the difference between the lower bound values for the best and second best assignment. The activity for which the maximal regret is realised and its currently best mode are chosen for branching.

In order to formalise the maximal regret concept, let us introduce $LB(\alpha)$ as a bound on the minimal objective function value of any schedule that can be developed from node α given the set of current domains $\Delta(\alpha)$. Additionally, let $LB(\alpha, \Delta_i = \{\mu\})$ denote the value of this bound if we bind a free activity $i \in \mathcal{V}^f(\alpha)$ to one of the modes μ in its current domain, i.e., replace $\Delta_{M_i}(\alpha) = \{\dots, \mu, \dots\}$ with $\{\mu\}$, and apply *CP* in order to evaluate the consequences of this assignment. The "best" mode for activity i given the domains Δ is the one with smallest lower bound value:

$$
m(i, \alpha) := \arg \min_{\mu \in \Delta_{M_i}(\alpha)} LB(\Delta, \Delta_{M_i} = \{\mu\})).
$$

The regret of not assigning the best mode to i can then be defined as:

$$
\begin{aligned}
regret(i, \alpha) \quad := \quad & \min_{\mu \in \Delta_{M_i}(\alpha) \setminus m(i, \alpha)} LB(\alpha, \Delta_{M_i}(\alpha) = \{\mu\}) \quad - \\
& LB(\alpha, \Delta_{M_i}(\alpha) = m(i, \alpha)).
\end{aligned}
$$

Finally, the function $act(\alpha)$ returns the unassigned activity $i \in \mathcal{V}^f(\alpha)$ with maximal regret:

$$act(\alpha) := \arg \max_{i \in \mathcal{V}^f(\alpha)} regret(i, \alpha)).$$

Summary of the Branching Scheme We can now define the branching scheme recursively. This is done in Figure 7.4. Recall that we only have to specify $\Delta(\alpha)$, since this determines all other sets and values.

The search tree is traversed in depth-first order until a leaf node is generated, i.e., until $\mathcal{V}^s(\alpha) = \mathcal{V}$. Backtracking occurs when a leaf node is reached, when bounding considerations allow to prune a branch, or when an inconsistency has been detected, i.e., when some domain becomes empty.

Because of the simple branching structure and the fact that constraint propagation only removes values which cannot participate in any feasible schedule that can be developed from a node, it is easy to see that the branching scheme is complete in the sense that it can generate any feasible mode assignment vector and reduce the start and completion time domains in such way that they contain all feasible start and completion times.

Start and Completion Times

Intuitively, the fact that two linked activities i and j, with i preceding j, are assigned to the same gate means that the precise value of the intermediate completion of i and the start of j becomes meaningless. This can be visualised in Figure 7.2 by moving the parking activity j to the arrival gate 1 or to the departure gate 2. In general, for any pair of linked activities $i, j \in \mathcal{V}$, with $(i, j) \in \mathcal{E}^{tow}$, that are assigned to the same gate, the values of $C_i = S_j$ can be arbitrarily chosen from the domains $\Delta_{S_j}(\alpha')$ or $\Delta_{C_i}(\alpha')$, where α' is a solution node of the search tree where values for all mode variables have been selected.

We use this observation in the following way. Let $i \in \mathcal{V}^a$, $j \in \mathcal{V}^p$, and $(i, j) \in \mathcal{E}^{tow}$; if, at any search tree node α, $M_i = M_j$ after the application of constraint propagation, then we arbitrarily set $C_i := \min \Delta_{C_i}(\alpha)$ and $S_j := C_i$. In analogy, let $j \in \mathcal{V}^p$ and $k \in \mathcal{V}^d$ and $(j, k) \in \mathcal{E}^{tow}$; if, at any search tree node α, $M_j = M_k$ after applying constraint propagation, then we arbitrarily set $S_k := \max \Delta_{S_k}(\alpha)$ and $C_j := S_j$.

The start and completion times of all other activities are not explicitly assigned in the branch-and-bound algorithm. The remaining degree of freedom is exploited in the subsequent solution for a VRSPTW for the tow crews.

7.2.6 Lower Bounds

Lower bounds for the objective function value of any schedule that can be developed from the current node are used to select activities and modes for branching, and to prune parts of the search tree based on the comparison of the current lower bound and

At the root ρ   Let ρ be the root of the search tree. Let $\Delta'_{M_i} := \mathcal{M}_i$, for all $i \in \mathcal{V}$, $\Delta'_{S_i} := [t_i^a]$ for all $i \in \mathcal{V}^a$, $\Delta'_{C_i} := [t_i^d]$ for all $i \in \mathcal{V}^d$, and $\Delta'_{S_i} := [0, T], \Delta'_{C_i} := [0, T]$ for all $i \in \mathcal{V} \setminus (\mathcal{V}^a \cup \mathcal{V}^d)$. Then

$$\Delta(\rho) := CP(\Delta').$$

In node α   Let α be a node of the search tree and let $\Delta(\alpha)$ be the set of current domains in α. If $\exists \{i, j\} \in \mathcal{D} : i, j \in \mathcal{V}^s(\alpha) \wedge EC_i + d^{setup}_{iM_i jM_j} \leq LS_j \wedge EC_j + d^{setup}_{jM_j iM_i} \leq LS_i$ then use disjunctive branching and create two child nodes $l'(\alpha)$ and $r'(\alpha)$, otherwise use mode branching and create two child nodes $l(\alpha)$ and $r(\alpha)$.

Disjunctive branching   Let $\{i, j\} \in \mathcal{D} : i, j \in \mathcal{V}^s(\alpha)$ be the activity pair chosen in α.

$l'(\alpha)$: Add the constraint $C_i + d^{setup}_{iM_i jM_j} \leq S_j$;
    then $\Delta(l'(\alpha)) := CP(\Delta(\alpha))$.

$r'(\alpha)$: Add the constraint $C_j + d^{setup}_{jM_j iM_i} \leq S_i$;
    then $\Delta(r'(\alpha)) := CP(\Delta(\alpha))$.

Mode branching   Let $i := act(\alpha)$ be the activity chosen in α and let $\mu := m(i, \alpha)$ be the currently "best" mode for i.

$l(\alpha)$:   Let $\Delta'(\alpha) := \Delta(\alpha) \setminus \Delta_{M_i}(\alpha) \cup \Delta'_{M_i}(\alpha)$, where $\Delta'_{M_i}(\alpha) := \{\mu\}$.
    Then: $\Delta(l(\alpha)) := CP(\Delta'(\alpha))$.

$r(\alpha)$:   Let $\Delta''(\alpha) := \Delta(\alpha) \setminus \Delta_{M_i}(\alpha) \cup \Delta''_{M_i}(\alpha)$, where $\Delta''_{M_i}(\alpha) := \Delta_{M_i}(\alpha) \setminus \{\mu\}$. Then: $\Delta(r(\alpha)) := CP(\Delta''(\alpha))$.

Figure 7.4: The branching scheme

the value of the best solution found so far, if any. Lower bounds LB_i can be derived for each of the individual goals z_i introduced in Section 7.2.3 in a straightforward way. Clearly, the bounds depend on the set of current domains $\Delta(\alpha)$, and the overall bound on $z(\Delta)$ is given by:

$$LB(\Delta) := \sum_{i=1}^{3} \alpha_i \cdot LB_i(\Delta).$$

Because this value must be frequently recomputed or updated, we will use rather simple bounds that can be calculated with low effort.

By considering the most preferred gate in the current domain of each activity, we obtain the following bound for the overall preference score:

$$LB_1(\Delta) = -\sum_{i \in \mathcal{V}} w_i \cdot \max_{\mu \in \Delta_{M_i}} u(i, \mu).$$

A lower bound on the total number of towing operations is obtained by testing the mode domain intersections of all linked activities:

$$LB_2(\Delta) := |\{(i,j) \in \mathcal{E}^{tow} : \Delta_{M_i} \cap \Delta_{M_j} \neq \emptyset\}|.$$

A lower bound for the deviation from a reference Schedule (S', C', M'), can be obtained by simply testing for mode domains that no longer contain the mode selected in the reference schedule:

$$LB_3(\Delta) := \sum_{i \in \mathcal{V}: M_i' \notin \Delta_{M_i}} w_i.$$

7.2.7 Problem Partitioning

Practical gate scheduling problem instances involve a large number of flights and gates. Although a gate schedule is in reality continuous, it is in many ways natural to partition the underlying flight schedule into one-day periods for which gate schedules have to be constructed; still, a limited interaction between successive days is caused by aircraft staying at the airport over night. Within one day at a large airport terminal, on the order of magnitude of 1000 activities must be scheduled at approximately 100 gates.

Problem partitioning, or decomposition, is a way to accelerate the process of solving these large problem instances by decomposing a problem into smaller sub-problems. The sub-problems can then either be solved independently, or, as we will see in Section 7.2.8, the information about the sub-problems can be used in some other way to enhance the overall solution algorithm.

A problem can be partitioned exactly or heuristically. While an exact partitioning splits a large problem into formally independent sub-problems, the sub-problems in a heuristic partition are not strictly independent but loosely coupled. For a general discussion of problem decomposition techniques for constraint satisfaction problems we refer to Tsang (1993).

Exact Partitioning Based on the Constraint Graph

An exact partitioning of any decision problem can be efficiently obtained in polynomial time by finding the connected components of the constraint graph, which is defined as the graph consisting of nodes corresponding to the decision variables and edges between any pair of variables (nodes) that appear in a common constraint (see Section 3.1.3 on page 21). A sub-problem is defined by the decision variables and constraints within a connected component of the graph. Solving all sub-problems to optimality is equivalent to solving the complete problem to optimality.

When using the exact partitioning approach on the practical gate scheduling problem instances which were used to test our algorithms and that are defined for twenty-four hour periods, it was sometimes possible to isolate some small sub-problems in the early morning or late evening of a day. However, the largest part of any problem could not be partitioned exactly, leaving a main sub-problem that still contained almost all decision variables. It is therefore interesting to look for ways to heuristically partition a problem.

Heuristic Problem Partitioning Using a Clique Partitioning Model

The Clique Partitioning Problem   A gate scheduling problem can be decomposed heuristically by partitioning a complete, edge-weighted graph $G(V, E, (w_{ij}))$ into non-overlapping cliques in such a way that the similarity of vertices within a clique is maximised. The node set V of the graph G corresponds to the activity set of the gate scheduling problem. The edge weights w_{ij} are a measure of the similarity or dissimilarity between the associated activities i and j and will be defined in the following way: If the two activities have similar gate preferences, then w_{ij} is positive, otherwise it is negative. The basic idea now is to partition the gate scheduling problem into loosely coupled sub-problems by partitioning G into an arbitrary number of cliques in such a way that the total edge weight within all cliques is maximised, or, equivalently, the total weight of all edges between different cliques, called the *cut*, is minimised. Minimising the weight of the cut is achieved by placing activities with similar gate preferences within the same clique.

Figure 7.5 shows an example of a complete graph with five vertices (activities) that is partitioned into two cliques (sub-problems) V_1 and V_2; in general, the number of cliques may be larger than two. In the following, we will first formally describe the partitioning problem and then explain how to derive the edge weights w_{ij}.

The problem of partitioning the graph $G(V, E, (w_{ij}))$ in such a way that the cut is minimised is known as *clique partitioning problem*, or CPP. Using the binary decision variables x_{ij} which take the value 1 if vertices i and j are in the same

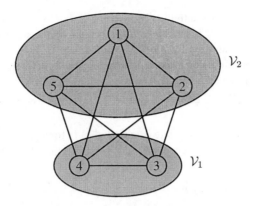

Figure 7.5: Example of a graph partitioned into two cliques

clique and 0 otherwise, the CPP can be formally described as follows:

$$\min \sum_{i,j \in \mathcal{V}: i<j} w_{ij}x_{ij}, \tag{7.9}$$

s.t.

$$
\begin{aligned}
x_{ij} + x_{jk} - x_{ik} &\leq 1, & \forall i,j,k \in \mathcal{V} : i < j < k, & \qquad (7.10)\\
x_{ij} - x_{jk} + x_{ik} &\leq 1, & \forall i,j,k \in \mathcal{V} : i < j < k, & \qquad (7.11)\\
-x_{ij} + x_{jk} + x_{ik} &\leq 1, & \forall i,j,k \in \mathcal{V} : i < j < k, & \qquad (7.12)\\
x_{ij} &\in \{0,1\}, & \forall i,j \in \mathcal{V} : i < j. & \qquad (7.13)
\end{aligned}
$$

Constraints (7.10) – (7.12) ensure that if two edges of a triangle (a clique of three vertices) in the graph belong to the same clique, then the whole triangle belongs to this clique.

If all edge weights are non-negative or non-positive, then the problem can easily be solved. However, if the graph has negative as well as positive edge weights then the CPP is NP-complete (Dyer and Frieze 1985). Exact and heuristic algorithms for the CPP have for example been described by Grötschel and Wakabayashi (1990) and Dorndorf and Pesch (1994). The CPP will be solved using a fast and effective heuristic algorithm proposed by Dorndorf and Pesch (1994).

A Similarity Metric   After the formal description of the CPP, we are left with the task of defining the edge weights w_{ij} in a way that is meaningful for the underlying gate scheduling problem. The weights are derived from the matrix (u_{ij}) of normalised activity-gate preferences. The basic idea is that two activities are similar if their two corresponding rows in the preference matrix have similar entries in all columns, which means that they prefer the same set of gates. We will measure the degree of similarity of two activities by looking at the average difference of their gate preferences. We will further take into account that a similarity with respect to a highly preferred gate (high preference values) is of greater significance than a similarity with respect to a barely acceptable gate (small preference values), or even with respect to an infeasible gate (preference values of zero). As all activities can be assigned to the fictitious gate 0, we will only consider the set of gates or modes $\mathcal{M}^0 := \mathcal{M} \setminus \{0\}$.

The relative importance $\widehat{w}_{ijk}$ of a gate (mode) $k \in \mathcal{M}^0$ for a pair of activities $i, j \in \mathcal{V}$ is the ratio of the sum of preferences of i and j for k to their total preference values:

$$\widehat{w}_{ijk} := \frac{u_{ik} + u_{jk}}{\sum_{l \in \mathcal{M}^0} (u_{il} + u_{jl})}.$$

For normalised preference values this implies that $\widehat{w}_{ijk} \in [0, 1]$ and $\sum_{k \in \mathcal{M}^0} \widehat{w}_{ijk} = 1$.

The normalised similarity s_{ijk} of a pair of activities $i, j \in \mathcal{V}$ with respect to gate $k \in \mathcal{M}^0$ is:

$$s_{ijk} := \begin{cases} 1 - |u_{ik} - u_{jk}| / \max\{u_{ik}, u_{jk}\} & \text{if } u_{ik} > 0 \lor u_{jk} > 0, \\ 0 & \text{otherwise.} \end{cases}$$

The similarity measure can take values in the interval $[0, 1]$; if the preference values of activities i and j with respect to gate k are equal, then $s_{ijk} = 1$.

The normalised weight of the edge between nodes representing activities $i, j \in \mathcal{V}$ can now be defined as:

$$\widetilde{w}_{ij} := \begin{cases} \sum_{k \in \mathcal{M}^0} \widehat{w}_{ijk} \cdot s_{ijk} & \text{if } \{i, j\} \in \mathcal{D} \quad \lor \quad (i, j) \in \mathcal{E}^{low}, \\ 0 & \text{otherwise.} \end{cases}$$

$\mathcal{D}$ is the set of disjunctive activity pairs introduced in Definition (7.8). The weight $\widetilde{w}_{ij}$ can only take a non-zero value if i and j are in disjunction or if they are linked, i.e., if i and j are two subsequent activities for the same aircraft. It follows from the definitions of $\widehat{w}_{ijk}$ and s_{ijk} that $\widetilde{w}_{ij}$ is normalised, with values close to 1 corresponding to a high similarity and values close to 0 to a low similarity of activities i and j.

Using a bias value $\beta \in [0, 1]$, the edge weights w_{ij} to be used in the Objective Function (7.9) can now simply be defined as follows:

$$w_{ij} := \widetilde{w}_{ij} - \beta.$$

The bias β is used to ensure that the weights take negative values for activity pairs of low similarity; because $\widetilde{w}_{ij}$ is normalised it follows that $w_{ij} \in [-\beta, 1 - \beta]$. For given preference values, a low bias leads to more positive weights and consequently to fewer cliques (partitions) than a high bias, which generally leads to a fine grained partitioning into many cliques.

We have now completely defined the CPP that can serve to heuristically partition a given gate scheduling problem. The following section shows how the resulting partition is used within the branch-and-bound algorithm.

7.2.8 Layered Branch-and-Bound

In tree search algorithms that use a chronological backtracking strategy, branching decisions are always undone in the reverse order in which they were made. If two successive branching decisions are only weakly related or even unrelated, this may lead to a weak performance of the search algorithm, because effort is wasted by searching futile branches repeatedly. A related, second problem is that the search tends to concentrate on a small area of the tree, in the proximity of a first solution.

There are many ways in which these two main problems can be addressed. To avoid concentration of the search on a narrow region of the search space, breadth-first search strategies can be used. The repeated exploration of similar, futile sub-trees can be avoided by using *dependency directed backtracking* (DDBT), some times also called *intelligent backtracking*. The idea of DDBT is to identify the culprit(s) that necessitate backtracking, so that the algorithm can backtrack to the relevant decisions only; however, the identification of the culprit(s) based on the constraints in the problem may not be easy, and DDBT may require great overhead. A repeated search within futile subtrees can to some extent also be avoided by choosing a favourable search order in which branching decisions are made. This is the approach that we will follow here. For a general and exhaustive discussion of issues arising in the design of tree search algorithms we refer to Tsang (1993).

In this section, we shall address the two problems by using the decomposition of the problem to guide a truncated branch-and-bound search. The search tree, which corresponds to the complete gate scheduling problem, is conceptually split into layers that correspond to the sub-problems that have been identified by solving the associated CPP described in the previous section. Within each layer, only branching decisions concerning the variables of the corresponding sub-problem are made. Before leaving a layer, the search chronologically backtracks within the current layer until a time limit expires or the layer is exhausted. It then continues from the best partial solution found within the current layer. The intuition behind this approach is that, by keeping decisions concerning strongly related variables close to each other, the distance one has to backtrack is reduced and the effectiveness of backtracking is increased. Additionally, backtracking within each layer leads to an in-breadth exploration of the current sub-problem.

The principle is best illustrated by an example. Figure 7.6 shows an example of a layered branch-and-bound tree with two layers which correspond to the partition of the example in Figure 7.5 into two subsets V_1 and V_2. On the first level of the tree, only decision variables related to the two activities in the set V_1 are considered for branching. For example, the search may begin by assigning modes to activities 3 and 4 at nodes 1 and 2, respectively; when reaching node 2, no more decisions concerning the sub-problem defined by V_1 can be made[3], and backtracking is initiated. Backtracking subsequently leads to the generation of nodes 3, 4, and so on. Backtracking continues until the sub-problem is exhausted or a time-limit expires. In the

---

[3] Assuming all disjunctions are oriented.

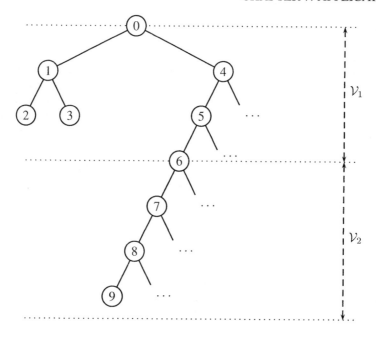

Figure 7.6: Example of a layered branch-and-bound tree

example, we assume that the solution with the best lower bound has been found at node 6, and the search therefore continues from node 6 and proceeds to the next layer. In the second layer, only decisions concerning the variables corresponding to the set V_2 will be made. The search continues to node 9, which corresponds to a solution, and then backtracks. When backtracking, the search does not leave the current layer: if the layer is exhausted, the search does not backtrack beyond node 6 to the previous layer, but instead stops, or, in general, continues to the next layer.

The sub-problems are selected for branching in the order of the total importance, or weight, associated with their activities, i.e., the sub-problem V_k for which $\sum_{i \in V_k} w_i$ is maximal is considered first, and so on.

The sub-problems influence the search order and the way in which backtracking is performed. By imposing a time-limit for the effort to be spent in each layer and by preventing a backtrack to the previous layer, the branch-and-bound search is no longer exhaustive but turns into a heuristic. It is worth mentioning that the sub-problems do not restrict the constraint propagation process, which does not only consider the variables of the current sub-problem but takes the complete problem into account.

7.2.9 Large Neighbourhood Search

An initial gate schedule found using the layered branch-and-bound approach is iteratively improved through Large Neighbourhood Search (LNS, Kilby et al. 1998, 2000). The central idea of LNS as a general search technique is to relax some of the decisions made during the construction of a solution and use a constructive method to reform the relaxed part of the solution at a lower cost.

Schedule Improvement

Given a feasible schedule $(\Delta_S^*, \Delta_C^*, \Delta_M^*)$, LNS for the gate scheduling problem proceeds as follows:

- Choose an activity $i \in \mathcal{V}$ with a "bad" mode assignment.

  A bad assignment M_i is an assignment to the ficitious gate 0 or one that causes a potentially avoidable tow for a pair of activities $(i, j) \in \mathcal{E}^{tow}$ or $(j, i) \in \mathcal{E}^{tow}$. A tow is required if $M_i \neq M_j$; it may be avoidable if the mode sets both include a common real gate, i.e., if $\mathcal{M}_i \cap \mathcal{M}_j \setminus \{0\} \neq \emptyset$.

- Choose a subset $\mathcal{V}(i)$ of activities of a given size n that includes activity i and other, "closely related" activities.

  The subset $\mathcal{V}(i)$ is constructed using the edge weights w_{ij} of the associated clique partitioning problem in the following way: Initially, $\mathcal{V}(i) := \{i\}$; the set is grown by greedily moving the activity $j \in \mathcal{V} \setminus \mathcal{V}(i)$ to $\mathcal{V}(i)$ for which the maximal increase, or minimal decrease, of the total weight within $\mathcal{V}(i)$ is obtained, i.e., for which $\sum_{k \in \mathcal{V}(i)} w_{jk}$ is maximal.

- Relax all decisions concerning the activities in $\mathcal{V}(i)$ but keep all other decisions.

  This is achieved by reconstructing the partial solution for all activities in the set $\mathcal{V} \setminus \mathcal{V}(i)$ by simply resetting the start time, completion time, and mode domains of all activities $j \in \mathcal{V}$ to their initial values and then making all mode assignment and disjunction orientation decisions that were made for activities $j \in \mathcal{V} \setminus \mathcal{V}(i)$ during the construction of the schedule $(\Delta_S^*, \Delta_C^*, \Delta_M^*)$; disjunctions concerning a pair of activities j and k with $j \in \mathcal{V} \setminus \mathcal{V}(i)$ and $k \in \mathcal{V}(i)$ remain relaxed.

- Complete the schedule by applying branch-and-bound search, using the value of the best full schedule found so far as upper bound.

- If the new schedule improves upon the current schedule then replace the current schedule with it. Repeat the previous steps until every "bad" assignment in the current gate schedule has been chosen for improvement.

The intuition behind relaxing the decisions corresponding to the activity set $\mathcal{V}(i)$ is to introduce a degree of freedom that will allow to fix the problematic assignment of i. The size of the set $\mathcal{V}(i)$ should be large enough to offer sufficient freedom, yet small enough to allow a fast branch-and-bound search. In computational experiments we found that a suitable size of the set $\mathcal{V}(i)$ was between twenty and thirty activities.

Reactive Scheduling

LNS cannot only be applied to improve a given initial schedule, but is also useful for adapting a gate schedule to flight schedule disruptions with only small changes in the gate schedule. In the following we shall briefly outline the LNS approach for reactive gate scheduling.

In terms of the gate scheduling model (7.1) – (7.7) a flight schedule disruption may lead to changes of arrival or departure times t_i^a and t_i^d, to changes of the mode sets $\mathcal{M}_i$ in case of aircraft changes, or to new or cancelled activities. These changes may lead to constraint violations and thus invalidate a gate schedule.

To adapt or "repair" a gate schedule that has become infeasible, a modified version of the LNS scheme described above may be used. Instead of selecting activities with unfavourable mode assignments, the search focuses on activities involved in a constraint violation. Because multiple constraint violations can occur simultaneously and because the reconstruction of partial solutions that contain an infeasibility is not useful, as the search would immediately fail when trying to continue, it is first necessary to relax enough decisions so that the remaining partial schedule becomes feasible. The set of violating activities for which decisions are relaxed is denoted with $\mathcal{V}'$. Depending on the type of violation, there may be more than one way to relax decisions so that a particular constraint violation is avoided. We can now proceed in an analogous way as when using LNS for solution improvement, the main difference being that instead of selecting activities with "bad" assignments, we repeatedly select violating activities from the set $\mathcal{V}'$.

7.2.10   Computational Experiments

Implementation and Test Data

The layered branch-and-bound algorithm including the generic constraint propagation algorithm and the consistency tests, the exact and heuristic problem partitioning algorithms, and the LNS improvement heuristic have been implemented in C++. All results reported below have been obtained on a PentiumPro/200 PC with the Linux operating system.

We have tested the algorithm on two problem sets:

1. The first set contains fourteen manually constructed small test problems with approximately ten to twenty activities. The instances where used to validate

the model and algorithm by comparing the results to manually built gate schedules. The instances can all be solved to optimality within a fraction of a second.

2. The second set consists of fourteen problems based on real flight schedules for two weeks at a large international airport. These instances contain approximately 800 activities per day that must be scheduled at 94 gates. The problem instances have been exported from a commercial gate scheduling decision support system (DSS); the gate preference values and activity priorities used were determined by a rule based sub-system of the DSS.

To evaluate our algorithm, the results for the second test set will be compared to gate schedules built by the commercial gate scheduling DSS that is in use at the same airport. The system has been developed in the past three years and represents the current state of the art. The decision logic of the system uses a rule based approach; it replaces and improves upon an older rule based DSS that takes an approach similar to the one in the prototype system described by Gosling (1990).

Results

The algorithm was evaluated with goal weights $\alpha_1 = \alpha_2 = 1$ and $\alpha_3 = 0$. The preference values for the large test problems were defined as follows: An assignment to the dummy gate 0 is penalised with a preference value $u_{i0} = -5$, for all $i \in \mathcal{V}$; all other preference values are normalised, i.e. $u_{i\mu} \in [0, 1]$, for all $i \in \mathcal{V}$ and $\mu \in \mathcal{M}_i \setminus \{0\}$. Intuitively, this means that a single assignment to the dummy gate is as bad as five tows; assigning an activity to a gate with the lowest possible preference value 0 instead of a gate with the highest possible preference value 1 is as bad as a single tow.

Because it is difficult to interpret the numeric objective function value, we report the results with respect to the number of activities assigned to the dummy gate, the number of tows, and the overall preference score for all real gates.

After initial experiments, the following run time limits were chosen: a total run-time limit of 500 seconds for finding an initial solution, and a time limit of 15 seconds for each LNS iteration, i.e. per attempt to fix a bad assignment. The total time limit for constructing the initial solution determines the time limits for each layer of the search tree; for a given layer, we simply allocate the fraction of the total time equal to the share of activities within the layer, i.e., the layer of sub-problem i, or activity set $\mathcal{V}_i$, receives a fraction $|\mathcal{V}_i|/|\mathcal{V}|$ of the run-time. The time required for finding an initial solution is therefore at most $t_{\max}$ but usually significantly smaller.

A problem is first partitioned exactly, and the resulting sub-problems are then partitioned heuristically. For the large test problems, exact partitioning leads to at most 3 independent sub-problems; however, the largest sub-problem always contains all but one or two activities, and the remaining sub-problems are of size one.

For heuristic partitioning, the associated clique partitioning problem is defined using a bias β of 0.05, which was empirically found to lead to useful partitions. On

Day	$|\mathcal{V}|$	Initial Solution					Large Neighbourhood Search				
		Layers	t_1	Open[a]	Tows[b]	Pref.	It.	$t_2{}^c$	Open[a]	Tows[b]	Pref.
						(sec)					(sec)
1	735	35	202	1	47	190	54	399	0	9	189
2	801	47	226	4	53	195	64	503	0	18	194
3	783	42	199	1	54	195	52	447	0	11	191
4	806	44	236	1	53	196	72	725	0	28	194
5	797	41	176	3	43	196	64	467	2	17	196
6	800	42	188	0	57	197	68	401	0	23	195
7	666	29	328	0	81	152	97	1098	0	33	149
Sum				10	388	1321			2	139	1308

[a]Number of activities assigned to the fictitious gate, excluding mandatory assignments.
[b]Excluding mandatory tows.
[c]Including t_1.

Table 7.1: Results of the branch-and-bound algorithm for the first test week

average, this resulted in 39 sub-problems, or search tree layers, with a minimum of 29 and a maximum of 47 sub-problems; the size of the sub-problems varied between three and approximately one hundred activities.

The LNS improvement of an initial solution uses subsets $\mathcal{V}(i)$ of size 24.

Tables 7.1 and 7.2 show the results for the two test weeks. For each day of the week, the tables show the number of activities to be scheduled and additional information on the initial solution found using layered branch-and-bound as well as on the final solution after the application of LNS. The columns shown for the initial solution contain the number of layers, or sub-problems, the time used for finding the solution, the number of *open* activities, which are assigned to the fictitious gate, the number of tows required, and the total preference score for all real gates. The same columns are shown for the final solution, except that the number of LNS iterations appears instead of the number of search tree layers. For the criteria related to the objective function value, the total values are shown at the bottom of the table.

For a given problem instance, certain mandatory tows may be required and it is possible that certain activities must remain unassigned, as any assignment other than the fictitious gate would lead to constraint violations. At the root of the search tree, lower bounds on the number of mandatorily unassigned activities and mandatory tows can be derived by applying constraint propagation; these numbers are shown in Tables 7.3 and 7.4 in the section "Mandatory" in columns "Open" and "Tows". Because these numbers cannot be influenced by the solution algorithm and are thus not useful for the comparison of algorithms, the columns for open activities and tows do otherwise not include these numbers.

Day	$\|\mathcal{V}\|$	Initial Solution					Large Neighbourhood Search				
		Layers	t_1	Open[a]	Tows[b]	Pref. (sec)	It.	t_2[c]	Open[a]	Tows[b]	Pref. (sec)
1	723	34	322	0	69	195	74	843	0	20	192
2	820	40	367	5	112	194	150	1456	1	51	195
3	799	39	372	4	101	194	134	1352	0	46	193
4	819	41	370	4	97	195	135	1369	2	52	194
5	815	37	326	7	100	196	137	1199	1	52	195
6	818	39	379	1	116	198	149	1536	0	57	198
7	635	29	379	0	86	149	102	1027	0	38	145
Sum				21	681	1321			4	316	1312

[a]Number of activities assigned to the fictitious gate, excluding mandatory assignments.
[b]Excluding mandatory tows.
[c]Including t_1.

Table 7.2: Results of the branch-and-bound algorithm for the second test week

Table 7.1 shows that, in the initial gate schedule found for day one of the first test week, one activity is assigned to the fictitious gate, or left open; the schedule requires 47 tows and the rounded total activity-gate preference score is 190. The search tree contains 35 layers. The required run-time of 202 seconds is smaller than the time limit of 500 seconds; this is caused by the fact that the overall time limit is distributed over the layers, and that some layers are exhaustively searched before their limit expires. The solution is then improved within 54 LNS iterations. The time required for the improvement is 399 - 202 = 197 seconds. In the improved schedule, no activity remains open, and the number of tows is reduced to 9; this is achieved at the cost of a slight decrease in the total preference score to 189. The number of LNS iterations seems small when compared to classic local search algorithms. However, it must be taken into account that the transition from one solution to an improving neighbour may affect many more decision variables than in typical local search neighbourhoods.

The results show that LNS can consistently reduce the number of open activities and the number of tows at the price of a slight decrease in the total preference score.

The results in Table 7.2 for the second test week, which has a different underlying flight schedule, are similar to those of the first week. However, the problems in the second week appear to be more difficult, as more activities remain open and the number of tows increases.

The results shown in Tables 7.1 and 7.2 can be slightly improved at the cost of an increased run-time by applying the algorithm multiple times with different control

Day	Branch-and-Bound			Rule-Based			Mandatory	
	Open[a]	Tows[b]	Pref.	Open[a]	Tows[b]	Pref.	Open	Tows
1	0	9	189	7	43	187	6	15
2	0	18	194	11	42	191	0	15
3	0	11	191	12	39	188	0	12
4	0	28	194	8	49	191	0	11
5	2	17	196	11	41	190	0	12
6	0	22	195	9	53	191	1	11
7	0	33	149	17	91	149	7	18
Sum	2	139	1308	75	358	1287	14	94

[a]Number of activities assigned to the fictitious gate, excluding mandatory assignments.
[b]Excluding mandatory tows.

Table 7.3: Comparison of results for the first test week

parameters, e.g., time limits, partitioning bias, and the size of the subsets used for LNS.

Tables 7.3 and 7.4 compare the results obtained with the proposed algorithm with the gate schedules calculated by a commercial rule-based system. The tables show that the branch-and-bound algorithm leads to substantial improvements. The gate schedules are significantly better with respect to the number of open activities and the number of required tows. In the first (second) week, the number of activities assigned to the fictitious gate can be reduced by more than 97 (96) %, and the number of tows decreases by more than 61 (46) %; at the same time, the total preference score is slightly improved.

Day	Branch-and-Bound			Rule-Based			Mandatory	
	Open[a]	Tows[b]	Pref.	Open[a]	Tows[b]	Pref.	Open	Tows
1	0	20	192	8	61	189	5	9
2	1	51	195	14	81	191	0	9
3	0	46	193	10	73	189	0	9
4	2	52	194	17	86	190	0	7
5	1	52	195	23	87	191	0	8
6	0	57	198	23	107	193	1	6
7	0	38	145	17	94	146	5	12
Sum	4	316	1312	112	589	1289	11	60

[a]Number of activities assigned to the fictitious gate, excluding mandatory assignments.
[b]Excluding mandatory tows.

Table 7.4: Comparison of results for the second test week

Chapter 8

Summary and Conclusions

This work has developed effective solution methods and described new applications for a very general class of deterministic, non-preemptive project scheduling models. The models studied in this book are concerned with the allocation of scarce resources over time to activities, the start of which may be constrained by minimal and maximal time lags; these lags allow to specify any possible temporal relation between pairs of activities. The single- and multi-mode models for resource-constrained project scheduling with generalised precedence constraints, or time windows, are very expressive and cover many requirements commonly found in practical applications. The basic single-mode problem is a generalisation of many well known, difficult problems studied in project and machine scheduling.

While we have mainly considered the objective of minimising the completion time of a project, most of the results hold for any regular objective function, and they are frequently also applicable for optimising non-regular measures of performance, as demonstrated by one of the applications proposed in Chapter 7.

A secondary objective of this work has been to investigate the application of constraint propagation techniques for project scheduling. Constraint propagation is an elementary problem reduction technique that transforms problems into equivalent problems which are hopefully easier to solve. This is achieved by repeatedly deducing new implicit constraints that allow to reduce the search space by removing inconsistent assignments that cannot participate in any feasible solution.

To provide a theoretical foundation for the constraint propagation approach, Chapter 3 has reviewed different concepts of consistency, which, roughly speaking, define a certain level of search space reduction. Because establishing full k-consistency, k-domain-consistency, or k-bound-consistency for an arbitrary number k of decision variables is difficult and generally requires exponential effort, approximations are required. To this end, a number of consistency tests are iteratively applied. Consistency tests are simple rules, or logical tests, that deduce additional, redundant constraints. By repeatedly applying the tests within a fixed point iteration, the derived knowledge is reused, or propagated, until no further conclusions can be drawn. As long as the tests satisfy a very natural monotony condition, the resulting fixed point is unique.

Chapter 4 has investigated consistency tests that may be applied in project scheduling. It has focused on interval consistency tests, i.e., tests that analyse the required and available amount of work within certain time intervals. Within this framework we have described tests for disjunctive scheduling with unit resource availabilities and requirements as well as tests for cumulative scheduling with discrete supply and demand in a unified way, using numerous examples for illustration.

Previous research, which has been confirmed in this study, has shown that difficult project scheduling problem instances are frequently characterised by low resource supply, which in turn leads to difficult disjunctive sub-problems. We have therefore first discussed how promising disjunctive sub-problems of a project scheduling problem can be isolated and then studied consistency tests originally proposed for disjunctive scheduling (sequencing). Our analysis has shown that these tests can be understood as special cases of a general sequence consistency condition. We have related the tests based on this condition to the concept of interval work, or energy, and have shown that in sequencing it suffices to test the required and available work within all activity intervals, i.e., time intervals with a start and end defined to be the earliest start and latest completion time of some activities. The search space reduction achieved by the sequence consistency tests has been related to the general concepts of consistency introduced in Chapter 3.

We have discussed how the sequence consistency condition can be generalised for cumulative scheduling, where, in contrast to the disjunctive case, it is no longer sufficient to consider only activity intervals. Chapter 4 has finally described how the consistency tests, which have been introduced for single-mode scheduling, can be applied for multi-mode problems to reduce the activity start time domains as well the mode domains.

Chapter 5 has integrated the constraint propagation techniques into a new branch-and-bound procedure for single-mode resource-constrained project scheduling with time windows. The algorithm implicitly enumerates activity start times by either starting activities as early as possible or delaying them in such a way that the construction of non-active, i.e., dominated, schedules is avoided. At each node of the tree, a fixed point is computed by repeatedly applying a number of consistency tests. The search space is further reduced by enforcing some necessary conditions that must be met by active schedules.

The procedure has been evaluated on several large test sets of benchmark problem instances, and the influence of the different building blocks of the algorithm and of a set of parameters characterising the test problems have been analysed. The experiments have demonstrated the effectiveness and efficiency of the approach.

On a test set of over thousand systematically generated instances with one hundred activities each of the problem with generalised precedence constraints, the time-oriented branch-and-bound algorithm can find feasible solutions for all solvable problem instances. It solves more problems to optimality than other exact procedures that have recently been proposed, while at the same time achieving a significantly smaller average deviation from a lower bound for the project duration. It is remarkable that with respect to the latter criterion, the simple time-truncated version of the branch-and-bound method yields solutions that improve upon the results of the best known heuristics, and that these solutions are found within average run times as small as ten seconds.Similarly good results for a second benchmark test set consisting of larger problem instances with five hundred activities per project have demonstrated that the branch-and-bound algorithm also scales very well.

The algorithm has additionally been evaluated on four large benchmark test sets for the well studied, special project scheduling problem with simple finish-start precedence constraints. The results show again that the algorithm scales very well; for larger instances, it is competitive to other exact procedures for this problem, and its truncated version may even be a useful heuristic. The good performance on the larger test sets is particularly interesting because the algorithm does not include certain features which enhance the performance on this special problem but that are hard to adapt for generalised or extended versions of the problem.

The branch-and-bound procedure has been extended in Chapter 6 for the multi-mode version of the project scheduling problem with time windows by combining the time-oriented branching over activity start times with a binary branching over mode assignments or restrictions.

We have finally dealt with two applications of project scheduling in airport operations management. Chapter 7 has first described how the scheduling of ground handling activities required for serving aircrafts while at an airport gives rise to a resource-constrained multi-project scheduling problem with time windows.

The focus of Chapter 7 has then been on airport gate scheduling which deals with the task of assigning flights to terminal gates or parking positions and scheduling the start and end times of the assignments. We have shown how this task can be modelled as a special multi-mode project scheduling problem with a non-regular objective function, specially structured temporal constraints, and disjunctive resources. The proposed solution method of the branch-and-bound type again relies on the use of constraint propagation techniques for search space reduction. For dealing with large practical problems with on the order of magnitude of thousand activities, the branch-and-bound procedure has been combined with additional problem decomposition and solution improvement techniques which both are of general interest beyond the application at hand. The problem has been decomposed into loosely coupled subproblems using a new generic problem partitioning approach, and the search tree is conceptually split into layers that correspond to the sub-problems. Initial solutions are iteratively improved by using the branch-and-bound algorithm within a large neighbourhood search scheme. Computational experiments with large real-life data sets have demonstrated that the modelling approach is well suited and that the proposed solution method is very effective and greatly improves upon the results of a modern rule based decision support system.

The approach followed in the gate scheduling application has been to adapt a successful standard project scheduling model and solution methods for a practical problem. Based on the experience gained, we believe that this way of starting from standard models and methods and extending them to cover even more realistic problem classes is an promising direction for future research as well as for the development of practical software applications.

Due to their generality, the basic project scheduling models studied here are very good starting points. The constraint propagation based solution techniques that we have investigated are also well suited for such an approach because most of the basic building blocks, i.e., the consistency tests, are not custom tailored for specific scheduling models and objective functions but cover a wide range of possible applications. Furthermore, the efficiency of the solution methods proposed in this work can to a great extent be attributed to the application of these techniques. The design of strong and efficient consistency tests therefore also remains a promising step towards the development of improved solution methods.

List of Figures

List of Tables

List of Symbols

Symbol	Description
$[t_1, t_2]$	Time interval $[t_1, t_2] := \{t_1, \ldots, t_2\}$.
$]t_1, t_2[$	Time interval $]t_1, t_2[:= \{t_1 + 1, \ldots, t_2 - 1\}$.
$i \leftrightarrow j$	Activities i and j are in disjunction, i.e. the constraint $S_i + p_i \leq S_j \vee S_j + p_j \leq S_i$ must hold.
$i \rightarrow j$	Activity i must be processed before activity j, i.e. $S_i + p_i \leq S_j$ must hold.
$i \rightarrow \mathcal{A}, \mathcal{A} \rightarrow i$	i must be processed before (after) the activities in $\mathcal{A}$.
(i, j)	Temporal constraint between activities i and j of the form: $S_i + d_{ij} \leq S_j$.
$\mathcal{A}$	Usually denotes a subset of activities that require the same resource.
$\mathcal{A}_i$	Shorthand notation for $\mathcal{A} \setminus \{i\}$.
$act(\alpha)$	Activity chosen in node α.
$C_i(\Delta)$	Completion time of activity $i \in \mathcal{V}^s(\Delta)$ given Δ: $C_i(\Delta) := S_i(\Delta) + p_i$.
$\mathcal{C}$	Set of all constraints.
γ	A consistency test.
Γ	Set of all consistency tests.
d_{ij}	Integral time lag in temporal constraint (i, j).
$d_{i\mu j\nu}$	Integral time lag in temporal constraint (i, j) in multi-mode models if activity i is processed in mode μ and activity j in mode ν.
d'_{ij}	Transitive minimal time lag between activities i and j.
Δ_{x_i}	Current domain (set of possible assignments) of variable x_i.
Δ_i	Shorthand notation for Δ_{S_i}, i.e., the current start time domain (set of possible start times) of activity i; $\Delta_i \subseteq \mathbb{N}_0$ and if an upper bound UB is given then $\Delta_i \subseteq [0, UB - p_i]$.

continued

Symbol	Description
Δ	Set of all current domains: $\Delta := \{\Delta_{x_i} \mid x_i \in \mathcal{V}\}$.
$\mathcal{E}$	Set of all temporal constraints.
$\mathcal{E}^{min}$	Set of all temporal constraints with minimal lags: $\mathcal{E}^{min} := \{(i,j) \in \mathcal{E} \mid d_{ij} > 0\}$.
$\mathcal{E}^{max}$	Set of all temporal constraints with maximal lags: $\mathcal{E}^{max} := \{(i,j) \in \mathcal{E} \mid d_{ij} \leq 0\}$.
$EC_i(\Delta)$	Earliest completion time of activity i: $EC_i(\Delta) := ES_i(\Delta) + p_i$.
$ES_i(\Delta)$	Earliest start time of activity i: $ES_i(\Delta) := \min \Delta_i$.
$EC^{pr}(\mathcal{A})$	Earliest time by which the activities in $\mathcal{A}$ can be completed if preemption is allowed.
H	A hypothetical constraint to be falsified by a consistency test.
LB_0	Precedence based lower bound for the makespan.
$LC_i(\Delta)$	Latest completion time of activity i: $LC_i(\Delta) := LS_i(\Delta) + p_i$.
$LS_i(\Delta)$	Latest start time of activity i: $LS_i(\Delta) := \max \Delta_i$.
$LS^{pr}(\mathcal{A})$	Latest time at which the activities in $\mathcal{A}$ must be started if preemption is allowed.
M_i	Mode variable or mode assignment of activity i.
$\mathcal{M}_i$	Set of possible modes in which activity i may be processed.
p_i	Processing time of activity i; $p_i \in \mathbb{N}_0$.
$p_i(t_1, t_2)$	Interval processing of activity i: smallest amount of time during which i must be processed in the time interval $[t_1, t_2[$.
$P(\mathcal{A})$	Total processing time of $\mathcal{A}$: $P(\mathcal{A}) := \sum_{i \in \mathcal{A}} p_i$.
$P(\mathcal{A}, t_1, t_2)$	Total interval proc. time of $\mathcal{A}$: $P(\mathcal{A}, t_1, t_2) := \sum_{i \in \mathcal{A}} p_i(t_1, t_2)$.
$pc_i(\Delta)$	Minimal start time of i if only precedence constraints (j, i) between activities in $j \in \mathcal{V}^s(\Delta)$ and i are considered.
$rc_i(\Delta)$	Minimal start time of i if only precedence constraints (j, i) between activities $j \in \mathcal{V}^s(\Delta)$ and i and, additionally, resource constraints are considered.
r_{ik}	Requirement of activity i for resource k; $r_{ik} \in \mathbb{N}_0$.
$r_{i\mu k}$	In multi-mode models: requirement of activity i for resource k if i is processed in mode μ; $r_{i\mu k} \in \mathbb{N}_0$.
$\mathcal{R}$	Set of all resources: $\mathcal{R} := \mathcal{R}^\rho \cup \mathcal{R}^\nu$.
$\mathcal{R}^\rho$	Set of renewable resources.
$\mathcal{R}^\nu$	Set of non-renewable resources.
$\mathcal{R}_i$	Set of all resources required by activity i: $\mathcal{R}_i := \{k \in \mathcal{R} \mid r_{ik} > 0\}$
R_k	Available capacity of resource k; $R_k \in \mathbb{N}_0$.
S	Vector of start time variables or start time assignments.
S_i	Start time variable or start time assignment of activity i.

continued

Symbol	Description
$S_i(\Delta)$	Start time of activity $i \in \mathcal{V}^s(\Delta)$ given Δ: $S_i(\Delta) := ES_i(\Delta) = LS_i(\Delta)$.
t	A time period.
$t(\alpha)$	Schedule time in node α: $t(\alpha) := \min_{i \in \mathcal{V}^{f'}(\alpha)} ES_i(\alpha)$.
$t^+(\alpha)$	Adjusted earliest start time in node α: $t^+(\alpha) := \min_{i \in \mathcal{V} \setminus \{j\}: \mathcal{R}_i \cap \mathcal{R}_j \neq \emptyset} \{EC_i(\alpha) \mid EC_i(\alpha) > t(\alpha)\}$, for $j = act(\alpha)$.
UB	Real or hypothetical upper bound on the optimal makespan.
$\mathcal{V}$	Set of all activities; also: set of all variables.
$\mathcal{V}(t)$	Set of all activities in process at time t.
$\mathcal{V}_k$	Set of all activities requiring resource k: $\mathcal{V}_k := \{i \in \mathcal{V} \mid r_{ik} > 0\}$.
$\mathcal{V}_k(t_1, t_2)$	Set of activities requiring resource k that must be completely or partially processed within $[t_1, t_2[$: $\mathcal{V}_k(t_1, t_2) := \{i \in \mathcal{V}_k \mid p_i(t_1, t_2) > 0\}$.
$\mathcal{V}^c$	A subset of activities which belong to the same maximal disjunctive clique, i.e. which are pairwise disjunctive. We often speak of an associated, possibly fictitious, resource with capacity one that is required by all activities in $\mathcal{V}^c$.
$\mathcal{V}^f(\Delta)$	Set of all free (unscheduled) activities given Δ: $\mathcal{V}^f(\Delta) := \{i \in \mathcal{V} \mid |\Delta_i| > 1\}$.
$\mathcal{V}^{f'}(\Delta)$	Set of free and non-delayed activities given Δ: $\mathcal{V}^{f'}(\Delta) := \mathcal{V}^{tc}(\Delta) \cup \{i \in \mathcal{V}^f(\Delta) \mid ES_i(\Delta) = rc_i(\Delta)\}$.
$\mathcal{V}^s(\Delta)$	Set of all activities scheduled given Δ: $\mathcal{V}^s(\Delta) := \{i \in \mathcal{V} \mid |\Delta_i| = 1\}$.
$\mathcal{V}^{tc}(\Delta)$	Set of *timemax-constrained* activities given Δ: $\mathcal{V}^{tc}(\Delta) := \{j \in \mathcal{V}^f(\Delta) \mid \exists i \in \mathcal{V}^f(\Delta) : (i, j) \in \mathcal{E}^{max}\}$.
$\mathcal{V}^{tu}(\Delta)$	Set of *timemax-unconstrained* activities given Δ: $\mathcal{V}^{tu}(\Delta) := \mathcal{V}^f(\Delta) \setminus \mathcal{V}^{tc}(\Delta)$.
w_{ik}	Work required by activity i from resource k: $w_{ik} := p_i r_{ik}$.
$W(\mathcal{A})$	Total work of $\mathcal{A}$: $W(\mathcal{A}) := \sum_{i \in \mathcal{A} \subseteq \mathcal{V}_k} w_{ik}$.
$W(\mathcal{A}, t_1, t_2)$	Total interval work of $\mathcal{A} \subseteq \mathcal{V}_k$ in time interval $[t_1, t_2[$: $W(\mathcal{A}, t_1, t_2) := \sum_{i \in \mathcal{A}} r_{ik} p_i(t_1, t_2)$.

References

ADV. 1997. Sicherung und Optimierung des Luftverkehrsstandortes Deutschland — Situationsanalyse und Beiträge zu Problemlösungen. Tech. rep., Arbeitsgemeinschaft Deutscher Verkehrsflughäfen.

AGGOUN, A. AND N. BELDICEANU. 1993. Extending CHIP in Order to Solve Complex Scheduling and Placement Problems. *Mathematical and Computer Modelling* **17**, 57–73.

AGGOUN, A., M. DINCBAS, A. HEROLD, H. SIMONIS AND P. VAN HENTENRYCK. 1987. The CHIP System. Technical Report TR-LP-24, ECRC, Munich, Germany.

AHN, T. AND S. ERENGÜÇ. 1998. The Resource-Constrained Project Scheduling Problem with Multiple Crashable Modes. *European Journal of Operational Research* **107**, 250–259.

ALLEN, J. 1983. Maintaining Knowledge About Temporal Intervals. *Communications of the ACM* **26**, 832–843.

ALVAREZ-VALDES, R. AND J. TAMARIT. 1993. The Project Scheduling Polyhedron: Dimension, Facets and Lifting Theorems. *European Journal of Operational Research* **67**, 204–220.

APPLEGATE, D. AND W. COOK. 1991. A Computational Study of the Job-Shop Scheduling Problem. *ORSA Journal on Computing* **3**, 149–156.

ASHFORD, N., H. M. STANTON AND C. A. MOORE. 1997. *Airport Operations*. McGraw-Hill, New York, 2nd edn.

ASHFORD, N. AND P. WRIGHT. 1992. *Airport Engineering*. Wiley-Intersience, New York, 3rd edn.

BABIC, O., D. TEODOROVIC AND V. TOSIC. 1984. Aircraft Stand Assignment to Minimize Walking. *Journal of Transportation Engineering* **110**, 55–66.

BAKER, K. 1974. *Introduction to Sequencing and Scheduling*. Wiley, New York.

BANDARA, S. AND S. WIRASINGHE. 1992. Walking Distance Minimization for Airport Terminal Configurations. *Transportation Research* **26A**, 59–74.

BAPTISTE, P. AND C. LE PAPE. 1995. A Theoretical and Experimental Comparison of Constraint Propagation Techniques for Disjunctive Scheduling. In *Proceedings of the 14th International Joint Conference on Artificial Intelligence*. Montreal.

BAPTISTE, P. AND C. LE PAPE. 1996. Edge-finding Constraint Propagation Algorithms for Disjunctive and Cumulative Scheduling. In *Proceedings of the 15th*

Workshop of the U.K. Planning Special Interest Group. Liverpool, UK.

BAPTISTE, P. AND C. LE PAPE. 2000. Constraint Propagation and Decomposition Techniques for Highly Disjunctive and Highly Cumulative Project Scheduling Problems. *Constraints: an International Journal* **5**, 119–139.

BAPTISTE, P., C. LE PAPE AND W. P. NUIJTEN. 1999. Satisfiability Tests and Time-Bound Adjustments for Cumulative Scheduling Problems. *Annals of Operations Research* **92**, 305–333.

BAPTISTE, P., C. LE PAPE AND W. P. NUIJTEN. 2001. *Constraint-Based Scheduling.* Kluwer Academic Publishers, Boston.

BARON, P. 1969. A Simulation Analysis of Airport Terminal Operations. *Transportation Research* **3**, 481–491.

BARTUSCH, M., R. MÖHRING AND F. RADERMACHER. 1988. Scheduling Project Networks with Resource Constraints and Time Windows. *Annals of Operations Research* **16**, 201–240.

BERGE, C. 1985. *Graphs.* North Holland, Amsterdam.

BESSIÈRE, C. 1994. Arc-Consistency and Arc-Consistency Again. *Artificial Intelligence* **65**, 179–190.

BESSIÈRE, C., E. FREUDER AND J.-C. RÉGIN. 1999. Using Constraint Metaknowledge to Reduce Arc Consistency Computation. *Artificial Intelligence* **107**, 125–148.

BIBEL, W. 1988. Constraint Satisfaction from a Deductive Viewpoint. *Artificial Intelligence* **35**, 401–413.

BIHR, R. 1990. A Conceptual Solution to the Aircraft Gate Assignment Problem Using 0,1 Linear Programming. *Computers & Industrial Engineering* **19**, 280–284.

BŁAŻEWICZ, J., W. DOMSCHKE AND E. PESCH. 1996. The Job Shop Scheduling Problem: Conventional and New Solution Techniques. *European Journal of Operational Research* **93**, 1–33.

BŁAŻEWICZ, J., K. H. ECKER, E. PESCH, G. SCHMIDT AND J. WĘGLARZ. 2001. *Scheduling Computer and Manufacturing Processes.* Springer, Berlin, 2nd edn.

BŁAŻEWICZ, J., J. K. LENSTRA AND A. RINNOOY KAN. 1983. Scheduling Subject to Resource Constraints: Classification and Complexity. *Discrete Applied Mathematics* **5**, 11–24.

BŁAŻEWICZ, J., E. PESCH AND M. STERNA. 1998. A Branch and Bound Algorithm for the Job Shop Scheduling Problem. In *Beyond Manufacturing Resource Planning (MRP II)*, A. Drexl and A. Kimms, eds. Springer, Berlin, pages 219–254.

BOCTOR, F. 1993. Heuristics for Scheduling Projects with Resource Restrictions and Several Resource-Duration Modes. *International Journal of Production Research* **31**, 2547–2558.

BOCTOR, F. 1996a. An Adaptation of the Simulated Annealing Algorithm for Solving Resource-Constrained Project Scheduling Problems. *International Journal of Production Research* **34**, 2335–2351.

BOCTOR, F. 1996b. A New and Efficient Heuristic for Scheduling Projects with Resource Restrictions and Multiple Execution Modes. *European Journal of Operational Research* **90**, 349–361.

BÖTTCHER, J., A. DREXL, R. KOLISCH AND F. SALEWSKI. 1999. Project Scheduling under Partially Renewable Resource Constraints. *Management Science* **45**, 543–559.

BRAAKSMA, J. 1977. Reducing Walking Distances at Airports. *Airport Forum* **4**, 135–142.

BRINKMANN, K. 1992. *Planung von deterministischen Projekten mit beschränkten Ressourcen und zeitlichen Maximalabständen*. Ph.D. thesis, University of Karlsruhe.

BRINKMANN, K. AND K. NEUMANN. 1996. Heuristic Procedures for Resource-Constrained Project Scheduling with Minimal and Maximal Time Lags: The Resource Levelling and Minimum Project-Duration Problems. *Journal of Decision Systems* **5**, 129–156.

BRON, C. AND J. KERBOSCH. 1973. Algorithm 457: Finding all Cliques of an Undirected Graph. *Communications of the ACM* **16**, 575–577.

BRUCKER, P., A. DREXL, R. MÖHRING, K. NEUMANN AND E. PESCH. 1999. Resource-Constrained Project Scheduling: Notation, Classification, Models, and Methods. *European Journal of Operational Research* **112**, 3–41.

BRUCKER, P., B. JURISCH AND A. KRÄMER. 1996. The Job-Shop Problem and Immediate Selection. *Annals of Operations Research* **50**, 73–114.

BRUCKER, P. AND S. KNUST. 1999. A Linear Programming and Constraint Propagation Based Lower Bound for the RCPSP. Tech. rep., University of Osnabrück.

BRUCKER, P., S. KNUST, A. SCHOO AND O. THIELE. 1998. A Branch and Bound Algorithm for the Resource-Constrained Project Scheduling Problem. *European Journal of Operational Research* **107**, 272–288.

CARLIER, J. 1982. The One-Machine Sequencing Problem. *European Journal of Operational Research* **11**, 42–47.

CARLIER, J. AND B. LATAPIE. 1991. Une Méthode Arborescente pour Résoudre les Problèmes Cumulatifs. *RAIRO Recherche Opérationelle* **25**, 311–340.

CARLIER, J. AND E. PINSON. 1989. An Algorithm for Solving the Job-Shop Problem. *Management Science* **35**, 164–176.

CARLIER, J. AND E. PINSON. 1990. A Practical Use of Jackson's Preemptive Schedule for the Job Shop Problem. *Annals of Operations Research* **26**, 269–287.

CARLIER, J. AND E. PINSON. 1994. Adjustments of Heads and Tails for the Job-Shop Problem. *European Journal of Operational Research* **78**, 146–161.

CASEAU, Y. AND F. LABURTHE. 1994. Improved CLP Scheduling with Task Intervals. In *Proceedings of the 11th International Conference on Logic Programming*, P. van Hentenryck, ed. MIT-Press.

CASEAU, Y. AND F. LABURTHE. 1995. Disjunctive Scheduling with Task Intervals. Tech. Rep. 95-25, Laboratoire d'Informatique de l'Ecole Normale Supérieure Paris.

CASEAU, Y. AND F. LABURTHE. 1996a. CLAIRE: Combining Objects and Rules for Problem Solving. In *Proceedings of the JICSLP'96 Workshop on Multi-Paradigm Logic Programming*. Technical University of Berlin.

CASEAU, Y. AND F. LABURTHE. 1996b. Cumulative Scheduling with Task Intervals. In *Proceedings of the Joint International Conference on Logic Programming*.

MIT-Press.

CHANG, C. 1994. *Flight Sequencing and Gate Assignment in Airport Hubs.* Ph.D. thesis, University of Maryland at College Park.

CHEN, Y. 1999. Arc Consistency Revisited. *Information Processing Letters* **70**, 75–184.

CHENG, Y. 1997. A Knowledge-Based Airport Gate Assignment System Integrated with Mathematical Programming. *Computers and Industrial Engineering* **32**, 837–852.

CLOWES, M. B. 1971. On Seeing Things. *Artificial Intelligence* **2**, 179–185.

COHEN, J. 1990. Constraint Logic Programming Languages. *Communications of the ACM* **33**, 52–68.

COLMERAUER, A. 1990. An Introduction to Prolog III. *Communications of the ACM* **33**, 69–90.

CONWAY, R., W. MAXWELL AND L. MILLER. 1967. *Theory of Scheduling.* Addison-Wesley, Reading, MA.

COOPER, M. C. 1989. An Optimal k-Consistency Algorithm. *Artificial Intelligence* **41**, 89–95.

DAVIS, E. 1987. Constraint Propagation with Interval Labels. *Artificial Intelligence* **32**, 281–331.

DAVIS, E. W. 1973. Project Scheduling Under Resource Constraints. *AIIE Transactions* **5**, 297–313.

DE REYCK, B., E. DEMEULEMEESTER AND W. HERROELEN. 1999. Algorithms for Scheduling Projects with Generalised Precedence Relations. In *Project Scheduling — Recent Models, Algorithms and Applications*, J. Węglarz, ed., vol. 14 of *International Series in Operations Research and Management Science.* Kluwer Academic Publishers, Boston, pages 77–105.

DE REYCK, B. AND W. HERROELEN. 1998. A Branch-and-Bound Procedure for the Resource-Constrained Project Scheduling Problem with Generalized Precedence Constraints. *European Journal of Operational Research* **111**, 152–174.

DE REYCK, B. AND W. HERROELEN. 1999. The Multi-Mode Resource-Constrained Project Scheduling Problem with Generalized Precedence Relations. *European Journal of Operational Research* **119**, 538–556.

DECHTER, R. AND J. PEARL. 1988. Network-Based Heuristics for Constraint Satisfaction Problems. *Artificial Intelligence* **34**, 1–38.

DEMEULEMEESTER, E. L. AND W. S. HERROELEN. 1992. A Branch-and-Bound Procedure for the Multiple Resource-Constrained Project Scheduling Problem. *Management Science* **38**, 1803–1818.

DEMEULEMEESTER, E. L. AND W. S. HERROELEN. 1997a. A Branch-and-Bound Procedure for the Generalized Resource-Constrained Project Scheduling Problem. *Management Science* **45**, 201–212.

DEMEULEMEESTER, E. L. AND W. S. HERROELEN. 1997b. New Benchmark Results for the Resource-Constrained Project Scheduling Problem. *Management Science* **43**, 1485–1492.

DOMSCHKE, W. AND A. DREXL. 1991. Kapazitätsplanung in Netzwerken: Ein Überblick über neuere Modelle und Verfahren. *OR Spektrum* **13**, 63–76.

DOMSCHKE, W. AND A. DREXL. 1998. *Einführung in Operations Research.* Springer, Berlin, 4th edn.

DORNDORF, U. AND E. PESCH. 1994. Fast Clustering Algorithms. *ORSA Journal on Computing* **6**, 141–153.

DORNDORF, U., E. PESCH AND T. PHAN-HUY. 2000a. A Branch-and-Bound Algorithm for the Resource-Constrained Project Scheduling Problem. *Mathematical Methods of OR* **52**, 413–439.

DORNDORF, U., E. PESCH AND T. PHAN-HUY. 2000b. Constraint Propagation Techniques for the Disjunctive Scheduling Problem. *Artificial Intelligence* **122**, 189–240.

DORNDORF, U., E. PESCH AND T. PHAN-HUY. 2000c. A Time-Oriented Branch-and-Bound Algorithm for Resource-Constrained Project Scheduling with Generalised Precedence Constraints. *Management Science* **46**, 1365–1384.

DORNDORF, U., E. PESCH AND T. PHAN-HUY. 2001. Solving the Open Shop Scheduling Problem. *Journal of Scheduling* **4**, 157–174.

DORNDORF, U., T. PHAN-HUY AND E. PESCH. 1999. A Survey of Interval Capacity Consistency Tests for Time- and Resource-Constrained Scheduling. In *Project Scheduling — Recent Models, Algorithms and Applications*, J. Węglarz, ed. Kluwer Academic Publishers, Boston, pages 213–238.

DREXL, A. 1991. Scheduling of Project Networks by Job Assignment. *Management Science* **37**, 1590–1602.

DREXL, A., W. EVERSHEIM, R. GREMPE AND H. ESSER. 1994. CIM im Werkzeugmaschinenbau: Der PRISMA-Montageleitstand. *Zeitschrift für betriebswirtschaftliche Forschung* **46**, 279–295.

DREXL, A. AND J. GRÜNEWALD. 1993. Nonpreemptive Multi-Mode Resource-Constrained Project Scheduling. *IIE Transactions* **25**, 74–81.

DREXL, A., R. KOLISCH AND A. SPRECHER. 1997. Neuere Entwicklungen in der Projektplanung. *Zeitschrift für betriebswirtschaftliche Forschung* **49**, 95–120.

DYER, M. AND A. FRIEZE. 1985. On the Complexity of Partitioning Graphs. *Discrete Applied Mathematics* , 139–153.

ELMAGHRABY, S. 1977. *Activity Networks: Project Planning and Control by Network Models.* Wiley, New York.

ELMAGHRABY, S. 1995. Activity Nets: A Guided Tour Through Some Recent Developments. *European Journal of Operational Research* **82**, 371–432.

ELMAGHRABY, S. AND J. KAMBUROWSKI. 1992. The Analysis of Activity Networks under Generalized Precedence Relations. *Management Science* **38**, 1245–1263.

ENDLER, J. AND C. PETERS. 1998. Flughäfen und Luftverkehr — Eine Branche im Umbruch. *Zeitschrift für betriebswirtschaftliche Forschung* **50**, 1048–1067.

FEST, A., R. H. MÖHRING, F. STORK AND M. UETZ. 1999. Resource Constrained Project Scheduling with Time Windows: A Branching Scheme Based on Dynamic Release Dates. Tech. Rep. 596, Technical University of Berlin.

FISHER, H. AND G. THOMPSON. 1963. Probabilistic Learning Combinations of Local Job-Shop Scheduling Rules. In *Industrial Scheduling*, J. Muth and G. Thompson, eds. Prentice-Hall, Englewood Cliffs, NF.

FOCACCI, F. AND W. NUIJTEN. 2000. A Constraint Propagation Algorithm for Scheduling with Sequence Dependent Setup Times. In *Proceedings of the 2nd International Workshop on the Integration of AI and OR Techniques in Constraint Programming for Combinatorial Optimization Problems*, U. Junke, S. Karisch and S. Tschöke, eds. University of Paderborn, pages 53–55.

FRANCK, B. 1999. *Prioritätsregelverfahren für die ressourcenbeschränkte Projektplanung mit und ohne Kalender*. Ph.D. thesis, University of Karlsruhe.

FRANCK, B. AND K. NEUMANN. 1998. Resource-Constrained Project Scheduling with Time Windows: Structural Questions and Priority Rule Methods. Tech. Rep. WIOR-492, University of Karlsruhe.

FRANCK, B. AND T. SELLE. 1998. Metaheuristics for the Resource-Constrained Project Scheduling Problem with Schedule-Dependent Time Windows. Tech. Rep. WIOR-546, University of Karlsruhe.

FREUDER, E. C. 1978. Synthesizing Constraint Expressions. *Journal of the ACM* **21**, 958–966.

FREUDER, E. C. 1982. A Sufficient Condition for Backtrack-Free Search. *Journal of the ACM* **29**, 24–32.

FULKERSON, D. 1962. Expected Critical Path Lengths in PERT Networks. *Operations Research* **10**, 808–817.

GAREY, M., R. GRAHAM, D. JOHNSON AND A.-C. YAO. 1976. Resource Constrained Scheduling as Generalized Bin Packing. *Journal of Combinatorial Theory* **21**, 257–298.

GAREY, M. AND D. JOHNSON. 1979. *Computers and Intractability. A Guide to the Theory of NP-Completeness*. W.H. Freeman and Company.

GOSLING, G. D. 1990. Design of an Expert System for Aircraft Gate Assignment. *Transportation Research* **24A**, 59–69.

GRAHAM, R., E. LAWLER, J. LENSTRA AND A. RINNOOY KAN. 1979. Optimization and Approximation in Deterministic Sequencing and Scheduling Theory: A Survey. *Annals of Discrete Mathematics* **5**, 287–326.

GRÖTSCHEL, M. AND Y. WAKABAYASHI. 1990. Facets of the Clique Partitioning Polytope. *Mathematical Programming* **47**, 367–387.

GÜNTHER, H.-O. AND H. TEMPELMEIER. 2000. *Produktion und Logistik*. Springer, Berlin.

HAGHANI, A. AND M.-C. CHEN. 1998. Optimizing Gate Assignments at Airport Terminals. *Transportation Research* **32A**, 437–454.

HAMZAWI, S. 1986. Management and Planning of Airport Gate Capacity: A Microcomputer-Based Gate Assignment Simulation Model. *Transportation Planning and Technology* **11**, 189–202.

HAN, C.-C. AND C.-H. LEE. 1988. Comments on Mohr and Henderson's Path Consistency Algorithm. *Artificial Intelligence* **36**, 125–130.

HARALICK, R. M. AND L. G. SHAPIRO. 1979. The Consistent Labelling Problem: Part I. *IEEE Transactions PAMI* **1**, 173–184.

HARALICK, R. M. AND L. G. SHAPIRO. 1980. The Consistent Labelling Problem: Part II. *IEEE Transactions PAMI* **2**, 193–203.

HARTMANN, S. 1998. A Competitive Genetic Algorithm for Resource-Constrained

Project Scheduling. *Naval Research Logistics* **45**, 733–750.

HARTMANN, S. 1999. *Project Scheduling under Limited Resources: Models, Methods, and Applications.* Springer, Berlin.

HARTMANN, S. AND A. DREXL. 1998. Project Scheduling with Multiple Modes: A Comparison of Exact Algorithms. *Networks* **32**, 283–297.

HAX, A. AND D. CANDEA. 1984. *Production and Inventory Management.* Prentice-Hall, New Jersey.

HEILMANN, R. 1998. A Branch-and-Bound Procedure for MRCPSP/max. Tech. Rep. WIOR-512, University of Karlsruhe.

HEILMANN, R. 1999. *Das ressourcenbeschränkte Projektdauerminimierungsproblem im Mehr-Modus-Fall.* Ph.D. thesis, University of Karlsruhe.

HEILMANN, R. AND C. SCHWINDT. 1997. Lower Bounds for RCPSP/max. Tech. Rep. WIOR-511, University of Karlsruhe.

HEIPCKE, S. AND Y. COLOMBANI. 1997. A New Constraint Programming Approach to Large Scale Resource Constrained Scheduling. In *Third Workshop on Models and Algorithms for Planning and Scheduling Problems, Cambridge, UK.*

HENTENRYCK, P. V. 1992. *Constraint Satisfaction in Logic Programming.* MIT Press, Cambridge.

HERROELEN, W., E. DEMEULEMEESTER AND B. DE REYCK. 1998. Resource-Constrained Project Scheduling: A Survey of Recent Developments. *Computers & Operations Research* **25**, 279–302.

HERROELEN, W., E. DEMEULEMEESTER AND B. DE REYCK. 1999. A Classification Scheme for Project Scheduling Problems. In *Project Scheduling — Recent Models, Algorithms and Applications*, J. Węglarz, ed. Kluwer Academic Publishers, Boston, pages 1–26.

HOVE, J. C. V. AND R. F. DECKRO. 1998. Multi-Modal Project Scheduling with Generalized Precedence Constraints. In *Proceedings of the Sixth International Workshop on Project Management and Scheduling*, G. Barbarasoğlu, S. Karabati, L. Özdamar and G. Ulusoy, eds. pages 137–140.

HUFFMAN, D. A. 1971. Impossible Objects as Nonsense Sentences. In *Machine Intelligence 6*, R. Meltzer and D. Michie, eds. Elsevier, pages 295–323.

IATA. 2000a. Airport Handling Manual. Tech. rep., International Air Transport Association, Montreal and Geneva.

IATA. 2000b. Freight Forecast 2000 – 2004. Tech. rep., International Air Transport Association, Montreal and Geneva.

IATA. 2000c. Passenger Forecast 2000 – 2004. Tech. rep., International Air Transport Association, Montreal and Geneva.

ICMELI, O., S. ERENGÜÇ AND C. ZAPPE. 1993. Project Scheduling Problems: A Survey. *International Journal of Operations and Production Management* **13**, 80–91.

JACKSON, J. 1956. An Extension of Johnson's Results on Job Lot Scheduling. *Naval Research Logistics Quarterly* **3**, 201–203.

JAFFAR, J., J.-L. LASSEZ AND M. MAHER. 1986. A Logic Programming Language Scheme. In *Logic Programming: Relations, Functions and Equations*, D. DeGroot and G. Lindstrom, eds. Prentice Hall, pages 441–468.

JAFFAR, J., S. MICHAYOV, P. STUCKEY AND R. YAP. 1992. The CLP($\mathcal{R}$) Language and System. *ACM Transactions on Programming Languages and Systems* **14**, 339–395.

JEAVONS, P., D. COHEN AND M. COOPER. 1998. Constraints, Consistency and Closure. *Artificial Intelligence* **101**, 251–265.

JOHNSON, T. 1967. *An Algorithm for the Resource-Constrained Project Scheduling Problem*. Ph.D. thesis, Massachusetts Institute of Technology.

KELLEY, J. 1961. Critical Path Planning and Scheduling: Mathematical Basis. *Operations Research* **9**, 296–320.

KILBY, P., P. PROSSER AND P. SHAW. 1998. Implementation of LNS for Constrained VRPs. Tech. rep., University of Strathclyde, Glasgow, Scotland.

KILBY, P., P. PROSSER AND P. SHAW. 2000. A Comparison of Traditional and Constraint-Based Heuristic Methods on Vehicle Routing Problems with Side Constraints. *Journal of Constraints* **5**, 389–414.

KLEIN, R. 2000a. Bidirectional Planning: Improving Priority Rule Based Heuristics for Scheduling Resource-Constrained Projects. *European Journal of Operational Research* **127**, 619–638.

KLEIN, R. 2000b. *Scheduling of Resource-Constrained Projects*. Kluwer Academic Publishers, Boston.

KLEIN, R. AND A. SCHOLL. 1999a. Computing Lower Bounds by Destructive Improvement — An Application to Resource-Constrained Project Scheduling. *European Journal of Operational Research* **112**, 322–346.

KLEIN, R. AND A. SCHOLL. 1999b. Scattered Branch and Bound: An Adaptive Search Strategy Applied to Resource-Constrained Project Scheduling. *Central European Journal of Operations Research* **7**, 177–201.

KLEIN, R. AND A. SCHOLL. 2000. PROGRESS: Optimally Solving the Generalized Resource-Constrained Project Scheduling Problem. *Mathematical Methods of OR* **52**, 467–488.

KOLISCH, R. 1995. *Project Scheduling under Resource Constraints: Efficient Heuristics for Several Problem Classes*. Physica-Verlag, Heidelberg.

KOLISCH, R. AND A. DREXL. 1997. Local Search for Nonpreemptive Multi-Mode Resource-Constrained Project Scheduling. *IIE Transactions* **29**, 987–999.

KOLISCH, R. AND S. HARTMANN. 1999. Heuristic Algorithms for the Resource-Constrained Project Scheduling Problem: Classification and Computational Analysis. In *Project Scheduling — Recent Models, Algorithms and Applications*, J. Węglarz, ed. Kluwer Academic Publishers, Boston, pages 147–178.

KOLISCH, R. AND R. PADMAN. 2001. An Integrated Survey of Deterministic Project Scheduling. *Omega* **29**, 249–272.

KOLISCH, R., C. SCHWINDT AND A. SPRECHER. 1999. Benchmark Instances for Project Scheduling Problems. In *Project Scheduling — Recent Models, Algorithms and Applications*, J. Węglarz, ed. Kluwer Academic Publishers, Boston, pages 197–212.

KOLISCH, R. AND A. SPRECHER. 1996. PSPLIB — A Project Scheduling Problem Library. *European Journal of Operational Research* **96**, 205–216.

KOLISCH, R., A. SPRECHER AND A. DREXL. 1995. Characterization and Generation of a General Class of Resource-Constrained Project Scheduling Problems. *Management Science* **41**, 1693–1703.

KUMAR, V. 1992. Algorithms for Constraint-Satisfaction Problems: A Survey. *A.I. Magazine* **13**, 32–44.

LAWLER, E. 1963. The Quadratic Assignment Problem. *Management Science* **9**, 586–599.

LAWLER, E. L. 1976. *Combinatorial Optimization: Networks and Matroids*. Holt, Rinehart, and Winston, New York.

LE PAPE, C. 1994a. Constraint-Based Programming for Scheduling: A Historical Perspective. Tech. rep., Operations Research Society Seminar on Constraint Handling Techniques, London.

LE PAPE, C. 1994b. Implementation of Resource Constraints in ILOG SCHEDULE: A Library for the Development of Constraint-Based Scheduling Systems. *Intelligent Systems Engineering* **3**, 55–66.

LE PAPE, C. 1995. Three Mechanisms for Managing Resource Constraints in a Library for Constraint-Based Scheduling. In *Proceedings of the INRIA/IEEE Conference on Emerging Technologies and Factory Automation*. Paris.

LE PAPE, C. AND P. BAPTISTE. 1996a. A Constraint Programming Library for Preemptive and Non-Preemptive Scheduling. In *Proceedings of the 12th European Conference on Aritificial Intelligence*.

LE PAPE, C. AND P. BAPTISTE. 1996b. Constraint Propagation Techniques for Disjunctive Scheduling: The Preemptive Case. In *Proceedings of the 12th European Conference on Artificial Intelligence*.

LHOMME, O. 1993. Consistency Techniques for Numeric CSPs. In *Proceedings of the 13th International Joint Conference on Artificial Intelligence*. Chambéry, France, pages 232–238.

LOPEZ, P. 1991. *Aproche énergétique pour l'ordonnancement de tâches sous contraintes te temps et de ressources*. Ph.D. thesis, Université Paul Sabatier, Toulouse. Cited after Lopez et al. 1992.

LOPEZ, P., J. ERSCHLER AND P. ESQUIROL. 1992. Ordonnancement de tâches sous contraintes: une approche énergétique. *RAIRO Automatique, Productique, Informatique Industrielle* **26**, 453–481.

MACKWORTH, A. K. 1977. Consistency in Networks of Relations. *Artificial Intelligence* **8**, 99–118.

MACKWORTH, A. K. 1992. The Logic of Constraint Satisfaction. *Artificial Intelligence* **58**, 3–20.

MACKWORTH, A. K. AND E. C. FREUDER. 1985. The Complexity of Some Polynomial Network Consistency Algorithms for Constraint Satisfaction Problems. *Artificial Intelligence* **25**, 65–74.

MALCOLM, D., J. ROSEBOOM, C. CLARK AND W. FAZAR. 1959. Applications of a Technique for Research and Development Program Evaluation. *Operations Research* **7**, 646–669.

MANGOUBI, R. AND D. F. MATHAISEL. 1985. Optimizing Gate Assignments at Airport Terminals. *Transportation Science* **19**, 173–188.

MARTIN, P. AND D. B. SHMOYS. 1996. A New Approach to Computing Optimal Schedules for the Job-Shop Scheduling Problem. In *Proceedings of the 5th International IPCO Conference*.

MESEGUER, P. 1989. Constraint Satisfaction Problems: An Overview. *AI Communications* **2**, 3–17.

MINGOZZI, A., V. MANIEZZO, S. RICCIARDELLI AND L. BIANCO. 1998. An Exact Algorithm for the Resource Constrained Project Scheduling Problem Based on a New Mathematical Formulation. *Management Science* **44**, 715–729.

MOHR, R. AND T. C. HENDERSON. 1986. Arc and Path Consistency Revisited. *Artificial Intelligence* **28**, 225–233.

MÖHRING, R. H., A. SCHULZ, F. STORK AND M. UETZ. 1998. Resource Constrained Project Scheduling: Computing Lower Bounds by Solving Minimum Cut Problems. Tech. Rep. 620, Technical University of Berlin.

MONTANARI, U. 1974. Networks of Constraints: Fundamental Properties and Applications to Picture Processing. *Information Sciences* **7**, 95–132.

MOORE, R. E. 1966. *Interval Analysis*. Prentice Hall, Englewood Cliffs.

NEUMANN, K. AND C. SCHWINDT. 1997. Activity-on-Node Networks with Minimal and Maximal Time Lags and their Application to Make-to-Order Production. *OR Spektrum* **19**, 205–217.

NEUMANN, K. AND J. ZHAN. 1995. Heuristics for the Minimum Project-Duration Problem with Minimal and Maximal Time Lags under Fixed Resource Constraints. *Journal of Intelligent Manufacturing* **6**, 145–154.

NEUMANN, K. AND J. ZIMMERMANN. 1999. Methods for Resource-Constrained Project Scheduling with Regular and Nonregular Objective Functions and Schedule-Dependent Time Windows. In *Project Scheduling — Recent Models, Algorithms and Applications*, J. Węglarz, ed. Kluwer Academic Publishers, Boston, pages 213–287.

NUDTASOMBOON, N. AND S. RANDHAWA. 1997. Resource-constrained Project Scheduling with Renewable and Non-Renewable Resources and Time/Resource Trade-Offs. *Computers and Industrial Engineering* **32**, 227–242.

NUIJTEN, W. P. 1994. *Time and Resource Constrained Scheduling: A Constraint Satisfaction Approach*. Ph.D. thesis, Eindhoven University of Technology.

NUIJTEN, W. P. AND E. AARTS. 1996. A Computational Study of Constraint Satisfaction for Multiple Capacitated Job-Shop Scheduling. *European Journal of Operational Research* **90**, 269–284.

NUIJTEN, W. P. AND C. LE PAPE. 1998. Constraint-based Job Shop Scheduling with ILOG SCHEDULER. *Journal of Heuristics* **3**, 271–286.

ÖZDAMAR, L. AND G. ULUSOY. 1995. A Survey on the Resource-Constrained Project Scheduling Problem. *IIE Transactions* **27**, 574–586.

PASCOE, T. 1966. Allocation of Resources — CPM. *Revue Française de Recherche Opérationnelle* **38**, 31–38.

PATTERSON, J. H., R. SLOWINSKI, F. TALBOT AND J. WĘGLARZ. 1989. An Algorithm for a General Class of Precedence and Resource Constrained Scheduling Problems. In *Advances in Project Scheduling*, R. Slowinski and J. Węglarz, eds. Elsevier, Amsterdam, pages 3–28.

PESCH, E. 1999. Lower Bounds in Different Problem Classes of Project Schedules with Resource Constraints. In *Project Scheduling — Recent Models, Algorithms and Applications*, J. Węglarz, ed. Kluwer Academic Publishers, pages 53–76.

PESCH, E. AND U. TETZLAFF. 1996. Constraint Propagation Based Scheduling of Job Shops. *INFORMS Journal on Computing* **8**, 144–157.

PHAN HUY, T. 2000. *Constraint Propagation in Flexible Manufacturing*. Springer, Berlin.

PRITSKER, A. AND W. HAPP. 1966. GERT: Graphical Evaluation and Review Technique — Part I: Fundamentals. *Journal of Industrial Engineering* **17**, 267–274.

PRITSKER, A. B., L. J. WATTERS AND P. M. WOLFE. 1969. Multiproject Scheduling with Limited Resources: A Zero-One Programming Approach. *Management Science* **16**, 93–107.

RADERMACHER, F. 1985/86. Scheduling of Project Networks. *Annals of Operations Research* **4**, 227–252.

ROY, B. 1962. Graphes et Ordonnancement. *Revue Française de Recherche Opérationelle* , 323–333.

SCHIRMER, A. 1999. *Project Scheduling with Scarce Resources*. Ph.D. thesis, University of Kiel.

SCHWINDT, C. 1996. ProGen/max: Generation of Resource-Constrained Scheduling Problems with Minimal and Maximal Time Lags. Tech. Rep. WIOR-489, University of Karlsruhe.

SCHWINDT, C. 1998a. A Branch-and-Bound Algorithm for the Resource-Constrained Project Duration Problem Subject to Temporal Constraints. Tech. Rep. WIOR-544, University of Karlsruhe.

SCHWINDT, C. 1998b. *Verfahren zur Lösung des ressourcenbeschränkten Projektdauerminimierungsproblems mit planungsabhängigen Zeitfenstern*. Shaker Verlag, Aachen.

SEIDEL, R. 1981. A New Method for Solving Constraint Satisfaction Problems. In *Proceedings of the 7th International Joint Conference on AI*. pages 338–342.

SLOWINSKI, R. 1980. Two Approaches to Problems of Resource Allocation among Project Activities. *Journal of the Operational Research Society* **31**, 711–723.

SLOWINSKI, R., B. SONIEWICKI AND J. WĘGLARZ. 1994. DSS for Multiobjective Project Scheduling Subject to Multiple-Category Resource Constraints. *European Journal of Operational Research* **79**, 220–229.

SPRECHER, A. 1994. *Resource Constrained Project Scheduling: Exact Methods for the Multimode Case*, vol. 409 of *Lecture Notes in Economics and Mathematical Systems*. Springer, Berlin and Heidelberg.

SPRECHER, A. 2000. Scheduling Resource-Constrained Projects Competitively at Modest Memory Requirements. *Management Science* **46**, 710–723.

SPRECHER, A. AND A. DREXL. 1998. Multi-Mode Resource-Constrained Project Scheduling by a Simple, General and Powerful Sequencing Algorithm. *European Journal of Operational Research* **107**, 431–450.

SPRECHER, A., S. HARTMANN AND A. DREXL. 1997. An Exact Algorithm for Project Scheduling with Multiple Modes. *OR Spektrum* **19**, 195–203.

SPRECHER, A., R. KOLISCH AND A. DREXL. 1995. Semi-Active, Active and

Non-Delay Schedules for the Resource-Constrained Project Scheduling Problem. *European Journal of Operational Research* **80**, 94–102.

SRIHARI, K. AND R. MUTHUKRISHNAN. 1991. An Expert System Methodology for an Aircraft-Gate Assignment. *Computers and Industrial Engineering* **21**, 101–105.

STORK, F. AND M. UETZ. 2000. On the Representation of Resource Constraints in Project Scheduling. Tech. Rep. 693, Technical University of Berlin.

TALBOT, F. B. 1982. Resource-Constrained Project Scheduling with Time-Resource Tradeoffs: The Nonpreemptive Case. *Management Science* **28**, 1197–1210.

TALBOT, F. B. AND J. H. PATTERSON. 1978. An Efficient Integer Programming Algorithm with Network Cuts for Solving Resource-Constrained Scheduling Problems. *Management Science* **24**, 1163–1174.

THESEN, A. 1977. Measures of the Restrictiveness of Project Networks. *Networks* **7**, 193–208.

TSANG, E. 1993. *Foundations of Constraint Satisfaction*. Academic Press, London.

TSANG, E. P. K. AND N. FOSTER. 1990. Solution Synthesis in the Constraint Satisfaction Problem. Technical report csm–142, Department of Computer Sciences, University of Essex, Essex.

VAN BEEK, P. 1992. Reasoning about Qualitative Temporal Information. *Artificial Intelligence* **58**, 297–326.

VAN HENTENRYCK, P. 1989. *Constraint Satisfaction in Logic Programming*. Logic Programming Series. MIT Press, Cambridge, MA.

VAN HENTENRYCK, P., Y. DEVILLE AND C. TENG. 1992. A Generic Arc-Consistency Algorithm and its Specializations. *Artificial Intelligence* **57**, 291–321.

VAN-HOVE, J. C., R. F. DECKRO AND J. T. MOORE. 1999. Multi-Modal Project Scheduling with Minimal Time Lag Constraints. Tech. rep., Air Force Institute of Technology, Wright Patterson AFB, Ohio.

WALTZ, D. L. 1972. Generating Semantic Descriptions from Drawings of Scenes with Shadows. Technical report AI-TR-271, Massachusetts Institute of Technology.

WALTZ, D. L. 1975. Understanding Line Drawings of Scenes with Shadows. In *The Psychology of Computer Vision*, P. H. Winston, ed. McGraw–Hill, pages 19–91.

WĘGLARZ, J. 1981. On Certain Models of Resource Allocation Problems. *Kybernetics* **9**, 61–66.

WIRASINGHE, S. AND S. BANDARA. 1990. Airport Gate Position Estimation for Minimum Total Costs — Aproximate Closed Form Solution. *Transportation Research* **24B**, 287–297.

XU, J. AND G. BAILEY. 2001. The Airport Gate Assignment Problem: Mathematical Model and a Tabu Search Algorithm. In *Proceedings of the 34th Hawaiian International Conference on System Sciences*. IEEE.

ZALOOM, V. 1971. On the Resource Constrained Project Scheduling Problem. *AIIE Transactions* **3**, 302–305.

ZHAN, J. 1994. Heuristics for Scheduling Resource-Constrained Projects in MPM Networks. *European Journal of Operational Research* **76**, 192–205.